S0-AEQ-636

Changing the Course of AIDS

A VOLUME IN THE SERIES

The Culture and Politics of Health Care Work

edited by Suzanne Gordon and Sioban Nelson

A list of titles in this series is available at www.cornellpress.cornell.edu.

Changing the Course of AIDS

Peer Education in South Africa and Its Lessons for the Global Crisis

David Dickinson

Foreword by Charles Deutsch

ILR Press
an imprint of
Cornell University Press
Ithaca and London

First published 2009 by Cornell University Press
Printed in the United States of America

Library of Congress Cataloging-in-Publication Data

Dickinson, David, 1963–
Changing the course of AIDS : peer education in South Africa and its lessons for the global crisis / David Dickinson; foreword by Charles Deutsch.
p. cm. — (The culture and politics of health care work)
Includes bibliographical references and index.
ISBN 978-0-8014-4831-7 (cloth)
1. AIDS (Disease)—South Africa. 2. Peer counseling—South Africa. 3. Change (Psychology)—Health aspects—South Africa. 4. Occupational health services—South Africa. 5. Health education—South Africa. I. Title. II. Series: Culture and politics of health care work.
RA643.86.S6D53 2009
362.196'979200968—dc22 2009016724

Cornell University Press strives to use environmentally responsible suppliers and materials to the fullest extent possible in the publishing of its books. Such materials include vegetable-based, low-VOC inks and acid-free papers that are recycled, totally chlorine-free, or partly composed of nonwood fibers. For further information, visit our website at www.cornellpress.cornell.edu.

Cloth printing 10 9 8 7 6 5 4 3 2 1

Contents

Foreword

A great deal has been written in the last two decades about HIV/AIDS, especially on the pandemic afflicting Southern Africa. What does this book add, not merely to our library of continuing tragedy, but to the hope that we can someday turn it into an archive helping us learn from the past?

In Southern Africa we are barely making a dent in rates of new infection. Prevention has always been grossly underfunded, and remains so. But now it is considered a priority to combine biomedical, structural, and social/behavioral prevention strategies. Two decades ago some virologists were confident that adequate investment in research would by now yield a vaccine preventing new HIV infection. Today, leading scientists say we may *never* have one. No one blames the scientists or the level of investment; science can't be forced. Similarly, structural solutions—alleviating poverty and providing equitable health care and education—are not things we can expect to happen quickly, in Southern Africa or anywhere else.

But expectations for social and behavioral strategies have been viewed through a different lens. The rhetoric of policymakers and donors is "behavior change communication" (BCC) and its staples are "messages." It derives from economists who posit rational actors who will act in their self-interest if they can only be given accurate information. Its leading advocates are mass media specialists who claim they can sell anything with the right images, jingles, and spokespersons. From a very different direction, preachers spout fire and brimstone and tell people what behavior God insists on; teachers pronounce facts about biology from the front of the room. None of these, individually or in chorus, has worked yet; and the suspicion is dawning that prevention education needs its perspective adjusted for realism.

Behavior changes such as delaying sexual debut, encouraging secondary abstinence, reducing the number of concurrent partners, and consistently using condoms are largely dependent on deeper changes in norms that sanction violence against women, transactional sex, and men's right to (and pride in) multiple sexual partnerships. If we expect broad and quick changes in these and related behaviors (drinking and drug use, for example) that are freighted with pleasure, power, custom, tradition, and economic desperation, then we will try the wrong things, and everything we try will look like a failure.

Yet norms and traditions of all kinds do change, everywhere and all the time. Certainly technologies such as computers and cell phones provoke dramatic changes, but changes in norms concerning gender, race, and ecology, different across countries and cultures, are no less dramatic. Not so many years ago, the streets of U.S. cities were decorated with dog litter and no one would have believed they'd all soon be walking their dogs with a plastic bag at the ready. We can't always see change coming and pinpoint the reasons, but it usually happens through a dynamic interplay between laws and policies, technologies, and our conversations. Fire hoses were turned against relatively few civil rights activists, but as their news filled the media, churches and universities' conversations about them kept rippling outwards. The words we use, and the words we stop using, matter. Indeed, activists supporting each of these changes found various ways to stimulate and guide conversations at dinner tables and water coolers everywhere.

Because AIDS is most closely associated with sex and death among people whose traditions and institutions (including schools) refrain from mentioning either, we have not made good use of our conversations. Since people of all ages usually talk, listen, think, and learn about sensitive issues such as sexuality on the quiet, with people like themselves, peer education is a leading social strategy to change the conversations and norms that surround behavior. What has been blurred by the myopia around BCC is that education is much more than information transfer and message transmission. Educators are better evaluated by the questions they ask than the answers they give. In this context, education is about *unsettling* the unexamined beliefs and traditional behaviors that are killing people, and doing these things, sometimes a little at a time, whenever the opportunity arises.

David Dickinson asks the question: How can we inject into the busy, distracted, difficult lives of the least educated and poorest among us the opportunity, and eventually the habit, to think critically about their social norms and behaviors; that is, about how to keep themselves and their loved ones healthy in a terribly dangerous environment? The answer is: Purposefully, persistently, with system and intent, through judicious infiltration of the social networks people live and act in. It requires intensive, sustainable face-to-face social strategies in which trusted people listen to what is being said and believed, and respond with stories that are not only accurate but also memorable and credible, and can compete successfully with the myths and beliefs that support dangerous norms. In some settings, such as schools, churches, mosques, and sports programs, peer education can be structured and scheduled. In other contexts, such as most workplaces, it is more informal and impromptu, but with many predictable opportunities to be prepared for.

It is the why, what, and how of these latter contexts that Dickinson so ably addresses. He is especially eloquent about the need to work below the surface and behind the scenes, where peer education has few rivals. He documents aspects of the struggle against AIDS that are not usually subject to disciplined scrutiny. He culls from the experiences and wisdom of hundreds of dedicated adult peer educators across South Africa, reconciling and contrasting their insights with theories that have been the basis of social strategies to contain and control new infection and test and treat those currently infected.

This book rests on a confidence in horizontal learning and a respect for what people who don't have much formal education can know and do for one another. Those beliefs are not widely and deeply owned by decision makers in the United States or South Africa. As we cast about for more realistic ways to approach prevention, and settle on strategies that help people think and talk together about what they believe and what they do, these insights into peer education at the workplace will remind us that we have the resources in our midst to change our conversations, our norms, and our behavior.

Charles Deutsch, ScD
Harvard School of Public Health

Acknowledgments

This book was a pleasure to write. I learned a great deal. For that I am grateful to many people.

Above all, I would like to thank the many HIV/AIDS peer educators who appear in this book (under pseudonyms) or contributed to the research in so many different ways. It would be hard to find a kinder, more interesting, or more dedicated group of people to research and write about. That, however, is not why I wrote a book about peer educators. I wrote it because I believe that peer education is a critical component of any effective response to HIV/AIDS and, indeed, to changing behavior beyond the challenge of AIDS. As such, the peer educators in this book are not simply research subjects but colleagues with whom I have worked and from whom I have learned. One peer educator whom I will name, since we have worked and published together, is Duncan Kabelo Kgatea who has taught me more than any other individual peer educator. Duncan, *ke a leboga!*

In addition to peer educators, many others involved in peer education programs—medical doctors, managers, trade union officials, nurses, and social workers—participated in the research; some appear (also under pseudonyms) in this book, and I am grateful to them all. The research would not have been possible without the HIV/AIDS managers at the companies I refer to as Autocircle, Autostar, Bestbuyco, Deco, Finco, and Mineco granting me research access—something that was not always easy for them given corporate fears over the reputational aspect of HIV/AIDS. I am also grateful to Brad Mears at the South African Business Coalition on HIV/AIDS (SABCOHA) for consistently and publicly supporting my research on peer education.

The research was funded from grants made by the University of the Witwatersrand (Wits) AIDS Research Institute and the Wits Faculty of Commerce, Law and Management's Research Committee. Professors Mukul Gupta and Mthuli Ncube at Wits Business School supported and approved the financing of working papers based on my research. Krish Sigamoney has consistently provided administrative support, while Gila Carter ably transcribed the many interviews.

The opportunity to take sabbatical leave during 2006–2007 greatly assisted in the production of this book. Grants from the Oppenheimer Memorial Trust and Wits' Anderson Capelli Fund allowed me to spend three months as a visiting scholar at the Institute of Industrial Relations, University of California, Berkeley. The opportunity to read and to reflect on my research was critical to the development of the arguments advanced. During my sabbatical I also spent two months living in a Free State township. There I conducted no research; my objective was to improve my Sesotho, but the experience of living in an African township helped me better understand the challenges faced by peer educators.

My exposure to the life of Africans started, long before I stayed in the Free Sate, in the township of Katlehong, southeast of Johannesburg. I am thankful to Daniel Morena Thulo and my many friends in Monise and other parts of Katlehong for accepting me as a part of their lives. The significance of African traditional healing plays a prominent part in this book. My understanding of this owes a great deal to Thapelo 'Touch' Hlahatse (Traditional Doctor Mosia) for which I am grateful.

My ideas on peer education have been both affirmed and challenged by Dr. Charles Deutsch of the Harvard School of Public Health/Centre for the Support of Peer Education (South Africa) who, in contrast to the "experts" pilloried in this book, is most certainly someone who understands the importance of peer-to-peer communication.

Pete Strauss and Karen Birdsall read and commented on earlier drafts of Chapter 1 and assisted in shaping my arguments into a comprehensible form. Suzanne Gordon, coeditor of Cornell University Press's Culture and Politics of Health Care Work series, took on what was still very much a work in progress. I could not have hoped for a better editor. The book is immeasurably more readable, and stronger, as a result of her input.

Finally, I dedicate this book to all peer educators and their fight for life. I hope that it contributes to their work and helps make AIDS everybody's everyday concern.

Changing the Course of AIDS

1

"Empowered with Information I Have Influenced a Lot of People"

The Quest for Behavioral Change

Robert Mokwena is a forty-five-year-old African miner who works for Mineco—a fictitious name for a large South African mining company. Over the past decade he has watched family and friends die. His best friend of many years, Benny Modise, died shortly after telling Mokwena that he was HIV-positive. At the time of his friend's death, antiretroviral treatment was unavailable. As he became more and more debilitated, Modise was unable to work and was put on medical disability. Admitted to hospital he grew increasingly despondent. Finally, Modise hung himself from a tree in the hospital grounds. Soon after this tragedy, Mokwena's niece died of AIDS and her infant daughter soon followed. Mokwena could do nothing for them but stand by helplessly and watch them die.

At work, after over twenty years underground, Mokwena had been promoted to a surface job as a training instructor for new recruits to the company. Part of his orientation program included a module on HIV/AIDS. People asked questions. Questions he couldn't answer.

So when the opportunity arose to enhance his knowledge of this epidemic, he took it. He became what is known as a *peer educator*—a commonly promoted communication channel that, in the context of AIDS means a lay person who helps educate coworkers, community members, and family and friends about HIV/AIDS, how to prevent infection and how to deal with the disease. "I became a workplace peer educator because I wanted to help my brothers and sisters," Mokwena explains. "Most of my colleagues cannot read and write. They need someone who knows their language and culture, someone with good communication skills." He wants to give his coworkers, family, and community not only education but also hope. There was no hope for his best friend, and that's why he believes Modise took his own life. "I think I would have convinced him to live if I was trained as a peer educator by then." On the death of his niece and her child he explains, "All the family was affected by this. I still believe I could have done something as a peer educator."

Becoming a peer educator was Mokwena's way of responding to the AIDS epidemic. "Fortunately I was chosen to be among the first volunteers to be trained [by the company] as a peer educator in the year 2000. I received a four-day course and a certificate. Empowered with information I have influenced a lot of people."

This book is about what happens when people like Mokwena decide to help those around them to deal with a catastrophic disease. It tells the story of South African peer educators and their quest to encourage behavioral change. The subject of this story—how to help other human beings change dangerous and destructive behaviors—is a very old one that has existed as long as there has been concern for others. Today, it is particularly urgent, acute, and pressing: a matter of life and death for millions of South Africans as well as for many millions more across the globe at risk or already infected with HIV.

In its sub-Saharan African epicenter, the AIDS pandemic presents a socially debilitating loss of life and a seemingly bottomless well of human suffering. Perhaps one in five adult South Africans is infected with HIV, and there is little evidence to show that the rate of new infections is slowing (Rehle et al. 2007). Only a fraction of those infected with the virus are aware that they are HIV-positive, and only a fraction of this fraction openly comes to terms with their status. Treatment, while increasingly available in South Africa, remains underutilized. Many people who are infected access treatment only when desperate and it is too late. To stem the epidemic, individuals at risk need to take steps to prevent infection, get tested for HIV, and, if infected, live openly with the virus and access available treatment. These are matters of individual behavior. Given the record so far, it is clear that, despite vast sums spent in combating the epidemic, there has been little progress. In the absence of a decisive medical response to AIDS, the quest to change individual behavior remains.

Although AIDS is an African tragedy, Africa is only one chapter of the pandemic. Beginning in San Francisco, its discovery in the early 1980s among the gay populations of world cities is well known. As are its transmission to hemophiliacs via contaminated blood and its spread into a range of vulnerable groups in developed countries: intravenous drug users, sex workers, and the inner-city poor. The pandemic continues. There are chapters still being written: on how the virus is entering into the vast populations of India and China and on how infection among drug users in the former socialist countries of Eastern Europe threatens the wider population. Given this, the quest for behavioral change in the era of AIDS is a matter of importance not only in South Africa, not only in Africa, but also globally.

Out of Africa, this book argues, comes something new. Something needed by all of us. The lessons we can draw from South African peer educators is relevant to stemming the AIDS pandemic beyond Africa. Preventing infection requires individuals to address and change the least manageable of human behaviors. For HIV infection is, for most, a question of sex: sexual behaviors that infection starkly exposes. Sexual behavior is embedded within beliefs about gender, faith, status, morality, identity, and more. Preventing infection, or coming to terms with being HIV-positive, requires individuals to take responsibility for themselves. Yet, this is not straightforward. Their actions and the actions of others with whom they coexist are enmeshed within a web of social understandings and responsibilities that can neither be ignored nor thrown out wholesale. The social worlds that we inhabit are shaped by the past as well as our own actions. In the story this book tells, a history of colonialism and apartheid have molded the life of individuals in South Africa, but many other institutions—such as churches, unions, and government—also play a role in shaping and reshaping the terrain of everyday life, and everyday sex. This book has lessons for regions as diverse as Asia and Eastern Europe where the epidemic is unfolding with, it would seem, little cognizance of what has happened elsewhere. Even in the advanced countries with their low rates of infection, there is much to learn from what peer educators are doing. For it may well be that the limits of managing this disease from above have been reached, and it is time to learn from below—where the parameters of risk are determined.

South African lessons are also relevant to other health-related problems, not just to HIV/AIDS. The quest for behavioral change is not, after all, confined to the AIDS pandemic. We are all acutely aware, from our own experiences, just how difficult it is to change what we do. Seemingly small decisions—what we eat, how much we drink, whether we light up a cigarette, how much exercise we get, or how fast we drive—make for big problems. Many of us manage, with only the occasional regret, miscalculation, or sense of guilt, lives not as well lived as we would like. For others, behaviors result in obesity, addiction, abuse, broken lives, illness, and premature death. We know all this, but we often stand powerless. *Telling* people what they should do to help themselves does not stop unhealthy eating, smoking, drinking, or reckless driving. Nor is it stopping AIDS.

In exasperation at our own stubbornness, we may resort to legal penalties. We may try to force people to change. That may moderate some behavior, perhaps speeding, but many choices lie beyond what we feel comfortable about legislating, are not amenable to legislation, can be legislated only at the margins, or will be driven underground by legal penalties. We remain with the problem of what to do after we admit that, for all the logic of our messages, individuals seem to be chained to behaviors that detract from their own and others' well-being.

This problem confronts us when we try to do something as seemingly innocuous as getting people to cut down on fat and salt in their diet—things that we know may add years to their lives and enhance their quality of life. If this is true, then the problem of getting people to change their behavior when it comes to AIDS is clearly enormous. Which is why the subject of this book—what has happened when HIV/AIDS peer educators try to get people to change their behavior—has much to teach us about getting people to change behaviors that have little to do with the HIV/AIDS epidemic. Even the slightest advances around AIDS can help us make progress in influencing the choices that have an impact on peoples' health and well-being and, by extension, escalating health care and social costs.

The choices people make are not simply individual ones. They exist in a web of social, workplace, family, and community relationships. Their individual choices are constrained by contexts in which they live and work. Typically, in thinking about the context of people's lives, we often focus on material conditions. There is a good reason for this. We know that many social and health problems are concentrated among the poor, and that their choices are restricted by difficult material conditions. Nonetheless, poor people can and do make choices. What we need to understand are the social factors that make it hard to enact these choices. A lack of resources is part of any answer, but not the only one. Consider, for example, the issue of alcohol abuse; we know that alcoholism is a major problem in many poor communities, but not all poor people are alcoholics and not all alcoholics are poor. This book looks at the psychological terrain that people inhabit and how the ordering of this psychological space can hamper attempts to change behavior. By this I do not mean probing the id, ego, and superego of South Africans but instead looking at the web of social relationships that influence behavior. Through an analysis of peer educator activity, we examine the texture of the social spaces of South African workers, their families, and their communities and how this constrains individuals' ability to respond to the epidemic. We will also see how peer educators, under the most difficult of contexts and with the most difficult of issues, labor to bring about behavioral change.

HIV/AIDS and Behavioral Change

Changes in sexual behavior could prevent most HIV infection and dramatically undercut the potency of the pandemic. Change in beliefs and behavior also play an important part in the effectiveness of providing antiretroviral treatment and in mitigating the impact of the disease, including the stigmatization of those who are infected or affected.

Early responses to AIDS assumed that knowledge about HIV/AIDS would be sufficient to change beliefs and bring about behavioral change (UNFPA 2002). This assumption promoted *top-down* or *vertical communication programs* that disseminate information from centers of expertise to target audiences. In short, the assumption was that information = knowledge = belief = behavior. Enough lectures, charts, illustrations, and graphs would change peoples' beliefs about the disease, which would, in turn, lead to lasting changes in their behavior. The general failure of such programs, evidenced by continued HIV infection and persistent stigmatization of those with the disease, has prompted a rethinking of such communication strategies (UNFPA 2002). Where success in changing sexual behavior and lowering infection rates has been observed, a number of authors have pointed to the contribution of horizontal, rather than vertical, communication processes (Low-Beer and Stoneburner 2003, 2004; Parker 2004; USAID 2002). A number of features characterize *horizontal communication processes,* including: embeddedness in local cultural contexts; dialogue, especially among similar individuals, rather than information delivered by experts; individuals as change agents, rather than as targets for change; and the importance of face-to-face, personal communication channels (Low-Beer and Stoneburner 2003; Panford et al. 2001; Parker 2004; USAID 2002).

Despite the potential of horizontal communication processes in changing beliefs and behavior around HIV and AIDS, Daniel Low-Beer and Rand Stoneburner (2003) point out that their value is rarely recognized. One important consequence of this neglect is that, beyond broad principles, we understand relatively little about horizontal communication processes around HIV/AIDS. This is not surprising. Apart from the vested interests of AIDS experts, who dominate vertical programs and are unlikely to voluntarily relinquish their role, horizontal communication throws up barriers to external observation because it is framed within local cultures and consists of face-to-face interaction between peers. Thus, even if the value of horizontal communication in changing beliefs and behaviors is acknowledged, how such communication takes place and why it works, if it works, remains opaque.

Workplace peer educators in South Africa operate within programs set up by companies that have become concerned about the impact of the AIDS epidemic on their public image and their ability to maintain a healthy workforce. Largely pushed by grassroots concern and activism—as well as frustration with the South African government's failure to come to grips with the epidemic—these companies have initiated workplace behavioral change programs in an attempt to stem the epidemic. Although workplace peer educators formally operate within vertically oriented company AIDS programs, they are best understood as grassroots change agents who operate within the specific cultures of their peer groups and utilize personal communication channels. Workplace HIV/AIDS peer educators are, thus, attempting, through horizontal communication processes, to change beliefs and behaviors around HIV/AIDS. Studying their activity provides insight into the process of peer-to-peer communication around HIV/AIDS and the challenges that this entails. This is important: There is much to learn about AIDS beliefs and behaviors from what is unfolding on the ground. This is perhaps especially so in South Africa where a colossal failure of leadership—across state, business, unions, and academia—in the face of AIDS has contrasted with responses from below.

HIV/AIDS in South Africa

AIDS presents a major challenge to South Africa. The primary means of HIV transmission in sub-Saharan Africa is unprotected heterosexual sex (UNAIDS 2003). Unless treated with antiretroviral drugs, the virus's destruction of the immune system results in increased illness and eventual death within nine to eleven years of infection (UNAIDS and WHO 2007). Antiretroviral drug treatment can control but not eliminate the virus for periods not yet established. The continuing incidence of HIV infection draws attention to the difficulties of responding to this disease. Stigmatization, fear, and discrimination—linked to sexual transmission and the disease's incurability—hamper efforts to promote prevention, testing, and treatment.

South Africa's antenatal HIV sero-prevalence surveys, measuring whether the person's immune system has "sero-converted" (i.e., produced antibodies) in response to the HIV virus, at public sector clinics have shown a rise in HIV prevalence among pregnant women from 0.7 percent in 1990 to 28.0 percent in 2007 (Department of Health 2008). A national sero-prevalence survey (Human Sciences Research Council [HSRC] 2005) indicated a wide difference in infection rates between the four racial categories used in South Africa: Africans, coloreds, Indians, and whites. These four racial categories were inherited from apartheid. They continue to be used in South Africa both for official purposes, notably Employment Equity legislation, and, with some variation, in popular discourse. Employment Equity legislation additionally groups Africans (indigenous people), coloreds (people of mixed origins), and Indians (people originally from the Indian subcontinent) as "black." All black people are regarded as being "previously disadvantaged" in comparison to whites, though it is recognized that the apartheid racial hierarchy resulted in greater discrimination against Africans than coloreds or Indians.

Among those two years and older, 13.3 percent of Africans, 0.6 percent of whites, 1.9 percent of colored, and 1.6 percent of Indians were found to be infected. While there is room to doubt the precise levels found in this survey, it is clear that HIV prevalence is much higher among Africans than other racial groups. Magnifying this racial dimension of the disease's distribution is the overwhelming numerical domination of Africans within the country's population. Statistics South Africa (2008a) estimated that of a population of 48.7 million, 79.2 percent were African, just over 9 percent white, 9 percent colored, and 2.6 percent Indian. Given the close correlation between race and socioeconomic status in South Africa, high prevalence rates among Africans equates to high HIV prevalence rates among the poor and poorly educated. The racial distribution of the disease, its causes, and its consequences are important issues that this book returns to a number of times.

There are also marked differences in the burden of the epidemic by gender. The HSRC survey found that while 8.2 percent of males (of two years and over) were HIV-positive, the rate among females was 13.3 percent. The intersection of race and gender leads to the highest infection rates among African women estimated at 24.4 percent of those between fifteen and forty-nine years of age. Perhaps the most frightening statistic, and the one that gives the best insight into how HIV/AIDS is affecting South Africa, is looking at the distribution by age. Since HIV is transmitted primarily by sex, prevalence peaks among people of working age: 33 percent among women aged twenty-five to twenty-nine and 23 percent among men aged thirty to thirty-nine (for all races). Among African women between twenty-five and twenty-nine, this peak spikes to 38 percent. Such peaks are disguised by much lower rates of infection among children, who are at little risk of infection until they become sexually active and older people whose most active sexual periods were before HIV was widespread. In the absence of behavioral change to reduce infection, over time the disease will be infecting approximately one in three women and one in four men in their twenties and thirties.

A plateauing of prevalence rates, which may now be occurring, does not indicate a slowing of the epidemic but rather that the number of new infections is offset by the deaths of those infected earlier. Demographic models predict that average life expectancy will drop to forty-six years in 2010, twenty-two years lower than it would have been in the absence of AIDS (Rehle and Shisana 2003). The effective provision and uptake of antiretroviral treatment will mitigate this drop in life expectancy. It will also increase the percentages infected with the virus because HIV-positive people will be living longer. Along with this will be the need for individuals and society to deal with the implications of a large proportion of the population relying on expensive, chronic antiretroviral medication.

The South African Context

An epidemic needs to be understood within the context that shapes the terrain on which the pathogen, and its host, exists. South Africa's HIV prevalence rates are not unique. However, it stands out as the most industrialized and most highly developed country with such high levels of infection.

It is impossible to tell the story of HIV/AIDS in South Africa without understanding the history and impact of *apartheid*—a legalized system of racial discrimination—and the transition to democracy that took place in 1994. In South Africa, Dutch and British settled the territory they occupied and thus the country was not, unlike many other imperial territories, governed only by means of a small colonial administration. These settler colonialists divided the country into a rich, white minority and an impoverished black majority. The story of South Africa's political miracle—the avoidance of an all-out race war—speaks to the eventual pragmatism of the white elite in stepping down from political power before the country descended into chaos. It also captures the agreement from leaders on both sides of the racial divide as to the desired future direction of the country: a modern, prosperous African state with legal equality for all and a transformation process designed to redress past discrimination.

This narrative of South Africa's apartheid era and democratic transition, however, misses important historical stages pertinent to understanding the country and its peoples today. Prior to European conquest, South Africa was populated by several Bantu-speaking societies. The term Bantu has picked up negative connotations in popular use. However, as a linguistic categorization of the majority of Africans in southern Africa, it remains a valid and useful category. These groups, as well as smaller populations of Khoe-San or Bushmen, were organized along family, clan, and tribal lines that in some cases solidified into larger nation polities. These indigenous societies had distinct political, military, economic, and social structures. The long process of colonization, which is usually dated with the arrival of Dutch settlers in 1652, subjugated these political entities. Thus, the construction of apartheid following the electoral victory of the Afrikaner (settlers of Dutch origin) National Party in 1948 was not the introduction of racial domination in South Africa but its brutal and open codification as an ideology subscribed to by the majority of whites and its systematic implementation through racist laws.

Yet despite centuries of colonialism and decades of apartheid, much of pre-colonial society remains—albeit often fragmented, devalued, and hidden. Belief in traditional African values often oscillates between pride and embarrassment. The truth is that these legacies are complex. In presenting itself as a modern organization, the African National Congress (ANC) has consistently striven to overcome tribalism as a division of black unity and a danger to its founding vision of a diverse but harmonious society. In part this was because of the apartheid government's deliberate policy of highlighting and supporting ethnic differences as a strategy of divide and rule. Precisely mapping ethnic groups is not possible (as the apartheid ethnographers found out). The fact that there are eleven official languages (two of European origin and nine indigenous), and that each of these are associated with a particular group that may itself be subdivided, highlights the complexity of ethnicity in South Africa. For all the ANC's ideal of racial unity, the question of ethnicity is of great significance to individuals' identities and loyalties, to social networks, and to the political need to craft not only a racial but also an ethnic balance of political power. However, beyond a public celebration of linguistic diversity, the legacy of the old within the modern is played out furtively.

To understand the context of the AIDS epidemic, we need to recognize how South Africa's difficult historical legacy shapes every facet of life. Given the subject of this book, we will need to bear in mind not only why the country's population has been particularly vulnerable to the transmission of the HIV virus but also how health care systems and access to those systems has been shaped by the broader processes that have constructed South Africa.

Pre-colonial Africa had extensive systems of indigenous healing. These attempted to address individual's health problems and were also responsible for public health and social stability though their influence on rights of passage to new social status and for maintenance of public health through prescribing and maintaining social and sexual relationships. These roles were (and remain) deeply linked to an African cosmology in which ancestors play a significant role for the living. Offending the ancestors—by failing to adhere to appropriate standards of behavior—brings problems to individuals and society. But these ancestors can also be used by traditional African healers to restore balance though processes of divination. Most commonly this is done by means of "throwing the bones" (tossing a collection of objects, including small animal bones, which are then interpreted). Mediating between the living and the ancestors, traditional healers seek to identify the root cause of problems and prescribe necessary corrective action. Typically, this combines paying attention to the ancestors and restoring, at least for a period, strained social relationships. Ceremonies in which an animal is slaughtered and eaten and traditional beer consumed are the most common way of rectifying ancestral neglect.

Steven Feierman (1985) describes the suppression of these indigenous systems of health care by colonial authorities across Africa who stripped away any serious roles of political or social control from subjugated populations. Witchcraft acts promulgated throughout the nineteenth and twentieth centuries in most African colonies eliminated the role of traditional healers in any form of social regulation. This change had public health implications. For example, traditions such as a cleansing period after the death of a spouse before resuming sex became a practice that relied on family subscription rather than a necessity backed by traditional healers forming part of the polity. This reduced the role of traditional healer to the provider of individual healing services—typically out of view (Chavunduka 1986). Alongside this suppression of traditional medicine, colonialists, notably in the form of missionaries, introduced Western medical practices. This kind of medicine has been of limited value across Africa for several reasons. Whether under colonial rule or after independence, insufficient resources have been available for doctors, nurses, hospitals, and clinics. Moreover, the narrow scope of Western medicine, even when available, largely ignores spiritual and social aspects of health. One result is that plural medical systems now exist in most African countries (MacCormack

1986) including South Africa. In such plural systems, people use different healing systems—such as Western, traditional, faith, and patent medicine—depending on accessibility, respectability, sympathy, cost, and perceived efficacy. Often, given doubt over efficacy and the multiple dimensions of health, more than one system is simultaneously consulted.

As the South African network of Western-based medical care extended, it did so in an uneven way. Health resources tend to be biased toward urban areas and to provide better service to richer sections of the populations. In South Africa, racial segregation reenforced this inequality with modern health care available, through public and private systems, for whites and limited poor-quality care available for blacks. Where health care was available for Africans, this was often based on economic expediency, as in the mining industry where an extensive system of health screening and interventions aimed at maintaining healthy workers was introduced with little regard for their families or, indeed, for workers beyond their period of service. Packard (1990) provides a detailed account of such a response in South Africa to tuberculosis among black migrant mine workers.

After the end of apartheid in 1994, the new government had to integrate a fragmented health service that had been divided both on racial and national (i.e., notionally independent, ethnically defined, black "homeland" states) lines—much of it squalid and underresourced. What it also inherited was a private health care system to which the richest 15 percent of the population had access via private insurance. While spending on health has been a priority for the ANC government, the public health care system remains distinctly second-class in relation to private care with limited facilities and poor services. Not surprisingly, despite the existence of extensive Western health care facilities, accessing plural health care options remains common in South Africa. While accessing what services are available from public-sector hospitals and clinics, Africans, in particular, consult traditional and spiritual healers or buy patent, often quack, medicines based on herbal formulas, which are available almost anywhere from street corners to large pharmacies.

The AIDS epidemic as a new health concern entered into this complex set of health systems operating in South Africa. Understanding the South African government's response to the epidemic, which we review shortly, requires placing the arrival of the disease within the wider tensions held within this complex system. The aspiration that all should have access to health services is undermined by the reality of limited and unequally distributed resources. Any hope that Africans, freed from colonial bondage, could draw on their own indigenous healing knowledge has not been fulfilled because of a fragmented and chaotic traditional health care system.

The story of AIDS in South Africa is, as this book emphasizes, much more than one of the state's response. It is also about how individuals, families, and communities have responded to the epidemic. In this regard, it is a question of understanding not only the legacy of publicly devalued traditional healing systems of Africans but also other dimensions of the African population. This is not to downplay the presence of other racial groups in South Africa. But the overwhelming majority of South Africans are Africans, and it is among this population that the epidemic is, at least currently, disproportionately concentrated. In South Africa there has been a long and deeply harmful process dehumanizing Africans. In response, Africans have, as oppressed people do everywhere (Scott 1990), learned to hide their true feelings, to dissemble, to steal advantage by stealth, and to undermine by petty, calibrated acts of sabotage what they dare not openly challenge. The need to overcome this public subservience to domination was the key to Steve Biko's call for black consciousness.[1] To the extent that this project remains unfulfilled, it feeds into typical responses to HIV/AIDS in which mostly white experts tell black Africans what they should be doing to protect themselves from AIDS, make sure they know their HIV-status, and, if infected, live healthfully and, when appropriate, start antiretroviral therapy. Many in the assembled audiences display a polite public reception, learn the correct responses, but do little more once the lecture is over. Away from such public performance, many rely on the alternatives explanations of HIV/AIDS that draw on African experience of their dehumanization with expert pronouncements commonly contradicted by a range of AIDS myths involving racial conspiracies that reflect a colonialized past as well as continued underdevelopment.

1. Steven Biko (1946–1977) founded the Black Consciousness Movement in South Africa. This movement stressed the need for blacks to take pride in themselves. Although black consciousness never rivaled the ANC as an organized opposition to apartheid, its influence in reshaping the cultural landscape of racial oppression and resistance was enormous. Biko was killed by police while in custody.

This book will explore not only the gulf between a handful of educated experts and an underdeveloped and undervalued African population but also the divisions within this population—divisions that have significant implications for any response to HIV/AIDS. Race dominates any evaluation of what divides South Africans, but within the four racial categories—Africans coloreds, Indians, and whites—there are further subdivisions. The African majority is divided by ethnic differences the salience of which depends on the situation, but which are readily available to justify actions or explain grievances that race alone cannot explain.

The gendered culture of South Africans, black and white, sets up another tension. While the South African Constitution is not infrequently referred to with pride, this coexists with widespread resentment among African men (and often women) of the rights that it gives to women and children. Religion further exacerbates divisions within the country. Although an overwhelming Christian country, South Africa has minorities of Muslims (among Indians and coloreds), Jews (among whites and the Lemba—a small African Jewish community found in South Africa and number of neighboring states [Le Roux 2003]), and Hindus (among Indians). Christians in South Africa are divided among a host of denominations, some linked closely to race. While almost 80 percent of South Africans describe themselves as Christians, they attend a range of mainline churches (e.g., Dutch Reformed, Catholic, Anglican, Methodist), as well as African Initiated, or Zionist, and Pentecostal churches. While very few Africans report that they subscribe to African traditional beliefs, in reality such beliefs coexist alongside Christian teachings and practice in most Zionist churches and, frequently, among the congregations of mainline and even Pentecostal churches despite hostile official stances.

Despite these differences within the African population, which the more public tensions of race conceal, there is a strong social ideology of unity—often expressed in the concept of *ubuntu* or the idea that people can only be people (that is fulfill their potential) with the help of other people. But while this ideal of unity is frequently espoused, any close observer sees what everybody knows: It is largely absent. While African children may grow up with the entire neighborhood acting as surrogate parents, the adult world of Africans, and South Africans generally, is a much harsher and individualistic competition for advantage and control. High levels of rape and child sexual abuse highlight the disregard for the welfare and dignity of others in South Africa. Africans often express nostalgia for what they claim to be the authentic social norms that prevailed in a pre-colonial golden age. At that time, neighbors supposedly rallied to help and care for one another. Today, the reality is that—with exceptions—below a pervasive culture of polite cheerfulness, there is frequent mistrust of neighbors' and even family members' real intentions. All this is, as we shall see, highly pertinent for how peer educators work in South Africa.

Poverty aggravates all these tensions and reduces opportunities for generosity or even reciprocity. It is hard to care for others when you are hungry. In post-apartheid South Africa hunger is not unknown, but the widespread provision of social security means that most families can put food, even if it is only pap (maize porridge) on the table. What constantly corrodes social fabric in South Africa is less absolute poverty than inequality, within families, within communities, and within the country. Despite a widened social security net, inequality is increasing (South African Institute of Race Relations [SAIRR] 2008). Using the internationally used Gini coefficient measure of inequality in which a score of zero reflects perfect income equality (everybody has the same level of income) and one complete inequality (one person receives the country's entire income), South Africa is one of the world's most unequal countries. South Africa's Gini coefficient of 0.7 reflects the reality of the top 10 percent of households enjoying 50 percent of national income while the bottom 40 percent of households received just 7 percent of income (Statistics South Africa 2008b). By comparison, Scandinavian countries (some of the world's most equal) have Gini coefficients at around 0.25, while the United States (one of the most unequal developed societies) has a Gini coefficient of 0.4. Inequality in South Africa stems in large part from a distorted labor market that has an intense shortage of skills, allowing a minority to earn high salaries, while a vast army of poorly educated, mainly African and colored, adults search unsuccessfully for employment. Although mitigated by extensive but largely unrecorded informal activity, South Africa's employment rate stands, depending on how it is measured, at between 20 and 40 percent.

Five Companies

Macroeconomic variables help us understand the broad terrain on which AIDS operates, but local conditions also shape the epidemic and responses.

This book focuses on workplace peer education. As well as having their own internal cultures, companies help shape the context of peoples' lives in many ways. In this book, we draw on the work of peer educators in five large South African companies: a mining company, two automobile manufacturers, a retail group, and a financial institution.

Above all other industries, the mining sector has shaped South African economic development and the country's social structure. Extracting the countries vast mineral wealth—gold, platinum, diamonds, and coal—has been the country's economic backbone. Much of this mining continues to use labor-intensive methods with profitability maintained by cheap labor. To achieve this, the mining industry has relied on migrant workers, both from neighboring states and within the country's borders. The flow of migrant workers set in motion by South Africa's mines endures to this day. Mining remains a high profile component of labor migration, but is now only the tip of the iceberg. Many apparently urbanized workers retain strong links with rural areas, or, looked at another way, many young men and women growing up in rural areas or small towns have little choice but to migrate to the urban areas if they are to find work. Approximately 55 percent of South Africa's population lives in urban areas. However, given widespread mobility, this is a gross simplification of where people live and work beyond providing a snapshot on census day.

A permanent system of labor migration provided a mechanism for the mining companies to de-link the costs of social reproduction and economic production. Without migration, companies must pay for the education, health care, and pensions of their workforce, either directly by salary levels that allow workers to pay for these themselves or indirectly though the state and taxation. With labor migration, workers could be superexploited because the cost of social reproduction—of raising families, of old age, and of disability—were transferred onto neighboring states and black homelands within South Africa. Not surprisingly, this system was resisted. Today the National Union of Mineworkers (NUM), one of the country's largest unions, still seeks to improve the working and conditions of black mineworkers—including campaigning for health and safety, an end to single-sex hostels that accommodate migrant workers, and the elimination of racial disparities within the workforce. White miners, long privileged by job and training reservation, are represented by separate unions that historically had been accommodated within the industry, at least from the

1930s onward. In 1922, white miners engaged in a violent insurrection on the Witwatersrand, known as the Rand Rebellion, in defense of privileges that management sought to undermine using cheaper black labor.

"Mineco," the mining company researched for this book, has 44,500 employees (out of an industry total of some half million). Like most large mining companies in South Africa, it is a rigid bureaucracy with a vast network of operations—including hostels, hospitals, management clubs, maintenance yards, and its own security force—supporting approximately ten mines, many with multiple shafts, and processing facilities spread across three of the country's nine provinces.

As we will see in Chapter 2, the mining industry was the first to respond to HIV/AIDS, and Mineco has a highly developed, though overstretched, HIV/AIDS program that includes a network of four hundred peer educators, testing facilities, and the provision of antiretroviral drugs for HIV-positive employees (but not their families). (Since the research for this book was conducted, Mineco has redesigned and greatly expanded its peer educator program with a target of over two thousand active peer educators.) The mining industry responded early to HIV/AIDS for a number of reasons. Given the extensive sexual networks created by the migrant labor system and single-sex hostels, there is a high level of HIV prevalence among mineworkers; this was detected relatively early as a result of annual medical checkups that all miners must, by law, undergo if they are to work underground.

Miners, whose families may live thousands of kilometers away from the mines, typically live in compounds while working. They may come from a neighboring country such as Mozambique or a former South African homeland such as the Transkei, the Xhosa-designated territory in what is now the Eastern Cape Province. Rather than living in homes or apartments, they live in single-sex hostels, where they bunk with many other miners. Previously, rigid social control limited their access to women, and homosexual relations (typically engaging in thigh sex rather than penetration) between older and younger mine workers were common (Moodie and Ndatshe 1994). Such homosexual relationships continue (Dickinson, Phillips, and Tau 2008) though almost certainly less commonly now that access to women is largely uncontrolled. In the past, miners returned home on an annual basis for perhaps six weeks between contracts. The workforce now has more permanent contracts, but frequently remains migratory.

Many miners still return only a few times a year when they have enough leave and enough money to justify the trip home. With the breakdown of apartheid's social order, informal settlements have mushroomed outside of mine accommodation. Away from their wives for long periods, miners frequently find other sexual partners, either prostitutes or girlfriends who live in these nearby settlements. While they are away, their wives may also find other sexual partners (Lurie 2004). This creates extended sexual networks through which HIV is rapidly transmitted.

At the Mineco operation in the North West Province that I researched in 2006, there was a large hostel with capacity for 1,300 men (one of seven hostels run by the company in the area). Previously the hostel had housed 3,000 employees. Wider social developments have dramatically changed the status of the hostel. There is a clear sense that managerial authority was—in contrast to the apartheid period—weak beyond the working environment. Despite the hostel theoretically providing everything required by migrant workers, hawkers had started to operate outside the hostel in 1994. Despite a management-erected sign forbidding it, there is now widespread informal economic activity around the entrance. Hawkers sell food, beer, pirated disks, and clothes along with patent and traditional medicines and, of course, sex.

Since 2000, a large informal settlement of tin shacks (or *mekhukhu*) has been (illegally) erected, partly on mine-owned land that abuts the hostel perimeter. (The settlement's nickname, Sondela, translates as "come closer.") Many mineworkers opted to leave the hostel and live in Sondela. By doing so, they are able to take advantage of the union-negotiated option of receiving a monthly living-out allowance in lieu of accommodation and meals that the hostel offered. Many live with girlfriends—usually unemployed women who are attracted to the concentration of employed and temporarily single men. Such girlfriends are maintained while keeping a family at "home" in the rural areas, predominantly, at this operation over one thousand kilometers away in the Eastern Cape Province.

At the end of their contracts, such miners typically return home. If they are injured or fall ill while working, a medical evaluation, known in South Africa as boarding, takes place. This procedure is outlined in the Labour Relations Act (Government of South Africa 1995) and allows for the disabled or sick employee to state their case in response to medical reports, assisted by a trade union representative or other employee. This process is conducted by a panel usually consisting of a company doctor, the employees' manager, and a union representative. The role of the panel (or medical board) is to assess the level of disability and decide whether it is temporary or permanent. Alternative employment within the company, that the employee would be capable of doing, should be offered. The increased use of subcontractors to carry out support services (such as catering and gardening) has constrained medical boards in this regard since employment in these, less physically demanding occupations no longer falls within the payroll of mining companies. If alternatives are not available, or recovery is unlikely, disability payments, usually three years of annual salary, are issued and the employment contract ended. As we shall see, the AIDS epidemic now plays a significant role in medical boarding with implications for both rural families and shack-based girlfriends.

Like all mining operations, the working environment is difficult and can be dangerous. Underground production pressures are intense—with supervisors pushing teams to raise production and achieve monthly production bonuses. This conflicts with a high sensitivity to occupational safety and the overall objective is to "produce ore with no blood on it." A focus on health and safety is one achievement that the NUM has helped to bring about in the industry. At this Mineco operation the NUM continued to be the dominant union among black workers, but its position was threatened by a number of splinter unions, some based on ethnic identity.

Another threat to NUM's influence is the large number of subcontractors operating in the mine. This also reduced the ability of the mine management to ensure operational procedures and to communicate with the workforce. Productivity is lower in subcontracted areas, but remains a profitable component of overall output because of lower costs. The morning shifts drill the rock face or *stope,* insert roof supports, and set blasting charges. Following blasting, the stopes are left clear while the smaller afternoon shift brings in materials and prepares for the night shift, which takes out the loosened rock for processing. The language of communication between whites and Africans is Fanagolo, a simplified language using mainly English, Afrikaans, IsiZulu, and IsiXhosa vocabulary used widely for instruction in the South African mining industry. The nearly all-male environment underground is tough, and requests are responded to only when you show that you can stand up for yourself. This is as true for peer education on the surface as it is for operations underground.

The manufacturing sector in South Africa initially developed because the mining industry needed to purchase plant, parts, explosives, cables, and pipes in large quantities. Unlike mining, developments in manufacturing processes required an increasingly skilled and therefore stable workforce. The result was the creation of an urbanized African workforce close to industrial areas—though one that was kept apart from white residential areas. Manufacturing diversified from supplying the mines to meeting the needs of the growing urban population. The growing South African consumer market attracted multinational companies seeking markets across the globe.

In the manufacturing sector, I researched two auto companies "Autocircle" and "Autostar." Both operate production lines in South Africa, and their output are integrated within the parent companies' global production and sales strategies. Both are much smaller than Mineco, one has 3,500 employees, the other 4,000 spread over a small number of sites (two for Autocircle and three for Autostar, which operates a separate distribution warehouse). While the usual racial division of labor is present in these companies' rank-and-file workers are noticeably better educated and skilled than in Mineco. Aware of the need for committed workers within a highly competitive global industry, Autocircle and Autostar's production line employees formed a relatively well-paid segment of the working class.

Global companies operating in South Africa had to negotiate international public pressure during apartheid and continue to be aware of the public pressure that can be brought to bear on them. This provided a further reason for both Autocircle and Autostar to provide extensive medical care for employees, something that extended to HIV/AIDS. Between them, the two companies have approximately 130 peer educators and extensive HIV/AIDS programs linked to strong occupational health departments.

Despite the relatively privileged position of Autocircle and Autostar's employees, these workplaces are far from models of industrial peace. Nearly every blue-collar worker in both companies belongs to the National Union of Metalworkers of South Africa (NUMSA) that dominates the engineering industry. When I interviewed production line workers in Autostar there was a clear sense of alienation and distrust of management (and sometimes the union). Even white-collar employees with whom I spoke, especially if they were black, alluded to workplace tensions. In line with the company's global policy, Autocircle had done away with the terms *employee* and *employer.* Reflecting a desire to have a high-involvement, high-performance workplace to which all contributed and which power relations were glossed over, now there were only *leaders* and *associates.* One African clerk whom I interviewed on her work as a peer educator maintained this jargon of leaders and associates throughout our hour-long interview. Only toward the end of our time together, when I goaded her with a question on management closing down the peer education program (a standard part of my interview schedule with peer educators, see Chapter 3) did she drop the "company speak."

> I don't think it [cutting the peer educator program] would work. First of all, peer educators are there to sort of suss out the feeling about things. Sometimes employees would not go to a manager and vent out their problems. They would want somebody who they can feel they can relate to, you know, on the same level... There was a time when some employees were feeling that they [couldn't] trust the medical station.... The only way that the medical station could know about that, was through us [peer educators]... Management sometimes see things from their perspective and not from the perspective of their subordinates.

Mistrust of management is widespread in South African workplaces. But given the countries racial past, this distrust is often enhanced and entrenched at what used to be known as the "color bar" that separates white managers and skilled workers from low-skilled black workers. At work, there is always the need to communicate, but real feelings can remain hidden behind a poker face or expressed only to coworkers in a vernacular that whites do not understand. If this is true for workplace instructions, it is even more so for issues of sexual behavior and HIV/AIDS.

If the expansion of a manufacturing sector required the growth of a black urban proletariat, this, in turn, helped to expand the market for consumer goods. The company I researched in the retail sector, which I call "Bestbuyco," has some 41,500 employees and is one of the largest retail companies in South Africa. It has approximately 15 hypermarkets (superstores selling clothes, furniture, appliances, and other goods in addition to groceries and household goods) and 120 supermarkets across the country selling groceries, household goods, and kitchenware. In some ways retail companies have a similar workforce profile as mining companies; a small, predominantly white, managerial corps and a vast workforce of low-skilled black workers (often colored as well as African in stores in the Western Cape or Gauteng provinces). However, there are also striking differences, noticeably in the smaller size of individual workplaces (though a hypermarket may have up to 1,000 employees). There is also a reversal of the gender bias with the most common jobs—shelf stackers, cashiers, and packers (who assist in bagging customers' purchases at the till)—filled by women. Like the low-skilled, black workforce of the mines, they are strongly unionized. Most are members of the national retail union: the South African Commercial, Catering and Allied Workers Union.

As a national company, operating largely within the borders of South Africa, Bestbuyco is under no international pressure to deal with HIV/AIDS. However, as a retail company selling directly to consumers, it recognizes its vulnerability to public opinion. Should it run foul of this, people can choose, with relative ease, to shop at rival stores. As a result, the company strives to project an image of involvement and support for community projects and good causes. This is true also for HIV/AIDS. Its own company program is, however, noticeably "cheap and cheerful" in comparison with Mineco, Autostar, and Autocircle. While it has an extensive network of some 800 peer educators, more costly interventions such as testing programs are limited and vary between stores while the provision of antiretroviral drugs to employees is limited to a tiny, but highly profiled, scheme.

"Finco," a financial institution with just under 30,000 employees in branches across the country as well as large offices in major urban centers, was the fifth company researched. While similar to other financial institutions in South Africa, Finco differs from the other four companies, notably in the higher levels of education and income, and lower level of unionization, of its employees. In contrast to the other companies, the majority of Finco's workforce is composed of white-collar, often middle-class, workers. This occupation profile is reflected, given the gendered and racial division of labor, in a workforce that is 42 percent white and 64 percent female. Although not all the researched companies had accurate estimates of the HIV-prevalence rates among their employees, Finco had taken part in an industrywide survey that had revealed a rate of around 3 percent (the exact prevalence rates in the companies that participated in this survey have never been publicly released). Such a "good" result, in the context of

South Africa's national prevalence rates, had not been expected and had taken the wind out of the sales of the HIV/AIDS program for a while.

Running an HIV/AIDS program with white-collar workers presents distinct opportunities and challenges. Such workers are easily able to access information for themselves. In Finco, every employee was on a medical aid scheme that gave access to antiretroviral drug treatment should they be HIV-positive. This achievement, proudly related by managers, was, however, only achieved by outsourcing lower-level jobs in the company such as canteen staff and security guards to subcontractors. Such workers remained without health insurance, but had become statistically invisible because they were no longer employees of Finco but of the subcontracting companies. Many middle-class employees assume that they are not at risk of contracting HIV. The problem for the company HIV/AIDS manager and the 450 or so peer educators in Finco was that any reduction of their activities as a result of the industrywide confirmation of low prevalence in the workforce would encourage perceptions that AIDS was not something that employees needed to think about. Peer educators in Finco worked against this perception, but it was often easier for them to promote "secondary awareness" by organizing community-based HIV/AIDS events and mobilizing staff to support AIDS projects in poor communities than directly address employees' own vulnerability to infection.

The South African Response to HIV/AIDS

To understand why these companies initiated peer education programs, we have to take a short detour to discuss the history of HIV/AIDS in South Africa. The first cases of HIV/AIDS in South Africa were in the early 1980s among homosexual men linked into the global network of gay communities. This first wave of the epidemic was overtaken by the late 1980s and early 1990s by a heterosexual epidemic that spread south from Central and East African countries with truck drivers, migrants, and returning exiles (Iliffe 2006). The apartheid state's early attempts to respond shared many of the mistakes of other national responses: limited action, shock tactics, and moral judgments. Additionally, messages from the apartheid government had little credibility among the majority, black population who saw this as another attack on them.

With the end of apartheid and the overwhelming electoral victory of the ANC in 1994, the opportunity to mount a comprehensive and credible response to the epidemic emerged. In 1994, HIV prevalence among pregnant women at state hospitals was around 7 to 8 percent. Despite the difficulties of managing the change of regime, the new government adopted a National AIDS Plan in 1994. This drew on all stakeholders in a comprehensive response to the epidemic (Leclerc-Madlala 2005). However, as Helen Schneider and Joanne Stein (2001) point out, implementation of the plan remained limited. The government's response was characterized alternatively by foot dragging (e.g., its reluctance to provide antiretroviral drugs for HIV-positive pregnant women until forced to do so by court rulings driven by the Treatment Action Campaign) and enthusiastic support for instant solutions (e.g., the Virodene cure that turned out to be little more than an industrial solvent).

A central feature of this confused national response to HIV/AIDS in South Africa has been denial and dissent around AIDS at the very highest levels. South Africa's first democratic president, Nelson Mandela, stated that he did not pay enough attention to AIDS during his five-year presidential term between 1994 and 1999. The dissident views of Thabo Mbeki, Mandela's successor, on HIV/AIDS are well known, if not well understood. While not denying the existence of AIDS, he dissented from the scientific consensus that AIDS results from HIV infection. Rather, Mbeki stressed the role of poverty as the cause of AIDS (rather than it simply increasingly vulnerability to HIV infection) and toyed with theories that antiretroviral drugs are an expensive scam perpetrated by multinational pharmaceutical companies. Many observers believe that Mbeki was reacting to the link made between the epidemic and racial discourses on African sexuality (Gevisser 2007); that is, just when Africans came to power, the epidemic was blamed on black Africans' uncontrollable sexual passions—a demeaning stereotype of Africans deeply embedded in European colonial ideology. Responding within this context, alternative explanations, especially those that promised a quick solution that would allow the new state to get on with its transformation project, were entertained while sobering mainstream explanations of the epidemic were questioned or downplayed.

Although willing to point to the failure of government, other leadership groups such as business, unions, academia, and religious organizations have been slow to fill the gap, in part because government failure has shielded their own inaction over costly or difficult decisions (Cairns, Dickinson, and Orr 2006; Dickinson 2004a). Along with high-level pronouncements often followed by little concrete action, the South African response to the epidemic has been characterized by grassroots activity. This has taken the form of pressure groups, notably the Treatment Action Campaign (TAC); support groups of those infected with the virus; community-based groups and charities providing home-based care for the dying and support for AIDS orphans; the nongovernmental organization (NGO) sector with community programs, often utilizing peer educators; and, as this book outlines, workplace-based responses that are in large part driven by employees.

Business, HIV/AIDS, and Workplace Peer Educators

The HIV/AIDS epidemic impacts South African business in terms of markets, investor confidence, and workforces and the skills they embody (Barnett and Whiteside 2002; Clarke and Strachan 2000; International Labour Organisation [ILO] 2000; Rosen et al. 2000; UNAIDS 2000; Whiteside and Sunter 2000). Despite this, the response of companies has been generally slow (Brink 2003; Dickinson 2004a). There is now widespread workplace responses to HIV/AIDS by large companies (Dickinson and Innes 2004; Dickinson and Stevens 2005), although the response of smaller companies lags behind that of larger corporations (Connelly 2004; South African Business Coalition on HIV/AIDS [SABCOHA] 2002; SABCOHA 2004; Stevens, Weiner, and Mapolisa 2003).

Considerable guidance is available to companies responding to HIV/AIDS, including codes that provide key steps and actions that should be taken (see, e.g., Department of Labour 2000, 2003; ILO 2001). These stress the need for stakeholder commitment to and involvement in drawing up a company's HIV/AIDS policy and implementation plan. Elements of workplace programs that are now standard in larger companies include education and communication, minimizing stigma and discrimination, distribution of condoms, voluntary testing and counseling, wellness programs, access to treatment, and assistance to families and communities.

In reality, while aspiring to conform to "best practice," company programs have often evolved in an ad hoc manner driven by the energy of lower-level champions, on the one side, and constrained by the skepticism of more senior management with a greater focus on production and profit, on the other. The uptake of recommended workplace HIV/AIDS program processes and elements is often selective and partial (Whelan, Dickinson, and Murray 2008). This reflects the very mixed set of economic and social factors pressuring companies to take action on HIV/AIDS (Dickinson and Stevens 2005). Despite this, the response of South African companies to HIV/AIDS is the most advanced internationally, given its position as the first highly industrialized country with high levels of HIV prevalence. Located at the forefront of global experience, the South African corporate response presents opportunities to learn about and improve company HIV/AIDS responses, including workplace peer education.

Workplace peer educators, the protagonists of this book, have become a standard component of company responses to HIV/AIDS in South Africa. Peer education is not confined to workplace HIV/AIDS programs but has been used extensively over a range of issues to educate and assist behavioral change across the globe (Kerrigan and Weiss 2000). The advantage of peer education, which uses peers rather than status-holding professionals, is thought to stem from the "similarity between message source and recipient [that] is vital to the ultimate impact of the message" (Wolf and Bond 2002, 362). However, the way in which peer educators change beliefs and bring about behavioral change remains inadequately understood (Turner and Shepherd 1999).

Large South African workplaces have peer educators operating within their HIV/AIDS programs for a number of reasons. These include enthusiasm from workers to take up this role, belief on the part of HIV/AIDS managers in their value, their availability to HIV/AIDS managers who may be otherwise resource constrained, and their inclusion in best practice guidelines. The South African Department of Labour (2003) recommends a ratio of one peer educator to every fifty workers. (See Table 1 in Appendix 1 for the actual ratio of peer educators to peers in the research companies and Dickinson [2006a] for a discussion of these ratios). If South Africa's formal sector companies (that is companies that largely comply with employment and other regulations and standards) were to follow this guideline, there would be approximately 150,000 peer educators nationwide, probably more than the national count of union shop stewards—in a country that has a union density (including the large but only marginally unionized agricultural and domestic sectors) of between 40 and 50 percent. This statistic alerts us to the significance of workplace peer educators as a response to HIV/AIDS in South Africa or wherever there is significant formal sector employment.

Workplace peer educators are formally positioned within vertically structured communication programs run by HIV/AIDS managers and are expected to give talks or training sessions to coworkers on assigned topics. Additionally, they are usually engaged in extensive horizontal-style communication with peers both inside and outside the workplace—efforts that are often categorized as "informal activity" (Dickinson 2006a). Moreover, as the "Jacks and Jills of all trades" within these programs, peer educators are expected to conduct a range of additional functions—articulated with different degrees of clarity—within company HIV/AIDS initiatives. These include assisting with companywide events, such as voluntary counseling and testing drives; condom distribution; providing a first line of support to coworkers; referring people to occupational health practitioners; and engaging in community projects, generally in the form of visits to institutions or talks to community groups. Workplace peer educators in South Africa are essentially volunteers. At best, there may be some time allocated for their activities with a token stipend provided. Initial training is usually limited, normally, to between two and five days. Previously, they were typically then left to their own devices. Increasingly, however, companies are attempting to organize refresher (or follow-up) training or workshops, set expectations on the activities peer educators should undertake, and require feedback from them.

Within companies, the industrial relations division between management and workers is recognized by the use of peer educators; messages on HIV/AIDS will be more effective if delivered by peers at all levels of the company. In practice, however, there is greater emphasis on employees in lower occupational levels, given the current distribution of the epidemic, and a greater response in taking up peer education among these employees, probably in large part because of the greater visibility of AIDS in their families and communities. This de facto allocation of communication responsibilities acknowledges the reality of differences in workplace status and social identity and means that peer educators work predominantly, from the perspective of management, on the other side of the industrial divide.

This industrial divide extends beyond the workplace. Peer educators do not limit their activity to coworkers, but are active with family, neighbors, churches, youth groups, and anywhere that opportunity for communication arises. But the horizontal division between management and workers, formally recognized by industrial relations practices such as collective bargaining, also divides communities. Workers' families and friends are unlikely to have contact with managers and their relatives outside the workplace. Thus, the social space within which workplace peer educators operate is not limited to companies' workforces but *is* bounded by the divisions of class and race that exist not only within companies but also throughout a society comprised of separate communities.

Despite this extensive arena of action, workplace peer educators have remained largely organized within their individual workplaces. This reflects both a commitment to their companies' HIV/AIDS programs and the value of these programs to peer educators as a platform for activity. While there is a strong desire to link up with peer educators from other companies, peer educators have taken limited steps in this direction. Thus, to date and excluding networks of NGO-organized, community- and faith-based peer educators (Centre for the Support of Peer Education [CSPE] 2008), there is no workplace peer educator movement.

Peer Educators and the AIDS Epidemic: The Quest for Behavioral Change

There are two key ways to bring about change: altering individual behavior and the wholesale transformation of social relationships through collective mobilization. This categorizing of social action in response to HIV/AIDS into individual behavioral change on the one hand and collective action on the other is, of course, a simplification. In reality, a rich spectrum of action including hybrid activities is taking place. Thus, for example, within AIDS campaigns there are often events that draw heavily on "confessional protest" (Young 2002) in which individuals make a public statement of personal responsibility for social ills. In the context of AIDS, this would include candlelit remembrance events for those who have, and who will, die of AIDS. Despite this diversity, this book focuses on the individual-change side of this key dichotomy, where peer educators are attempting to alter the beliefs and behavior of their peers. Collective change, the other side of this dichotomy, is where individuals are mobilized to apply pressure, or *collective action,* on another social agent able to concede procedural or material claims (Kelly 1998; Olson 1965). This latter realm is about changing the system, in favor of those groups able to mobilize their collective power. There is an extensive literature—including industrial relations, political science, development, and social movements—that deals with the question of collective action.

Collective action has been and continues to be relevant to key areas of the epidemic in South Africa. The first area has been access to antiretroviral treatment, achieved in large part by collective mobilization and public pressure driven by the TAC. This campaign has had success in widening access to antiretroviral drugs. Collective action is also clearly appropriate in addressing underlying factors that fuel the epidemic, notably poverty, inequality, and the migrant labor system (Colvin 2000; Hunter 2007; Marks 2002; Nattrass 2004; Shisana et al. 2005). Factors that emerge from the social and economic structure of the country, and indeed the global system, require a response based on collective mobilization to bring about change. To date, responses along these lines have been limited (De Waal 2006).

If there is little sign of structural change in response to HIV/AIDS, then the limits to individual volition in avoiding HIV infection within a life shaped by want, powerlessness, and social disruption need to be recognized (Parker 2004). Nevertheless, the AIDS epidemic demands, with extraordinary clarity, that individual behavioral change is necessary for survival. Central to this is behavior that prevents HIV infection, such as practicing safe sex on a consistent basis and reducing the number of sexual partners. Changes in individual behavior are also necessary for HIV testing to take place and for the accessing of treatment. A critical point made in this book is that *behavioral change requires that the epidemic be "normalized."* By this I do not mean that we accept infection and premature death as the norm. Rather, I refer to the normalization of HIV and AIDS as an ordinary topic of conversation in intimate spaces. That discussion needs to be taking place in intimate, rather than public, space needs to be emphasized. All too often, there is a public discourse on AIDS that bears little if any resemblance to what goes on backstage, in people's daily lives. Yet, such backstage normalization is central to defeating AIDS.

To argue that success against AIDS is not possible until we end poverty, inequality, and the mass disruption of personal relationships—in other words, until we change the social system—has great merit, but also significant dangers. This argument overlooks the fact that individual behavioral change will not be automatic even within a reformed system. More pressing, the response to HIV and AIDS cannot wait while utopia is built.

Collective action can have little impact on these basic behavioral practices. Neither marches nor petitions nor legal reform can ensure that people will use condoms. Testing and even treatment can be made compulsory, a collective response enforced by legislation, but the dangers of such approaches are generally deemed to outweigh the benefits. Such a decision may come from weighing human rights implications against the value of enforced public health measures. Alternatively, the same decision can be reached within a public health paradigm where there is a danger of compulsory measures increasing stigma and driving the disease underground. Attitudes are not something that can be easily legislated. Given this, there is a need for us to better understand and support individual behavioral change processes.

Our understandings of how individuals change is heavily influenced by diffusion theory. This field of study, which owes much to Everett Rogers (1962, 2003), who generalized diffusion theory from his own work in the 1950s on the adoption of agricultural technologies, such as new seed varieties, by American farmers. Rogers seeks to explain how new ideas are incorporated into people's repertoires of action. In the first edition of his textbook (1962), Rogers draws on 500 publications reporting on the diffusion of innovations; the fifth edition (2003) draws on over 5,000. These publications cover a wide range of innovations including, but not limited to, the adoption of technologies in manufacturing, agriculture, transport and communication; new ideas about teaching; new products and services; and a range of health-promoting behaviors, including diet, drug use, vaccinations, family planning, and AIDS prevention.

Distilled from this data is a model of how "an innovation is communicated though certain channels over time among members of a social system" (Rogers 2003, 11). Four elements are analyzed: (1) the innovation, (2) its communication, (3) the social system in which it is diffused, and (4) the time it takes to do this. Rogers' classic diffusion model is vertical in nature, with change agents or experts at the top of a hierarchy of actors who conceive or develop new innovations and who are "usually professionals with a university degree in a technical field" (2003, 28). The observable patterns of innovation adoption within a community reveal patterns of influence, which may well be different from the community's formal political or social structures. On this basis, individuals can be categorized along a scale of innovation adoption from the early to the late. Plotted on a graph, this produces an S-shaped curve that, Rogers argues, is common across the adoption of innovations. Initially, only a few bold and more far-sighted individuals experiment with the innovation. When its success is demonstrated—the *threshold level*—there is an acceleration of adoption within the community and, finally, the traditionalist holdouts come on board, completing the innovation's adoption.

Turning his attention to how to expedite the process of innovation adoption, Rogers (2003, 369) puts forward the following seven steps: (1) developing a need for change among community members, (2) exchanging information, (3) getting community members to understand the problem (of not adopting), (4) creating the intent to change, (5) translating intent into action by adopting the innovation, (6) stabilizing the new behavior, and (7) with mission accomplished, exiting the relationship.

A key challenge to successfully and rapidly achieving diffusion is a lack of similarity between the initiating expert and the intended beneficiaries of the innovation, affecting the second, third, and fourth step in particular. Rogers (2003, 302) states that "the exchange of ideas occurs most frequently between individuals who are alike." Consequently, it is necessary to overcome barriers of difference. This can be achieved either by experts winning over opinion leaders within the target community or by recruiting "change agent aides" who are similar to members of the target community and whose role is to "spread the word." Rogers argues that such agents—in this case, peer educators—are able to bridge the gap between otherwise very different innovator and potential beneficiaries.

HIV/AIDS campaigns have drawn on diffusion theory. Notable examples have included the STOP AIDS project among gay men in San Francisco (Singhal and Rogers 2003; Wohlfeiler 1997) and its extension as a randomized controlled intervention in a number of U.S. cities (Kelly et al. 1997). Despite measured success (in decreasing unprotected anal intercourse and the increased use of condoms), little is known about why it worked. What is clear is what the opinion leaders (peer educators) recruited into the intervention were asked to do. What is less clear is what actually took place to bring about the recorded changes. This reflects the emphasis, within diffusion theory, on mapping the path, rather than process, of diffusion. Glenn Turner and Johnathan Shepherd's (1999) attempt to link claims for peer education to theory comes, in part, from their own research that initiated and ran a peer-led HIV prevention project with young gay and bisexual men in the United Kingdom (Shepherd, Weare, and Turner 1997). They noted that "studies . . . in which peer educators 'seek out' people and conduct conversations on safer sex with them, have tended to place greater emphasis on the measurement of outcomes and have failed to identify the effective processes associated with these interventions" (205).

Thus, what remains largely unknown is exactly how people change their beliefs and behaviors. This is not because we do not have theories that outline how this process should happen. We do. And Roger's seven-step process is only one of many variations. These theories are generally rooted in transferring of information that will, via some internal algorithm, tip the balance in an individual's decision-making process so that that individual will follow through with behavioral change. The problem with such theories, demonstrated again in the failure to stem HIV infections in southern Africa, is that they don't work in practice. Which does not stop them being trotted out on a regular basis. Many peer educator manuals have a section comprised of potted accounts of theories of behavioral change. Rarely do they attempt to link these theories to how peer educators should work. Instead, the more thoughtful ones focus on how peer educators can improve formal educational activity. Less thoughtfully, some simply lay out the content that they expect peer educators to communicate.

There is an important point here. Daniel Low-Beer and Rand Stoneburner (2003, 2004) and Warren Parker (2004) among others argue that vertical communication is of limited value and we need to understand how horizontal processes of communication can bring about behavioral change. If they are right, then we are currently doing peer educators a disservice. First, we do not have a clear theory as to how behavior is changed. Second, while failing to fully acknowledge this, we do our best to make peer educators better at formal teaching in classroom situations or just ply them with reams of information. That is, we ask them to participate in and to replicate vertical communication methods. Third, despite only weak links among what might bring about behavioral change, their training, and their prescribed activities, we then evaluate their effectiveness and pass judgment.

Those explicitly or implicitly arguing for and implementing vertical communication strategies believe that peer educators are valuable because they are able to transmit messages conceived by experts. Those operating such interventions also surmise that the chosen target audience will then make appropriate decisions based purely on the logic of the messages, as understood by these experts, that the peer educators have introduced on their behalf.

Largely outside the field of health, there has been increasing interest in participatory, rather than top-down, development processes. The value of drawing on peoples' knowledge of their own situation, through "participatory rural [development] appraisal" is now widely recognized (Chambers 1994) and forms a standard tool for organizations such as the World Bank (1996). Tapping the knowledge of those whom we seek to work with should be a "no-brainer," though as Robert Chambers (1994) outlines, each generation of [university-trained] researchers seem to need to rediscover this for themselves. This book draws heavily on what participants, in this case peer educators, know about their own situation.

Beyond tapping the locals for knowledge, there is the question as to how participation can empower communities (Mayo and Craig 1995), since "participatory approaches [to development] do not necessarily seek emancipation or empowerment" (Laverack and Wallerstein 2001, 182). While those concerned with empowering communities recognized the importance of both individuals and collectives, the emphasis on individual empowerment is as a stepping-stone to community mobilization and collective action (Laverack and Wallerstein 2001; Labonte 1994). Thus, the UNDP's Human Development Report *People's Participation* (United Nations Development Programme 1993, 21) argues that, "the important thing is that people have constant access to decision-making power... People can participate as individuals or as groups... Often, however, they participate more effectively through group action—as members of a community organization, perhaps, or a trade union or a political party." Not infrequently, community empowerment is rendered down solely to its "ability to take collective action" (Williams, Labonte, and O'Brian 2003, 35). Falling back on the certainties of collective action as a means of empowerment occurs even when addressing intimate questions of sexual health (see Gordon 1995).

This book avoids gliding over the importance of individuals' behavior, how this is constructed and constrained, and how it can be changed. Collective action, alone, is inappropriate for the problem. Rather, what is explored in this book concerns horizontal communication processes and the argument that the value of peer educators lies not in their ability to take collective action (which is limited), nor in their activity as translators of expert messages within vertical communication programs. Rather, the value of peer educators is as protagonists in a struggle over the construction of belief in their communities. Success in this enterprise will be achieved by a reconfiguration of beliefs not predetermined by expert opinion but rather through an embedded process of interaction that provides a genuine platform for behavioral change. This book describes and theorizes these processes undertaken by HIV/AIDS workplace peer educators in South Africa.

Background to the Research

This book draws on six years of research into workplace response to HIV/AIDS in South Africa. In addition to a survey of twenty-eight large companies, I conducted a number of case-based research projects involving a total of eleven companies. The companies represent a wide range of economic sectors and were mainly large operations (see Table 2 in Appendix 1). The principle methodologies used in the research were questionnaires, interviews, participatory observation, and research diaries kept by peer educators. The research began broadly, by pursuing wide-ranging questions across the scope of existing (but often new) company HIV/AIDS programs. At the time, there was little independent analysis of these programs, and one key objective was to map out company programs and assess how these operated. This often produced a different picture from those optimistically put forward by managers. While doing this, it was also possible to capture the processes by which programs were emerging within companies. This earlier phase of the research underpins key sections of Chapter 2, which describes the company context within which workplace peer education typically operates.

Later my research increasingly focused on peer educators. I first interviewed rank-and-file peer educators during research projects conducted during 2003 and 2004. Only in 2005 and 2006 did I focus exclusively on peer education in Mineco, Autocircle, Autostar, Bestbuyco, and Finco. I focused on one component of workplaces responses to HIV/AIDS—peer education—for several reasons. Reviewing company responses to HIV/AIDS was becoming repetitive, and it was frustrating not to be able to go deeper into some of the issues that constituted these responses. There were, however, many choices for specialization. These included (and remain) the uptake of testing, treatment programs, stigma, extension into communities, migrant labor, occupational health practitioners, and union responses. Of course, none of these areas of specialization can be studied or understood properly in isolation from the others. While focusing on peer educators, this book necessarily touches on and refers to many of these other aspects of workplace responses. In this regard, the earlier, more holistic research is of value beyond being able to paint a realistic background to workplace peer education. Appendix 2 gives more detail on fieldwork methods used for the research that this book is based on.

My decision to study peer educators, rather than other equally interesting options, was driven by my admiration for what peer educators were trying to achieve. I had begun to appreciate just how important—and complex—their labor of love, for that is what it is, might be. It was also driven by a continued desire to know "what was really happening." The clearest signs pointed down the company hierarchy, and I headed in that direction. When it comes to peer education, peer educators themselves are the most obvious source of knowledge and understanding. This book seeks, though evidence-based or phenomenological research, to explain the actual practice of workplace peer education in South Africa.

An Outline of the Book: The Key Arguments

Following this introduction, Chapter 2 examines why companies are responding to the AIDS epidemic. Given that AIDS forms a core business issue only for specialized industries, primarily those involved in health and death, the fact that South African companies across the economic spectrum are responding to HIV/AIDS requires explanation. Of course, one can explain this response simply by pointing to the magnitude of the epidemic and its impact among people of working age. One view of company HIV/AIDS programs is that they are rational economic responses that seek to protect and prolong the lives of employees. While this understanding has some validity, high levels of unemployment and the current concentration of the epidemic among lower-skilled sections of the workforce means that company-level, cost-benefit calculations rarely propel AIDS programs into the boardroom. Despite this, wider implications—including market growth, expenditure shifting, social stability, and the country's international image—along with pressure from internal and external stakeholders exposed to the human rather than economic impact of AIDS, mean that companies have had little choice but to respond, or at least be seen to do so.

The complex set of forces that has compelled companies to implement HIV/AIDS programs also helps explain the nature of these programs, which are often run with limited resources largely outside of companies' key reporting lines. Chapter 2 illustrates this by examining how an HIV/AIDS program in a large South African company was established. As we shall see, it was initiated largely as the result of activism on the part of lower-level managers, occupational health practitioners, and rank-and-file employees.

Limited leadership and resources from senior management helps clarify why workplace peer education, while formally part of company HIV/AIDS programs, is better understood as a response from below. What drives most peer educators has little to do with concern for the company as a commercial operation; it is, as one peer educator put it, "for the love of people." Chapter 3 looks at workplace HIV/AIDS peer educators and the activities that they undertake. As a result of motivations that are often intense and personal, such as seeing family members die of AIDS, peer educators' activity tends to be extensive, energetic, and wide-ranging in nature. It also takes place in different settings with a high proportion of activity conducted outside the workplace, in families, churches, and other community locations. This indicates that, while peer educators may be anchored within a company setting that provides them with training and other resources, they are active in all facets of their lives rather than limiting themselves to the workplace.

One of the most fluid elements of peer educators' work is informal activity, which, while taking a wide range of forms, is characterized by raising awareness; giving information, advice, and support; and setting an appropriate example on HIV/AIDS issues within everyday contexts. Thus, for example, informal activity can include a quiet chat with a coworker during the lunch break, drawing attention to a television program on HIV/AIDS in conversation with friends, or providing a model of values and behavior as the coach of a boys' football club. It is not always easy to separate formal from informal activity, as private interactions spin out from public activity. Despite this linkage between formal and informal activity, the latter can usually be distinguished from the former by its more casual, low-profile, and often intimate formats.

Informal activity by peer educators can be understood within the paradigms of both vertical and horizontal communication processes. From the perspective of a vertical HIV/AIDS communication strategy, in which experts are attempting to impart information to targeted audiences, informal activity on the part of peer educators can serve as a valuable means by which information is reinforced, clarified, or elaborated in ways that are not easy within the formal and public context of a presentation.

However, the thrust of the research findings reported in Chapter 3 indicates that informal activity is best understood as a horizontal, rather than vertical, process of communication in which peer educators are engaged in ongoing dialogues with peers. Such as when members of a workplace peer educator group responded to an encounter with a new AIDS myth—that HIV-positive people on antiretroviral treatment need not use condoms. The peer educator who initially heard the story from a coworker immediately brought in another peer educator to quickly rebut the myth. The incident was then raised at a peer educators' meeting, where it was confirmed that this had not been an isolated incident. There and then, an easily understood parable to counter the myth was developed in the local vernacular (Setswana), and it was agreed that each peer educator would use this parable should they encounter the myth in the future. This process rested on expert-generated information (that HIV-positive individuals on antiretroviral treatment should continue to use condoms), but in its specific formulation and enactment, this response was entirely autonomous of the company's HIV/AIDS management structures or even the occupational nurses who were based in an adjacent building.

Since communication must play a role in effective prevention strategies, the informal work of peer education merits attention. This book focuses on the informal activity—of horizontal communication—between peers because this emerges as a difficult and far-from-natural process despite peer educators' advantages of similarity and familiarity. Almost every peer educator whom I interviewed expressed how difficult it is to change people's behavior. Some then indicated that, having provided information on HIV/AIDS to their peers, the onus lay with each individual to make their own choices. But many peer educators were utilizing a range of lay theories and practices to reach out to peers in ways that they hoped would promote behavioral change. Sometimes these theories and practices were sophisticated. For example, some used various tactics to ensure that, despite the need to be proactive with peers, they were not labeled as the "AIDS Lady" or "Mr. Condom," which they felt would allow peers to discount their inputs as arising from vested interests or fanaticism. Since they engaged with peers on an ongoing basis, these theories and practices are evaluated and adapted on a trial-and-error basis. What might, from a distance, appear to be a natural and easy process of horizontal communication between peers is, in fact, something that is challenging and requires considerable effort.

Chapters 4 and 5 build on this recognition to explore the environment in which peer educators operate and what informal activity tells us about horizontal communication processes that seek to change beliefs and behavior around HIV/AIDS. The environment in which peer educators work is illustrated in Chapter 4, focusing on issues of gender, race, and belief in traditional healing. Gender, race, and belief in traditional healing all make it difficult for peer educators to convince those they work with of key messages around HIV/AIDS. Age and different generational values also complicate communication, while religious belief systems make diverse claims over almost every aspect of HIV and AIDS. But gender, race, and belief in traditional healing illustrate some of the core problems faced by peer educators as they conduct horizontal communication.

Taking into account this complex ordering of social space within which horizontal communication takes place, Chapter 5 describes peer educators' modus operandi. This is done by using and elaborating on sociologist Erving Goffman's (1958) dramatic conceptualization of social interaction. In short, this consists of formal, front-stage interactions between different individuals and groups, and more relaxed backstage interactions between those sharing similar social positions. Many managers and other observers recognize that highly ritualized and highly charged front-stage interactions that typify industrial relations between management and workers make it difficult to convey important messages about HIV/AIDS. They value peer educators because they can move into backstage spaces both inside the workplace and in the community. They do not, however, recognize the complexity of this backstage work. When it comes to HIV/AIDS as well as many other behavioral change initiatives, backstage social order and its social rules also present barriers to peer education—barriers that we will explore.

Gender differences that occur in all sexually mixed social spaces make peer education work difficult. Janet Bujra (2006) describes how in the smallest backstage space of all—the couple—the micro politics of sex are linked directly to the power relations of gender that are referenced to wider social values. Thus, for example, peer educators dealing with a peer's concern over condoms bursting during intercourse with her husband may realize that this is not about the quality of the condoms but about a lack of sexual foreplay and the woman still being dry when intercourse begins. Typically in South Africa, a woman is unable to raise this, or other, sexual issues with her partner (Abdool Karim et al. 1994; Klugman 2000; Newmann et al. 2000), let alone reveal that she has discussed it, and possible solutions, with somebody else—especially if the somebody else is male. Consequently, in such situations the peer and peer educator need to work around the central issue of gender relationships and acceptable intergender communication to find a way of innocuously introducing lubrication and avoiding burst condoms, even if nothing more fundamental changes.

While gender relationships are present in the backstage spaces of both workers and management, race sharply aligns with and is often a key marker of the industrial relations and social divisions in South Africa. In this situation, it could be assumed that, in contrast to gender, the racial status of peer educators allows unproblematic access to peers given their similarity. Given the legacies of racial division and conflict, however, racial similarity allows deflection of any need to change behavior and can result in problems being externalized. Although there can be variations, the standard pattern for this externalization is for whites to see AIDS as a problem of blacks, and blacks to see AIDS as a problem to which whites are indifferent or even instigator. The limited visibility of white peer educators, an issue described in Chapter 3, is both a symptom and driver of these socially constructed explanations of the epidemic. For whites, the lack of white peer educators confirms that the epidemic does not affect them and that blacks have brought it among themselves through promiscuity. For blacks, whites' absence in peer education programs indicates that they are happy to see blacks die or indeed are behind the epidemic in some way. On the issue of race, front-stage social cleavages undermine the value of similarity for HIV/AIDS peer educators. Increasing the number and visibility of white peer educators is a structural response that would help. Nonetheless, for our purposes we need to accept that a backstage space without racial difference may still be a difficult space for HIV/AIDS peer educators to work. Their often-unwelcome messages of the need for personal change can be swiftly undercut, and their own credibility as peers questioned, by easy and more palatable explanations of the epidemic in which someone else is responsible. These explanations often resonate with what appears to be common sense in a racially divided country.

While race is immediately visible, a belief in traditional values, including healing, is more difficult to see. Among whites, traditional healing effectively does not exist (though the use of other alternative health systems is widespread). Among Africans, the existence of traditional healing is very real and highly controversial; there are believers, opponents, and many shades in between. There is an ongoing cultural war over traditional beliefs within the African population that divides communities, families, and, indeed, peer educators. Traditional healing is not simply an alternative to Western medicine but part of a cosmology of traditional belief. The failure of Western medicine to decisively demonstrate superiority over AIDS means that the disease has become an important front in this struggle between Western and traditional values. The peer educator, operating at least formally within the company's HIV/AIDS program and putting forward explanations of HIV/AIDS drawn from Western medicine, steps directly into these conflicts.

Given that backstage spaces are far from relaxed when issues around HIV/AIDS are raised, peer educators must sometimes remove themselves and peers from these constraints. They do this by "slipping out of order" and creating a space that is at least temporarily insulated against social pressures. The peer educator must take into this space not only the interests of the peer but also an awareness of external constraints that the peer faces. The space must be private and there must be guaranteed confidentiality. Without these conditions, honest conversation is not possible. Slipping out of order can only be of limited duration; both peer and peer educator must return to their everyday lives. Slipping out of order, and the necessity of returning, can take place in many different ways. One illustration comes from David Abrams, a peer educator working as a uniform clerk in a large supermarket, whose office provided confidentiality for those seeking information on HIV/AIDS. As he explained, "they say 'yes' they need to see me about uniforms, but [once the door is closed] it's about this sickness. Then there is talk, then tears, then more talk." Often the talk was about a family member; at other times, it was about the worker's own HIV status. These confidential talks sometimes resulted in decisions by peers to test for HIV and a request that Abrams accompany them during the procedure. This Abrams did, recognizing the fear and stigma around HIV/AIDS and his own position as a peer educator, by "going to check the post box" and then meeting up with them at the local clinic.

Slipping out of order is a form of liminality (Turner 1974) in which normal social rules are relaxed. The periods of collective liminality described by Turner allow new social formulations to be reached. However, the steps out of order described in this book are individualized, filled with realism, often emotionally stressful, and must conclude with pragmatic, sometimes devious strategies that equip peers to deal with social relationships that have not been altered while they have been out of order.

Conceived within this model of social space, peer educators are bona fide members of backstage spaces to which nonpeers or experts do not have access. Yet they need to operate out of order since the backstage spaces of workmates, friends, and family do not provide an intimacy to discuss HIV and AIDS openly or honestly. The achievements originating out of order are often small. In part this is because a plurality of interests interlock to form a system of values, status, and material interests that are invested in particular ordering of backstage space. Given this, some peer educators have come to realize that they need to move beyond the limits of working out of order if they are to accelerate more widespread behavioral change.

The problem of interlocking beliefs, the constraints these place on individuals' ability to change their behavior, and peer educators' evolving attempts to overcome these is the subject of Chapter 6. From the perspective of some peer educators, their work needs to expand from dealing with individuals to the varied social institutions that construct belief. By "turning" these institutions so that they incorporate concerns over HIV/AIDS, they will increasingly "speak with one voice" and reduce the psychological escape routes for peers who would rather not confront difficult issues of personal behavioral change.

This task is illustrated by examining the relationship of South African trade unions with peer educators. Unions are primarily concerned with the central front-stage industrial relations conflict between their members and management. Given the burden of the AIDS epidemic, we might expect unions, especially those representing African workers, to be at the forefront of dealing with AIDS and closely allied, if not seeking to lead, peer education. This has not been the case, and unions' failure to add their voice means that peer educators—fully cognizant of the importance of unions in constructing the belief of many of their peers—need to work to bring unions around. In addressing why unions have not responded as might be expected and why peer educators have to expand their work into bringing unions into an alliance, two issues are explored.

The first returns us to the issue of contested backstage order. What emerges is that unions concerned with front-stage conflicts do not welcome the backstage chaos that confronting AIDS threatens to unleash. Marshaling power is as much about suppressing internal divisions as it is about confronting an external opponent. Beyond passing pro forma resolutions, responding to AIDS means opening up suppressed divisions within trade unions' constituencies. Issues of gender and traditional beliefs are two of the most obvious fault lines that would threaten rank-and-file unity. The second issue returns us to another central concern of this book—the question of individual behavioral change and collective action to change structural constraints. Unions are organizations based on the principles of collective action. With this in mind, it is perhaps obvious that they have struggled to understand and to work with peer educators whose focus is the individual. These two issues help illustrate the challenge facing peer educators in trying to harmonize the voices of other social institutions around AIDS, such as traditional healers and churches.

The final chapter summarizes what we have learned from the quest of workplace peer educators to change behavior. Their activities point us toward a new way of thinking about behavior and how it can be modified. For experts, looking always from the outside, the challenges peer educators are responding to are difficult to see. Grasping what peer educators are doing, and why, will assist us more than a plethora of studies conceived in centers of expertise and administered on study populations. Whatever we can learn about changing behavior is of immense importance in efforts to bring the AIDS epidemic to heel. What HIV/AIDS peer educators in South African companies are demonstrating is of value in changing behavior in other societies grappling with HIV/AIDS and in understanding how to alter other behaviors that compromise our health and limit the full potential of our lives.

2

"People Are Dying, but They Don't Listen When We Tell Them"

The Corporate Response to HIV/AIDS in South Africa

Many outside of South Africa may be puzzled that businesses that are not in health care are responding to the AIDS epidemic. Why are South African businesses—slowly at first and now more visibly—responding to the problem of HIV/AIDS, and how is that response unfolding?

When questioned, many company managers and management consultants initially offer an economic rationale. Since HIV/AIDS primarily affects those of working age, it makes business sense to prevent HIV infection of workers and ensure, through the use of antiretroviral drugs, that those already infected continue working so that companies don't lose labor, accumulated skills, and experience. In this view, a cost-benefit analysis should demonstrate the financial value to a company of mounting HIV/AIDS programs. Yet, the business case for aggressively responding to HIV/AIDS in South Africa is not compelling—at least not yet.

Expanding cost-benefit calculations from the level of individual companies to the national economy provides another possible explanation for business's desire to counter the epidemic. In this scenario, the macroeconomic implications of the epidemic distinguish it from other diseases and have prompted private-sector action aimed at staving off macroeconomic decline or even collapse; businesses are voluntarily putting their shoulder to the wheel now to avoid economic catastrophe later. However, studies predict only marginal declines in gross domestic product (GDP) growth as a result of the disease within South Africa.[1] Moreover, as described in this chapter, company responses don't look, smell, or feel as though corporate South Africa is throwing its resources at HIV/AIDS in either a patriotic or far-sighted attempt to mitigate the epidemic's national impact.[2]

Rather, just as social activists have spawned a corporate social responsibility movement and mobilized public pressure to address a variety of social issues, company managers in South Africa have responded to pressures to do something about HIV/AIDS. If they are responding to the human

1. While some studies indicate a loss of GDP growth due to AIDS (e.g., ING Barings 2000), the overall consensus is that "there is currently no clear evidence of the actual economic impact of HIV/AIDS in South Africa" (South African National AIDS Committee [SANAC] 2007). Nevertheless, there remains uncertainty over the long-term economic impact. As Pieter Fourie (2007, 293) puts it, "Macroeconomic models focus on the size of economies and tend to neglect changes in the overall long-term structures of economies—not because of a weakness inherent of the discipline; the reality is that economists (like all AIDS analysts) simply do not have any clear understanding of how AIDS is impacting on the systemic variables that drive patterns and events in various societies." What is certain is that at the household level, the advent of AIDS in a family member frequently has catastrophic implications for household welfare (Desmond, Michael, and Gow 2000).

2. Two additional arguments seeking to explain why companies are responding to HIV/AIDS in South Africa can be put forward. First, that health and safety legislation (the origins of which may lie in social pressures) mean that occupational diseases, or diseases that affect safety, need to be responded to by business. HIV/AIDS does have implications for workplace health and safety, but generally only in specialized working environments such as hospitals where needle-stick injuries present an occupationally related danger of HIV infection. While health and safety structures are sometimes used as a vehicle for HIV/AIDS programs, it is not because of health and safety concerns that South African companies are responding to HIV/AIDS.

Second, many companies, especially larger ones, already make health-related interventions beyond that required by health and safety legislation. These take the forms of subsidized health insurance schemes, the provision of primary health care by company occupational health practitioners, and wellness programs. Such interventions may be the result of union pressure for employee benefits and social protection, recruitment competition, or arguments that a healthy workforce is more productive and that such interventions make business sense. The advent of HIV/AIDS has impacted on such interventions and has often been a stimulus for their expansion. Moreover, the structures responsible for company-based health systems form part of most companies' response to HIV/AIDS. However, to argue that company HIV/AIDS responses have resulted from such structures would, as illustrated in this chapter, be a misrepresentation.

suffering that the AIDS epidemic inflicts, it is because they have been forced to do so by internal and external pressures.

An Overview of Business, Labor, and the Economy

South Africa, with a population approaching fifty million is a middle-income, developing country. Historically, the powerhouse of the economy has been the mining industry, which started with the discovery of diamonds in Kimberly in 1867 and gold in Johannesburg in 1886. Gold and diamonds continue to be mined along with coal, platinum, and a range of other minerals. A few mining houses, loosely federated in the Chamber of Mines, have dominated the mining industry. Standing head and shoulders above them all for many years were the linked giants of Anglo American Corporation and De Beers. Restricted from investing overseas by anti-apartheid sanctions (and apartheid legislation), the mining houses diversified into massive industrial conglomerates that contributed to the creation of a large manufacturing sector. Alongside mining and manufacturing, agriculture has historically been a major sector of the economy. Like mining, agriculture has operated on a low-skilled labor-intensive basis. More recently, with the decline of all three of these sectors as job creators, the service sector—including South Africa's advanced financial institutions—has become the largest provider of employment. This service sector also includes over a million domestic workers working in the houses and gardens of the country's richer citizens.

Industrialization in South Africa was consciously promoted by the apartheid state, partly though the creation of a number of "parastatal" companies that were owned, but not directly run, by the state. These included the electricity company Eskom, the Iscor steel company, and Sasol, which converted coal to petrol in part to provide energy independence for a country that has few reserves of oil or gas but massive coal fields.

Many foreign companies set up shop in South Africa's growing economy—Unilever, Ford, Volkswagen, and the General Electric Corporation (GEC) among them. However, as the apartheid regime came under increasing international pressure, so too did these companies. A number disinvested—often a process of selling out to a domestic companies. Since the end of apartheid most have returned, and while the South African market is small by global standards, a base in South Africa that doubles up as a gateway to the southern African region is an important component of many companies' global strategies. In a reverse process, most of South Africa's conglomerates have been broken up into their component industries some of which, such as AngloGold Ashanti, the paper company Mondi, and South African Breweries (SABMiller) (all emerging from the Anglo American Corporation) have pursued their own aggressive globalization strategies.

The development of the South African economy has been integrally linked to policies of racial domination—that long predate the election, by an almost exclusively white electorate, of the National Party government in 1948 on a platform of apartheid (separate, racial, development). Many components of the apartheid economy were developed by the mining industry. Critical among this was the use of Africans as low-skilled, low-paid laborers while more skilled and better-paid jobs were reserved for whites. The migrant labor system also perpetuated low wages by separating economic and social reproduction. By relegating Africans to homelands, or drawing them from parts of Africa, to which they had to return once their employment contracts were over, employers and the state did not have to take responsibility for the true costs of maintaining a labor force. While working on the mines, Africans were accommodated in huge single-sex hostels while their wives and families remained in foreign countries or apartheid homelands that carried the costs of raising and caring for families.

The Group Areas Act, which legislated who could live where (down to the smallest detail), supported this system of labor migration between rural and urban/industrial areas. However, the development of manufacturing industries, requiring higher-skilled workers, created the need for more permanent settled labor. Townships or "locations" housed this workforce in vast developments of cheaply built houses—to which tenants added numerous shacks. South African cities came to represent a microcosm of the apartheid system. Whites lived in well-serviced leafy suburbs around the city center while Africans—or in the Western Cape, coloreds—lived in dusty neglected townships connected to factories (for company employees) and the town (for domestic workers) by railways or roads by which Africans commuted daily. Suburbs and townships were kept apart by industrial zones acting as buffers, by natural features such as valleys, or simply by being built miles apart.

The urbanization of Africans was a reluctant concession on the part of the custodians of apartheid—and with good reason. It was from the ranks of the growing black urban workforce that South Africa's powerful independent trade union movement emerged in the early 1970s. By the end of the decade, despite resistance, the power of the black unions was acknowledged with their incorporation into the industrial relations system of collective bargaining, which had previously been reserved for white workers. The most powerful grouping within this surge of black unionization was the socialist Congress of South African Trade Unions (COSATU) federation that aligned itself with the exiled African National Congress (ANC) and the South African Communist Party (SACP). By the 1990s some 50 percent of workers in South Africa were unionized.

In many ways the granting of African, colored, and Indian workers "industrial citizenship" by permitting their unions to bargain with management prefigured the wider processes of democratic change that would come to a head with the overwhelming election of the ANC in the first democratic elections of 1994. A raft of new labor legislation was promulgated by the new ANC government with the intention of rectifying workplace inequality and exploitation. The Labour Relations Act established rights for trade unions and, along with the Basic Conditions of Employment Act, working conditions for individual workers. The Skills Development Act sought to redress the country's massive skills shortage, something that was integrally linked to racially allocated education and job reservation for whites. Finally, the Employment Equity Act established a system of monitoring and processes by which companies were expected to deracialize workplaces.

This raft of new laws represented a decisive shift in the relationship between business and labor in comparison to previous legislation that allowed white-owned businesses, with the compliance of white unions, to keep blacks, and Africans especially, economically subservient. In shifting this balance, great efforts were made to implement these changes in an orderly and consensual way. The newly created National Economic, Development and Labour Council (NEDLAC) was made up of equal representation from government, labor, and business, and all labor legislation had to be approved by NEDLAC before being ratified by parliament.

Despite this institutional ability to influence new labor laws, business was in a precarious position after the fall of apartheid. Other than a few tentative discussions with the ANC in exile, it had gone along with the apartheid regime. South Africa's Truth and Reconciliation Commission (1998, 4:58) concluded that, "Business was central to the economy that sustained the South African state during the apartheid years.... Most businesses benefited from operating in a racially structured context." Given this, business chose not to confront new labor legislation head on. Recognizing the increased costs that this legislation represented, it sought to maintain profitability by moving to more capital- (and less labor-) intensive processes.

The resulting shedding of jobs in a country with a still-growing population has kept union power in check and produced mass unemployment. Between 1995 and 1999 unemployment (using the expanded definition) rose from 27 to 36 percent (Stats South Africa 2002) These figures, however, hide wide discrepancies: Those with less education and training are more vulnerable to unemployment. In practice, given the enduring legacies of apartheid's racially separated schooling systems, this means blacks in general and Africans in particular. By contrast, at the high end of the skills market there are chronic shortages—something that supports continued wage inequality in one of the worlds' most unequal nations. The plight of the unemployed is, however, mitigated by two factors. The first is extensive informal economic activity, such as hawking goods at street corners, that provides survival incomes for those without work. Additionally, the ANC government has extended the country's social security system. While this remains far from comprehensive, social grants for pensioners, the disabled, and children provides much-needed cash for many poor families that would otherwise face starvation.

In addition to the capitalization of production, business has resorted to the extensive use of temporary contract workers to combat the increased cost of labor. While labor legislation provided standards and protection for employees of the company, this can be circumvented by the use of labor brokers who create "triangular employment relationships." The labor broker is the employer of the worker. These brokers provide a labor service (via a commercial contract) to the company, and the contract worker provides labor to a company of which they are not an employee. The use of such arrangements confuses the lines of the employment contract and increases the vulnerability of workers. Despite efforts by the Department of Labour to close the loopholes that allow this practice, the rise of labor brokering has resulted in a two-tier labor market: company employees, usually unionized and enjoying relative security and a range of benefits and unorganized contract workers employed by labor brokers, who receive lower wages and few, if any, benefits.

The government has had to walk something of a tightrope in regard to labor market policy. On the one hand, the bulk of the ANC's electoral support comes from workers and their families. On the other hand, as the ruling party its fortunes are tied up with the South African economy. Thus, pro-labor legislation has gone along with an otherwise pro-business ideology. The rise of a small number of African business barons along with attempts to open economic opportunities to the previously disadvantaged through Black Economic Empowerment legislation is beginning to produce a change in the racial composition of management and ownership in the private sector. As much as the speed of this black economic empowerment should not be overestimated, it raises the question of whether class tensions will start to dominate over race politics in South Africa. There may be some truth in the idea that class will start to trump race, but what it overlooks is the demographics of the country. Although South Africa's business class may be starting to take on a multiracial complexion, South Africa's working class remains, and will largely remain, African.

The Corporate Response to HIV/AIDS

The earliest company response to HIV/AIDS was in the mining industry, which, in 1986 discovered 4 percent HIV prevalence rates among Malawian migrant workers. The Chamber of Mines' reaction was that "no known carriers [of HIV] will be engaged [i.e. employed] [and] all recruits from high risk areas will be tested at [the] source [of recruitment]" (Brink and Clausen 1987, 15). The union argued against pre-employment testing for HIV and eventually won an agreement with the Chamber of Mines to this effect. However, the Chamber rapidly scaled back the recruitment of Malawians (Campbell and Williams 1999). Such pre-employment testing (or profiling and avoidance of high-prevalence groups) was designed to minimize companies' risk and did nothing constructive to respond to the epidemic.

Outside the mining industry the first major company to deal with disease was Eskom, the state-owned electricity corporation, which adopted an HIV/AIDS policy in 1988. Until 1993 Eskom conducted pre-employment testing for HIV (Department of Health 1999; New Academy of Business 2001). Eskom dropped pre-employment testing as counterproductive in 1993, but other South African companies continued to use this as a "solution" to the threat of HIV/AIDS. Only in September 2000 did the Labour Court, responsible for interpreting labor law, rule against the routine use of pre-employment HIV testing in the case of *"A" v. South African Airways* (AIDS Law Project 2000).

In the late 1990s, large companies in South Africa launched comprehensive HIV/AIDS policies or consolidated their previous ad hoc responses. These included the Ford Motor Company (1998), Ilovo Sugar (1999), and Daimler Chrysler (2000) (Global Business Council on HIV/AIDS 2002; Randall 2002). In 2000 the tripartite National Economic, Development and Labour Council negotiated a *Code of Good Practice on Key Aspects of HIV/AIDS and Employment* (Department of Labour 2000). This document focused on the rights of HIV-positive employees and provided a broad overview of what company HIV/AIDS policies should include. In 2003, the Department of Labour's *HIV/AIDS Technical Assistance Guidelines* provided detailed suggestions on workplace HIV/AIDS programs.

South African mining companies have remained at the forefront of corporate efforts to check HIV/AIDS because their workforce is the most vulnerable to the disease. This vulnerability stems from the extensive migrant labor system in which male workers are separated from their families for long periods of time and from the low socioeconomic and educational status of most mine workers. The mining sector introduced large-scale antiretroviral drug provision for employees without health insurance. Arguing that such an initiative was cost-effective, Anglo American announced drug provision for all its employees, on 6 August 2002. The first pilot program, in Anglo America's gold mining subsidiary, began in November 2002 (Keeton 2003). De Beers and the Old Mutual insurance company followed suit by announcing their own antiretroviral drug programs on 12 August and 10 September 2002 respectively. In relation to the government's slow-changing policy on antiretroviral drugs, such announcements allowed South Africa's *Business Day* to argue—in a September 12 editorial entitled "Taming the Hurricane"—that "It is increasingly clear that corporate SA is beginning to take the initiative in getting to grips with the disease...Corporate South Africa is stepping into the breach where government has so obviously and tragically failed." Since then, corporate action on HIV/AIDS has continued to grow in scale and scope with most large companies now having specialized HIV/AIDS managers. Key aspects of recommended workplace HIV/AIDS responses in corporations include the following (Department of Health 1998; Department of Labour 2000, 2003; Family Health International 2002; ILO 2001; NOSA 2003):

- Identify and understand the risk HIV/AIDS poses.
- Establish commitment from management and employee representatives for the workplace response.
- Draw up an HIV/AIDS policy.
- Establish implementation structures that include management and employee representatives.
- Ensure good internal and external communications.
- Establish partnerships with groups able to assist the workplace program.
- Run awareness and education interventions.
- Encourage and assist behavioral change that will prevent HIV infection.
- Encourage voluntary HIV testing and provide counseling.
- Offer wellness programs, HIV/AIDS treatment, and care (subject to resource availability).
- Extend programs to families of employees and the community (subject to resource availability).
- Create an environment in which fear, stigma, and discrimination around HIV/AIDS is minimized.
- Monitor, evaluate, and review the program.

South Africa's *Business Day* argued that the corporate reply to HIV/AIDS demonstrated the triumph of private-sector decision making over a bungled state response to one of the greatest challenges South Africa has had to face. It is certainly true that some large companies were ahead of the state in providing antiretroviral drugs and that some company HIV/AIDS programs are far ahead of what is being done outside of the corporate environment. But focusing on these strengths hides the excruciatingly slow business response to AIDS.

As early as 1987, sections of South Africa's intellectual and political elite were aware that AIDS would have major implications for the country (Grundlingh 2001; Marais 2000). South African business even had its own AIDS "prophet" in the form of Clem Sunter, who used the Chairman's Corporate Social Responsibility (CSR) Fund of South Africa's largest company, Anglo American, as a platform to raise issues of national importance. In 1987 he identified AIDS as a "wild card" in a global scenario exercise. By 1992 it was portrayed as a significant threat to South Africa, although one that could still be averted. By 1996, the threat to productivity that AIDS posed was addressed in detail, and by 2000 Sunter coauthored a book on AIDS with an entire chapter on "AIDS in the Private Sector" (Sunter 1987, 1992, 1996; Whiteside and Sunter 2000).

In theory, the widespread use of strategic planning tools such as SWOT (Strengths, Weaknesses, Opportunities, and Threats) analyses and scenario exercises that businesses use to understand the environment they operate in should have identified HIV/AIDS as a potential threat at an early stage. Had this happened, companies could have begun to investigate this risk by measuring HIV prevalence in the workforce. There are several ways in which HIV prevalence in a population can be established—with different degrees of certainty. Anonymous prevalence testing takes unlinked samples of blood or saliva from, ideally, every member of the workforce and tests for the presence of antibodies to the HIV virus. Individuals cannot access their results, but this method allays concerns over being identified as HIV-positive and increases participation rates. However, to the extent that individuals cannot, for whatever reason, be persuaded to provide a sample, there remains uncertainty as to the true level of prevalence. Actuarial risk assessments take the demographic profile of the company workforce and, on the basis of data drawn from HIV prevalence surveys elsewhere, estimate prevalence among this group of employees. Alternatively, though only where companies, at a minimum, provide antiretroviral therapy to employees that will provide an incentive for testing, the prevalence rate can be estimated using data collected from voluntary counseling and testing programs.

However, risk assessment, as measured by the HIV prevalence in the workforce, did not happen. In May 2002, the South African Business Coalition on HIV/AIDS' (SABCOHA) survey of business' policies and programs revealed that the majority of companies had yet to assess the risk of HIV/AIDS within their own workforces, let alone mount a response to this risk. Even more surprising was that only 22 percent of companies with over five hundred employees had conducted anonymous HIV testing—the only sure way of knowing the levels of infection in the workforce. While only 52 percent of them had commissioned an actuarial risk assessment, a far less intrusive but also far less reliable method of assessing the scale of the problem in an organization (SABCOHA 2002). A survey of five hundred South African companies in September 2002 presented an even bleaker picture. More the 75 percent of companies had no idea of the prevalence rate in their organizations, and more than 60 percent of these firms had no strategy to manage the disease in their workplaces (Rusconi 2002).

The fact that the South African government failed to lead and coordinate a national response to AIDS is often used to rationalize South African business's slow reply to the threat of the disease. Some observers have argued that the government's failure to respond to the crisis confronted business with such a massive problem that their isolated actions would be ineffectual (Jelly 2003; Jordan 2001; SAPA 2001). Indeed, as in other countries, initial action by the South African government was often ill informed. Whenever the apartheid regime had attempted to deal with HIV/AIDS, it suffered from a lack of credibility with the majority of the population. The advent of a democratic government in 1994 made a national response to HIV/AIDS, involving all relevant stakeholders, a possibility (Leclerc-Madlala 2005). However, the demands of political transition and the ambitions of the new regime to develop South Africa into a modern economy deflected attention and resources away from HIV/AIDS (Marais 2000). Additionally, and significantly, intellectual skepticism at the heart of the post-apartheid government on the link between HIV and AIDS confused the national response (Willian 2004).

Yet government failure as an explanation for business inaction overlooks the fact that with or without a state-led effort to deal with HIV/AIDS, business would still have needed to respond to the epidemic. So why did business wait to do so until 2002 (the year that the first large companies introduced antiretroviral treatment), sixteen years after the first studies had identified HIV among workers and antenatal HIV prevalence rates had risen to 26.5 percent (Department of Health 2003a)?

One reason for this inaction was that corporate attention was focused elsewhere at the end of apartheid. If the post-1994 government has faced the enormous task of transforming society, so too business has been preoccupied with protecting its place within this new order. Because of its central role within the apartheid system (Truth and Reconciliation Commission 1998), South African business started this effort from a weak position. Adding to its problems, as it moved out of its apartheid isolation, South African business has also had to cope with increased competition from abroad. Despite these challenges, it seems hardly convincing to argue that these tasks preoccupied business to the extent that it was unable to evaluate its own interests in the face of the AIDS epidemic. Business leaders, for example, did not hesitate to raise AIDS when they attacked the government for mishandling the epidemic because it discouraged investment. By the end of the 1990s in the business press, AIDS was routinely added to lists of social challenges that "need[ed] to be tackled seriously through a comprehensive programme in order . . . to achieve a higher rate of growth in the long run" (De la Dehesa 1999). Prominent business leaders such as Julian Ogilvie Thompson, Chair of Anglo American, cited President Thabo Mbeki's open questioning of the link between HIV and AIDS as an area where South Africa had "stumbled badly" (SAPA and I-Net Bridge 2000).

To understand the true reasons for a slow reaction from South African business to the AIDS epidemic, it is important to move beyond the glaring failures of government and examine the actual business dynamic around the crisis. To get a close look at how corporations have dealt with AIDS, we will explore the case of one large South African company, "Deco," which illustrates how company responses to HIV/AIDS have been stimulated by social, rather than business, concerns. This case makes it clear that company action on HIV/AIDS has been driven from below rather than above and has been only weakly supported by legislated or voluntary regulation. All this has profound implications for the nature of company responses to HIV/AIDS and workplace peer education.

Getting Companies to Respond to HIV/AIDS: The Story of Deco

Background to Deco

Deco is a large South African corporation with over 25,000 domestically based employees. The company is divided into several major "divisions" that operate a number of diverse production processes including mining, processing, and manufacturing. These divisions, some of which are divided into smaller "business units," are located within a number of large industrial complexes. The largest division, in terms of employees, is Mining. Deco's management is predominantly Afrikaans and male, and its top management, until recently, almost exclusively so. Its structure is strongly hierarchical with fifteen grades of employee within the company. One human resources manager, when questioned about the lack of HIV/AIDS programs in his business unit, explained how this structure discouraged action: "I would have to fight the Deco system and that would just disrupt relationships. It would be jumping grades to take the initiative."

An engineering background is highly valued within the company, and this technical orientation supports a formidable capacity for project development which has seen the company expand operations dramatically in the last ten years. While the company is proud of its technical prowess, which has translated into high profit margins, management tends to struggle with "softer" workplace issues, such as employment equity legislation designed to bring the profile of the company's workforce into line with national demographics.

The company employs a large number of predominantly white, skilled, blue-collar workers. Lower grades, such as miners and machine operators, are predominantly African. Only 12 percent of the company's workforce is female. Approximately 55 percent of the workforce is unionized.

Short-Sighted Strategists

In the late 1990s Deco conducted a scenario planning exercise to map the "road ahead" between 2000 and 2010. This exercise drew on insights from thirty-six Deco managers and eleven "remarkable people" from outside the company. These managers and notables came up with four company scenarios, only one of which identified AIDS as a major factor. Even here, the scenario strategists contended that HIV/AIDS was a challenge to an underresourced economy rather than to the company itself. While the Deco document cautioned against overemphasizing individual scenarios, the fact that HIV/AIDS did not feature as a component of all four scenarios is telling. Certainly, the scenario exercise had no impact on the company's response to HIV/AIDS, which was already gaining traction elsewhere in the company. For all their managerial acumen and remarkableness, when it came to HIV/AIDS, the assembled think tank had failed to map the road ahead.

A Response From Below

Deco's response to HIV/AIDS began in a low-key fashion in some of its divisions, notably Mining, around 1997–1998. In 1999, Kay Smit, a mid-level manager in the company's central Human Resources (HR) office in Johannesburg, established a Corporate AIDS Forum. Smit's role as HIV/AIDS Coordinator was only one of a number of portfolios for which she was responsible. The Forum drew up a brief set of guidelines on HIV/AIDS, but these did not amount to a company policy. In the absence of central direction, individual Forum members, or AIDS Champions as we will call them, independently developed a number of HIV/AIDS policies for their own division or business units. Membership of the Forum was informal and consisted of Deco employees who were already active around HIV/AIDS in the company.

It was apparent from my very first contact with Deco in 2001 that HIV/AIDS was an issue that was being driven from below. The company's AIDS Forum was recognized, but it functioned without clear lines of communication to the rest of the company and was essentially voluntary. Smit encouraged those already working on HIV/AIDS in the company to attend. An invitation from corporate headquarters was enough to justify to divisional or business unit superiors that other responsibilities could be set aside to attend the Forum's monthly meetings. Few Forum members had a mandate to speak on behalf of their divisions or business units and decisions had to be taken back to individual workplaces for approval.

Around twelve AIDS Champions attended each meeting in late 2001 and early 2002. The members of the group ranged from Leon Nel, a mid-level HR manager in the company's Mining Division, through a range of junior managers, administrators, and company occupational health practitioners, down to Hillary Botha, a secretary in a divisional business unit. Botha had been a secretary since 1990 and had become involved with HIV/AIDS because she had "a passion for people." Deco was a "wonderful company," but she believed it wasn't responding to HIV/AIDS as it should. So she got things moving in her workplace. Siphelo Ganga, a junior HR manager in a different business unit, also illustrated the bottom-up nature of countering HIV/AIDS in Deco. When he came to Deco in 1998, he had been given the HIV/AIDS portfolio for his business unit not, he wryly pointed out, because of any previous experience on HIV/AIDS, but because he was new to the company and couldn't say "no" when the responsibility was delegated downward.

Given this downward delegation of responsibility, Ganga could, of course, have done nothing: Nobody was going to check up on him. But he had enthusiastically taken up the task and after drafting an HIV/AIDS policy for his business unit recruited a group of fifteen peer educators for whom he had organized training. Although the company didn't know it, he had come face to face with AIDS in his previous job at a mining company in South Africa's North West Province: "We buried people [who had died of AIDS]," he said. "As an HR manager it was my job to attend funerals [on behalf of the company]." He knew it would be the same for Deco and had decided to do what he could.

Other AIDS Champions had also been motivated by seeing the human impact of AIDS. Linda van den Burg blended her role as an industrial nurse at Deco with compassion. HIV/AIDS extended what she undertook beyond her formal responsibility for occupational health and first aid. Her first AIDS case in Deco was in the late 1990s. The union had brought a man who was being disciplined for absenteeism. Van den Burg got his permission for an HIV test. When it came back positive, it was clear the man was dying. She ended up taking ration packs, provided by the company for overtime shifts, to his home.

Grassroots Activism within the Company

Without any formal company policy on HIV/AIDS, it was necessary for AIDS Champions to operate in unorthodox and unauthorized ways. These included bootlegging resources and finding ways to navigate around the barriers presented by the structure and culture of the company. As more employees came to Van den Burg's office with apparently minor complaints, such as diarrhea, she started to offer them counseling and HIV testing. However, even when people knew their status, they didn't always act. Although most employees had health insurance they could not always afford the required copayments or time off work to visit the doctor. Worse still, contract workers did not have medical aid. One day a contract worker had staggered into Van den Burg's office and pulled up his shirt to reveal massive herpes zoster blistering across his chest and abdomen. She sent him to a doctor with instructions to bring back a prescription and utilized a trick her manager had taught her (for different purposes) to transfer funds within the company's accounting system to pay for the drugs the contract worker needed. When the manager confronted her because she had used the money to pay for a worker's medications, she reminded him that he had taught her the trick. If she was now doing something wrong then he was to blame.

Botha also learned that results could be achieved in unorthodox ways. As the 2001 World AIDS Day approached, one manager sent an e-mail to her warning that company vehicles were not available to transport workers to an HIV/AIDS educational event. When she got no reply to her e-mails questioning this, Botha ignored company protocol and walked straight into the manager's office. The vehicles were released: "It's the verbal that gets through to people," she explained. From then on Botha bypassed company etiquette and would arrive directly at managers' offices whenever she needed something.

Like other AIDS Champions in Deco, Botha had realized that, in the absence of a centralized company HIV/AIDS program, they needed to initiate structures within their own workplaces. She had set up an AIDS Action Team of peer educators in her business unit. This team met every month and conducted activities ranging from condom distribution to school art competitions. Report-back sessions at the AIDS Forum shared what these AIDS Champions were doing in their own parts of the company. Successful events and the recruitment of peer educators were always received with enthusiasm and congratulations. However, resistance to HIV/AIDS activities from management convinced many AIDS Champions that they needed to move beyond their individual workplaces.

Developing a Shared Technical and Emotional Understanding of HIV/AIDS

Collectively the Forum's members began to drive the grassroots action in Deco upward. This started with the development of an accurate understanding of HIV/AIDS, a shared emotional position, and the development of tactics and strategies that could be used to stimulate the company into taking HIV/AIDS seriously.

Although Smit convened and chaired Forum meetings, they were remarkably participatory, and there was a strong sense that the Forum belonged to all the AIDS Champions. In contrast to the larger corporate culture, decision making was collective with long discussions and involvement over details. The entire Forum participated in drawing up a deck of HIV/AIDS playing cards—each card had a humorous illustration and snippet of information about the disease—that was to be distributed on World AIDS Day 2001. Such involvement was in itself educational with, for example, long discussions over the messages and pictures on the playing cards. Many of the AIDS Champions also attended a university-based HIV/AIDS training course that Smit paid for from the HR budget—a joint activity that built further knowledge and camaraderie.

Their collective learning over HIV/AIDS provided frequent opportunities for employees not only to work together but to laugh together. On one occasion, when Smit was reporting back on the content of the university course to members of the Forum who hadn't attended, Nel interrupted, exclaiming that Kay's account was "Not true! We just talked about sex!" Amid the hilarity that followed Nel was asked with mock seriousness, "Were you corrupted?" But in addition to fun and laughter, there were also deeply sobering moments when the warmth created by the group was punctured by the cold reality of the epidemic. At one meeting Nel shared the results of a prevalence survey that had revealed an adult infection rate of over 30 percent in a township near his workplace. The meeting descended into a grim silence that was broken only when Botha quietly summed up their consensus: "That's the reality out there, it's a disaster." For Forum members this emotional understanding of the disaster that was breaking over the country constituted the rationale for an escalated company reply to HIV/AIDS.

Driving the HIV/AIDS Agenda in the Company

Technically mastering the details of HIV/AIDS was for AIDS Champions a means to an end; knowledge would support and/or prompt action. During a session in which they worked through "Ten Questions and Answers on HIV/AIDS," the group shared tips on how they could avoid confusion and get messages across clearly within their workplaces. For example, to explain that unprotected sex didn't automatically result in infection, Nel used the analogy of people racing through red traffic lights or in South African English, "jumping the robots." Jumping the robots didn't always mean a collision, but everybody could agree that eventually there would be an accident. For this reason it was best to be safe every time. Many of the other Forum members noted that they could also use this analogy.

Increasingly, the Forum developed a collective understanding that their disparate individual efforts, while valuable, were not enough: The company had to respond systematically. As this conviction grew so did the understanding of the immediate obstacle they confronted. It was management. This was not a great leap for AIDS Champions who had already found themselves frustrated by their immediate managers who often knew little about HIV/AIDS and were willing to do even less. A Knowledge, Attitudes, and Practices (KAP) survey conducted in Mining across all employment levels had generally received a good reception. But many managers at company level six and above (level six formed supervisory management, five and above middle- to top management) had refused to participate, even though the survey was anonymous. Although a number of AIDS Champions were themselves higher than level six, they agreed that "the problem is six and higher: that's where the attitudes are." Ganga volunteered that this was because managers "think they're immune."

As the 2001 World AIDS Day approached and managers would have to acknowledge the epidemic, the group collectively strategized about how they could confront managerial attitudes. Having decided that people should be encouraged to wear an item of red clothing on that day, someone suggested, to much laughter, that "we should unleash a hot, blond, white chick in a tight red dress on the fourth floor [where senior management had their offices] to distribute condoms! It would challenge their psychological perceptions that it's [only] gay and black people [who have HIV/AIDS]."

Although campaigning to bring about policy changes, AIDS Champions generally did not consider themselves to be social activists, such as Treatment Action Campaign (TAC) members. "Activists simply demand," they insisted. "We want to see this [HIV/AIDS response in the company] through. [For example,] there is no good getting treatment provided if you don't have a way of making it work."

Notwithstanding this intention to do as well as to demand, AIDS Champions were still in no position to implement a companywide program to make things work. It was not even clear what communication channels were available to them or if anyone would listen. While a managerial line ran from Smit through her superior to Deco's HR manager, on the issue of HIV/AIDS this connection was weak. However, as the Forum began to assert itself, new members started to join what looked like something of a corporate bandwagon. Not surprisingly, these new members sometimes clashed with the culture that founding members of the Forum had established. At one meeting Botha reported back on an AIDS orphanage project. She said that her workplace was supporting it and circulated a list of items that could be donated. Kobus Bezuidenhout, who was at his first Forum meeting on behalf of Group Health & Safety, worried because the list included farmyard animals. What would happen, he asked pragmatically, "if somebody gives them a cow?" For older Forum members niggling over details, rather than expressing a spirit of support, was not helpful. Botha quickly dispatched the matter: "What a pleasure! The children would have milk!" Amid giggling, Bezuidenhout's point was lost. Such clashes were usually passed over quickly, and the newcomers were generally welcomed as a sign of success in widening the company's response to HIV/AIDS.

Persuading the Company to Act

A key lesson for many AIDS Champions in Deco was that numbers would win arguments around HIV/AIDS in the company. In a profit-driven, engineering-dominated culture, one had to prove one's project both technically and financially. For AIDS Champions, responding to HIV/AIDS was not about profit. They viewed drawing up plans and anticipating difficulties as "talk" when what was needed was "action." However they also realized that if the company was to respond they needed to make the case in ways that management would understand. As a nurse on the Forum explained, "People are dying, but they don't listen when we tell them. We need to give them statistics."

In Mining, Nel had been putting these together as best he could. As an HR manager, he had teamed up with a mine doctor to champion HIV/AIDS. With the advantage of annual medical checkups for underground workers, the rising number of AIDS-related illnesses had been easy to spot. The first case was picked up in 1994. In 1998 they put together a simple model that doubled new HIV cases each year, presenting it to management with the message that: "A bomb's exploded. The first bits of shrapnel are coming past us now and the big bits are on the way. We've got to put plans in place." Although the Mining management had expressed skepticism, they nonetheless gave the go-ahead for Nel to work on HIV/AIDS. As a result, Mining had the most advanced HIV/AIDS program within Deco. Nel's voice, an inspiration to other AIDS Champions, carried considerable weight within the Forum. He advised his colleagues that one first needed to "make an economic argument and then back it up with a moral case. Then they [management] see the point."

Smit did the same for the company as a whole. In 2001 she commissioned an HIV prevalence and costing exercise that allowed her to compile a simple economic case for intervention in which savings outstripped costs. The calculated savings over a six-year period were a miniscule fraction of the company's annual profits. Nevertheless, the argument that the company was being financially responsible in dealing with AIDS served as a useful fiscal fig leaf that allowed it to respond to mounting pressure. We can see that cost-benefit analyses serve an almost ritualistic role when we consider the fact that a 1999 HIV-prevalence estimate whose conclusions almost mirrored those of the 2001 study was universally ignored within the company. Moreover, the decision to escalate Deco's response in 2002 continued when a third, and more comprehensive, study indicated that economic benefits of a company HIV/AIDS program were likely to be neutral; that is, for each Rand spent on interventions, one Rand would be saved in terms of reducing the cost of HIV/AIDS—a return on investment of 0 percent.

Pressure from Inside and Outside

In addition to the cost-based arguments, Smit identified and tested a raft of other reasons for dealing comprehensively with AIDS, in the road shows that she took to divisional managers in an attempt to build support for intervention. Pressure was mounting, she outlined, both internally and externally for the company do to something, and it needed to create a comprehensive program. She argued that employees expected the company to do something about HIV/AIDS. She hoped that Forum members would back up her appeal as they brought their own concerns from their divisions and business units to upper-level management. She also emphasized that rising concern about the pandemic meant the company would be coming under greater public scrutiny.

Inside the company, employees and their unions were echoing public pressure in their calls for the provision of antiretroviral drugs. A consultant who assisted Deco in drawing up its response to HIV/AIDS in 2002 explained that, when developing the business case for the intervention, there had been little option but to address the perceived gap of antiretroviral drug provision in the company's program: "It felt like a trap. We either had to make a business case for providing antiretroviral drugs, or we had to find some other way of justifying them. There was no way we [the consultancy company] were going to come out against antiretroviral drugs... [T]he solution had to include antiretroviral drugs."

Perceiving public concern about HIV/AIDS, senior management sought to project an appropriate image. The company chairman asked Smit, through a number of intermediary levels, to provide information that could be publicly presented. Subsequently, in his annual statement, he reported that the company was implementing "a series of non-intrusive and proactive measures to educate and protect our employees from this disease [HIV/AIDS]." These comments were reprinted in advertisements placed in the national press in October 2001. Of course, this series of interventions was nothing more than what AIDS Champions had organized—largely without management assistance or knowledge.

Despite the lack of any clear channel for the AIDS Champions to push their message upward in the company, it nonetheless got through. Growing unease around the epidemic had justified Smit's establishment of the Forum, which was able to link the previously isolated actions of individual AIDS Champions throughout the company. Now a realization that the company would not be allowed to ignore the epidemic ensured that senior managers were willing to listen to voices from within the company.

In the absence of structures that linked the Forum and senior management, senior management itself had to come to the Forum. In March 2002, after the Forum had been meeting for over two years, the Company HR manager "dropped in" at their monthly meeting. His imminent arrival, preceded by a phone call from his secretary, reduced the Forum to a collective state of excitement. Between the phone call and his arrival, Van den Burg reduced the group to peals of laughter when she asked, "Should I put on more lipstick?"

Understanding Company Responses to HIV/AIDS

Even after senior management officially approved the Forum's activity, it was far from plain sailing. Nevertheless, this recognition of rising managerial concern marked a turning point. From then on, AIDS Champions could build programs with much greater attention to what was needed rather than what could be slipped into the spaces between "real" company activities.

The story of Deco helps us better understand that company responses to HIV/AIDS are far from straightforward products of cost-benefit analysis, social concern, or compliance with recommended best practice or national legislation. Rather, they are a messy outcome of internal activity, social pressures, and a pragmatic recognition from senior management that it is best to make a virtue out of a necessity. Deco's reply to HIV/AIDS can, with variations, be generalized to South African companies. Companies must build a business case that legitimates creating a program to deal with HIV/AIDS. Legislation and best practice guides play a minor, and rarely proactive, role, while the visibility of the epidemic combined with internal and external social pressures encourage action. This matrix of factors sculpts company responses as well as their limitations.

In many South African companies it was AIDS Champions who commissioned the studies that helped promote positive action. Often these studies didn't make a convincing case. Unresolved questions included the exact prevalence rate among the workforces; how lost productivity could be accurately measured; to what extent the price of antiretroviral drugs would drop; how many HIV-positive employees would access treatment; and whether workers could continue to be cheaply replaced if the national impact of the disease was considered. Nor could studies take into account the unknown future trajectory of the epidemic in the workforce; if HIV infection were to move into the more-skilled section of the population then the sums would stack up very differently. But these uncertainties aside, studies did at least demonstrate that the cost of intervention would pay for itself. (Sometimes with a little massaging, because by the time these studies were being commissioned in earnest nobody, mindful of public concern over HIV/AIDS, was going to produce a report that said "Do nothing; it's cheaper to let the epidemic run its course.") That was hardly going to galvanize company boardrooms seeking double-digit returns on investments, but it did get everybody off the hook. Managers could respond to demands for action on AIDS while at the same time plausibly arguing that it made business sense.

Although there was a raft of national legislation that could be applied to HIV/AIDS in the workplace, none of this forced companies to be proactive in confronting the epidemic.[3] The protection of HIV-positive individuals' rights was important in blocking pre-employment testing. Otherwise legislation has been of little value in driving company action on HIV/AIDS. Beyond stating what should *not* be done, the law says very little. The Department of Labour's *Code of Good Practice on Key Aspects of HIV/AIDS and Employment* (2000) is no more than a code and joins a number of other such guidelines that companies are free to use, adapt, or ignore as they wish (Whelan, Dickinson, and Murray 2008).

If financial and legal pressures have not compelled companies to deal with the crisis, then it is clear that corporate action has largely been a reaction to social pressures brought to bear on senior management. The story of Deco illustrates how AIDS Champions—lower-ranking managers and in some cases rank-and-file employees—mobilized within their own workplaces and campaigned within their company until they were taken seriously. The stories of other companies vary in detail, but are broadly similar in this respect. Not infrequently, early attempts at internal mobilization failed as AIDS Champions became discouraged or left companies without their programs being institutionalized. Later, new employees would start all over again. Only toward the end of the 1990s and early 2000 did grassroots responses inside companies start to link up, as in Deco, with concerns of executive management.

---

3. The Department of Labour's (2000) *Code of Good Practice on Key Aspects of HIV/AIDS and Employment* lists, in addition to the country's Constitution, eight relevant pieces of national legislation. These are: The Employment Equity Act, the Labour Relations Act, the Occupational Health and Safety Act, the Mine Health and Safety Act, the Compensation for Occupational Injuries and Diseases Act, the Basic Conditions of Employment Act, the Medical Schemes Act, and the Promotion of Equality and Prevention of Unfair Discrimination Act.

These executive concerns stemmed from the realization that, however weak the legal and financial arguments for responding to HIV/AIDS might be, inaction carried penalties. The threat to South Africa's corporate image was even more serious given employers' previous role within the apartheid system. Employees expected corporate leaders to do something about the epidemic. The TAC and unions were also critical in exerting external pressure, notably around the provision of antiretroviral drugs. As the managing director of one of Deco's divisions put it, "There isn't a business case for antiretroviral drugs on labor supply grounds. But there's a case in terms of the company's image."

Many company programs were motivated by concerns about image, as illustrated by this frank assessment from a senior Deco manager: "It's now a corporate image issue, but if we're late [in responding to HIV/AIDS] we're not going to be killed for it. Who's ahead on this issue? [i.e., nobody]. So we're in the club. There is little competitive image difference on HIV/AIDS." This calculated evaluation from senior management reflects not only the limited value that workplace responses to HIV/AIDS would bring to the bottom line but also their own social distance from the epidemic. By contrast, those campaigning for more robust corporate action had, for one reason or another, come into direct contact with the human consequence of AIDS. In a survey of 383 companies in late 2002 with an average workforce of 580 employees, 50 percent of managerial respondents reported that HIV/AIDS had no impact on their company. However, among the 33 percent of these managers who knew of somebody who was HIV-positive in the company, 72 percent thought that HIV/AIDS was having an impact on the company (Stevens et al. 2005), suggesting a causal link between personal knowledge of HIV-positive employees and the perceived impact of HIV/AIDS.

The visibility of HIV/AIDS in companies often varied widely. In a manufacturing company with around 250 employees researched in 2004, uncertainty about prevalence extended to visible indicators of impact, such as AIDS-related deaths within the company. When interviewed, three managers—all members of the company HIV/AIDS committee—gave different figures in this regard. One, the most senior, said he knew of no such deaths, a second cited a figure of four, and the third (the most junior of the three) claimed seven such deaths—producing copies of death certificates euphemistically indicating "natural causes" and "diarrhea" to support this (Dickinson 2005). More broadly, given the distribution of HIV prevalence among different socioeconomic groups outlined in Chapter 1, there is a clear inverse relationship between those who have firsthand experience of HIV/AIDS and their power within companies.

Not surprisingly then, AIDS Champions were self-selected from among those who, while not members of socioeconomic groups bearing the brunt of the epidemic, nonetheless came into direct contact with AIDS in their daily work. Thus, predominantly lower-ranked managers, notably in HR departments, and occupational nurses have driven company HIV/AIDS programs.

One outcome of this self-appointed set of AIDS Champions was the process of internal lobbying that the story of Deco illustrates. Despite their frustrations with company leadership, the Champions objective remained to "turn" management rather than to force it to concede to a set of demands. In getting senior management to take AIDS seriously, they recognized the value of having the TAC and unions make or threaten to make demands on companies. Given that these pressures were independent of their own work, they could position themselves as helping senior management to understand the imperative of responding to the epidemic. They provided managers—who knew next to nothing about HIV/AIDS, other than that it was becoming a corporate image issue—with actions that could be economically justified and made moral sense.

While managers realized that they had to be seen to be responding to HIV/AIDS and came to appreciate that they had employees keen to put programs in place, that did not mean they threw themselves unconditionally behind company HIV/AIDS programs. While some components of such programs were cheap and easy to sanction, others elements could be much more costly. What quickly became obvious was that it was not possible to easily limit the company's response. The sexual transmission of disease means that the success of any workplace program depends on the success of programs in the communities in which employees live. The provision of antiretroviral drugs to employees was something that could be justified financially, especially as drug prices dropped. But the cost would escalate if drugs were provided to employees' spouses who would very likely also be HIV-positive. Further, managers questioned whether treatment could be continued if the HIV-positive employee were laid off or retired. The problem of how far companies should go in providing antiretroviral drug treatment was considerably eased by the state's August 2003 decision to roll out treatment in the pubic sector. But, beyond the question of payment for drug therapy, if the epidemic is fueled by poverty, then company management—while wanting to project an image of corporate responsibility—also looked nervously at surrounding communities and their socioeconomic needs. Responding to *these* needs could overwhelm their resources.

In a survey of twenty-eight of South Africa's largest companies, with a total workforce of 547,000 employees in 2002–2003, 48 percent of responding managers said the most important reason for responding to HIV/AIDS was "to act as a responsible corporate citizen" (Dickinson and Innes 2004, 39). In practice, however, companies' policies circumscribed the extent of this corporate citizenship. Thirty-eight percent of the surveyed companies agreed that their company's HIV/AIDS policy recognized that the "whole of society must be considered." However, when it came to contract workers, who were not payroll employees but walked in and out of the company gates every day, only 19 percent of the companies included them in their programs (Dickinson and Innes 2004).

At Deco, managers raised considerable doubts about the potential cost and complexity of Deco's taking responsibility for HIV/AIDS in the community. The Deco managers interviewed highlighted the company's corporate social responsibility projects with local communities, but saw any move beyond this as something that was neither practical nor affordable. The managing director of one division explained, "There is a fear that we could be sucked into this kind of thing," while a senior HR manager thought that, "If we try to grapple [with HIV/AIDS] beyond the immediate family [of employees] it could become enormous."

Company Managers, AIDS Champions, and Peer Educators

Workplace peer educators operate in environments that are similar to that of Deco where the writ of legislation or guidelines around HIV/AIDS is limited. They also have to accept senior management's reluctance to deal aggressively with HIV/AIDS beyond efforts to project a good corporate image. This reluctance is due, in part, to managers' limited exposure to the human impact to AIDS. By contrast peer educators, even more than

AIDS Champions, are confronted with the tragedy of AIDS within their own families and communities. Another reason for managerial inaction was that when the sums were finally calculated, they didn't amount to a compelling bottom-line argument. This may yet change, but for the moment those seeking to lobby for company responses to the epidemic have to be content with a financial fig leaf of cost neutrality to justify a HIV/AIDS program. Yet, for peer educators, drawn from the ranks of company employees—most in lower occupational levels with limited education or resources—these programs, for all their limitations, are important.

This chapter, in describing how AIDS Champions catalyzed company responses, may have given the impression that Champions, as middle-level employees, both lobbied upward and organized downward. There is some truth in this; in addition to raising consciousness about the problem and arguing for a more comprehensive company reply to the epidemic, they were also busy organizing, as best they could, within the company. But, as we shall see in Chapter 3, their efforts to recruit and deploy peer educators rode on the enthusiasm and spontaneous activity of peer educators themselves. AIDS Champions did not call peer educators into being, nor can peer educators be seen as merely grassroots implementers of company HIV/AIDS programs. Instead peer educators represent a vast response to AIDS from below.

3

"For the Love of People"

Peer Education as a Response from Below

A People's Response

In June 2005, at the South African AIDS Conference, a biannual event in the country's AIDS calendar, I presented some preliminary ideas on workplace peer education at a session on HIV/AIDS workplace programs. The session was one of the best attended of the conference; around four hundred people in a large auditorium of the Durban International Conference Centre listened to half a dozen papers. Two of them, including my own, dealt with workplace peer educators. The other, a "meta-analysis" or study-of-studies, drew on statistical evaluations of the impact of workplace peer education on infection rates. On the basis of the handful of studies that met the demanding scientific criteria required for entry into the meta-analysis (a "gold standard" of trials in which the incidence of new infections among one workforce exposed to a peer educator program would be monitored against a similar, controlled, workforce without peer education), the author suggested that the effectiveness of peer education could not be proved. The audience, many of whom were AIDS activists or involved in company HIV/AIDS programs, was distinctly uncomfortable. There was polite applause when the speaker finished. My own paper was tentative. I had little data at that point. Nonetheless, I suggested that peer educators appeared to be doing many things within complex environments and argued that we needed to understand them better. I concluded by expressing my hopes about the potential of peer education. The audience responded with thunderous applause. By now the room was polarized on the issue. Another speaker, presenting a paper on her workplace HIV/AIDS program, deviated from her prepared script to describe her peer educators as "the eyes and ears of the [company] program," without whom she would be unable to function. Her spontaneous rebuttal of the doubts cast over peer education was immediately rewarded with a round of applause.

Despite the popular affirmations of peer education, there was dissent. Some attendees were skeptical about peer education and, despite risking unpopularity, were confident enough to make their point from the floor. Notably, these speakers had scientific and medical backgrounds, and their interventions were couched in the language of evidence, statistics, and tangible results. They were outnumbered, but with the power of expertise they refused to be cowed by the prevailing sentiment.

I came away from the session convinced that it was important to know more about workplace peer education. I was beginning to see that it was a "people's response" to the epidemic and the fact that it was generated from below partly explained why so many experts were skeptical of peer education. In addition, what was becoming clear was that neither scientists, nor doctors, nor company managers, nor AIDS activists really knew what peer educators were doing. On the one hand, there were powerful decision makers ready to evaluate peer education with what could easily be the wrong tools; as long as the tools were shiny and sharp. On the other hand, those involved or close to this grassroots action intuitively felt it was valuable and worthy of support but struggled to justify in precise terms why this was the case. So, what do we know about workplace HIV/AIDS peer educators? What do they do? And, why do they do it?

The Role of Workplace Peer Educators

The Official View...

One way to start answering the questions of what peer educators do and why they do it is to look at how managers and institutions define the ideal workplace peer educator and imagine his or her role. As with much within organizations, the "institutional imagination"—created with job titles, policy documents, organograms, and value statements—provides but a starting point for grasping realities. But a starting point is useful. While no HIV/AIDS manager would claim that their peer educator programs was perfect, they clearly have a vision of what they would like it to be.

First, the ideal peer educator would share identities of race, gender, age, occupation, and more with those they wished to educate. This means that if a group of peer educators were working with men and women of different ethnicities or races, collectively they would mirror this diversity. The next important qualification would be commanding the respect of those with whom they interacted. They would be good communicators who could talk easily and would have good listening skills. They would understand the need for confidentiality and would not gossip. Willing to go the extra mile, they would volunteer for the role and, based on a passion for this vocation, they would return from training as a full-fledged peer educator.

Their training, despite being only a few days, would have conveyed all necessary information about HIV/AIDS, infection, testing, treatment, and care. It would also outline and teach a range of communication skills. The training would establish some form of mutual peer educator support. Finally, it would explain the expected level of activity (which no doubt peer educators would surpass) and how to report this so that the company HIV/AIDS manager would know precisely what activity was taking place across the organization. Given the fast-changing nature of information around HIV/AIDS, peer educators would be highly motivated. They would be willing to attend regular updates or refresher training that would cover new developments in the field.

In the workplace, peer educators would initiate talks with coworkers on a range of issues, particularly HIV/AIDS and other sexually transmitted diseases. They would also learn and convey information about other health and wellness topics that would benefit peers. These would be given in the languages with which peers were most comfortable. To have access to their peers during work hours, the peer educator would establish a good relationship with their supervisor. This would facilitate the peer educator giving talks at team or shift meetings. The peer educators would draw materials for their talks from a company-provided manual, but would also respond to questions from the audience. The fielding of any questions coworkers might have would be done thoughtfully. Our ideal peer educator would not be ashamed to say that they didn't know the answer, and would either access their own reference material or would initiate a query to more professional staff within the company HIV/AIDS program, and get back with the answer. Their interventions would support broader company initiatives linked to events in the AIDS calendar, such as World AIDS or Valentines' Day. Coworkers who thought that they might be at risk of infection would approach the peer educator for guidance. In such situations the peer educator would encourage testing and provide support if the result was positive. However, if the situation ever moved beyond what they could handle, they would refer to professionals such as occupational health practitioners, company social workers, or psychologists.

Our ideal peer educator would take their activity beyond the workplace. They would assist organizations in the community responding to the epidemic: hospices, AIDS orphanages or day care centers, and home-based care organizations among others. In this, they would not only assist the community but also act as ambassadors for the company. In return, the company would, within reason, support their efforts with donations and publicity.

All of this activity on the part of the peer educator would be conducted with the minimum of fuss. Indeed peer education would enter into the normal business of the company with hardly a ripple. Even though the ideal peer educators would be passionate about their work, they would have a clear sense of proportion and would balance their commitment with competing work responsibilities.

They would be the salt of the earth.

…and Divergence

This ideal portrait of a company peer educator bears more than a passing resemblance to real peer educators. During my research I met many remarkable peer educators who would fulfill at least some, possibly many, of these criteria. But in reality, there were wide gaps between ideal and actual peer education programs in the companies I researched. This was not a surprise. One reason that company HIV/AIDS managers granted me research access was because they wanted to find out what peer educators were actually doing in their organizations. Some candidly told me, they didn't know. This chapter outlines how the reality of peer education differed from the ideal—quite possibly in greater detail than some managers really wanted to know.

Organization

The organization of peer educators within company HIV/AIDS programs varies enormously—both between and within companies. Organizational structures managing the activity of peer educators in the five researched companies included: HR management, Health & Safety structures, Occupational Health practitioners, Corporate Social Responsibility officers, multi-stakeholder HIV/AIDS committees, dedicated HIV/AIDS management, and line management.

Often these different forms of organization were a result of who within management had picked up the challenge of organizing peer educators and what organizational resources were available to them. As one HIV/AIDS manager jokingly, but tellingly, put it, "If X was in Building Maintenance, we'd be organizing the peer educators from there." Given this evolving process there are often gaps in organizational coverage within companies.

In some companies, managers attempted to remain in contact with peer educators and set expectations for their activities. Generally, however, links between those running company HIV/AIDS programs and peer educators were weak. Even when monitoring systems were in place they often failed to function. It was clear to many peer educators that nobody read the reports they filed. To test his suspicion, one peer educator in Mineco let his reports pile up in his desk drawer. No one ever asked for them.

Some peer educators mobilized independently. A number of mine shafts in Mineco had their own committees that coordinated peer educator activity. In theory these shaft-based groups were linked to the company's HIV/AIDS program, but in practice this link was often tenuous. Within Bestbuyco, peer educators in one of its regional divisions, feeling the need for greater coordination of their thirty-five company sites, established a regional peer educator committee.

Apart from training, which we examine shortly, many, perhaps most peer educators were largely unaware of the larger organizational structure to which they supposedly belonged, were often vague as to the details of the company's HIV/AIDS program, and had contact only with other peer educators with whom they worked. By and large, peer educators are self-driven rather than components of a larger, coordinated program.

Motivations: For the Love of People

Management may be uncertain about peer education, but peer educators are not. They felt an urgent need to respond to AIDS, in most cases, because they had witnessed firsthand the impact of HIV/AIDS on families, friends, and communities. Watching people die of something that they did not understand and that was talked about only in whispers propelled many into becoming peer educators. Not infrequently, these workers explained that becoming a peer educator was the only way they could find out about the disease. With this information, they felt they could help themselves and those around them. They would not again have to helplessly stand by. Kgomotso Maluleka, an African woman in her twenties, is an underground loco driver in Mineco. She echoed other peer educator's desire to overcome helplessness in the face of the epidemic.

> I became a Peer Educator ... because at the time we were growing up we saw people getting ill and we didn't know anything about HIV and I joined it [the peer educator program] to get information and to help others and to help myself. And then as I was [already] a Peer Educator in 2003 my aunt died of AIDS. She called us and told us, "I think you should be aware of this. I am dying and I am [HIV]-positive and now I am fully blown [i.e., in final AIDS stages; effectively she is making a deathbed confession that she is HIV-positive] so could you please take care of some of the children and those

> I am leaving in this world." And that was the thing that made me stronger as a Peer Educator.... Even if I was not infected I was affected by that time. I was hurt, and I asked myself some questions "If I don't help other people and don't help myself with this information, who will do that?"

Nicol Manuel, also in her twenties, works in the warehouse at Autostar and has a similar story. She became a peer educator after seeing how people in her community were "branded as going to die" if they had HIV. Since then, she watched her divorced father die of AIDS. Being able to help other family members and explain what was happening confirmed that becoming a peer educator was the right choice.

Some peer educators had graduated into giving advice on HIV/AIDS as part of a wider informal advisory role. Sonia Hendricks, a colored woman in her mid-forties, had been a nurse before she had joined Finco eighteen years ago where she is a supervisor in the Credit Card division. She is deeply involved in the life of her church and its community activity (which includes HIV/AIDS work) in her township. She proudly explains that relatives have to ring ahead to see if they should visit because she is so often "out and about." At work she described herself as the "Yellow Pages" (because she can help on any issue). Three years ago, the hundred or so staff on her floor—who call her "aunty" (a term of familiar respect in South Africa)—selected her to be a peer educator. But as she explained, she's "being doing it [giving advice on HIV/AIDS] without management for years."

Despite this passion on the part of established peer educators, the evidence on peer educator turnover, when it was available, suggested that many of those trained as peer educators failed to take up an active role or quickly dropout. Peer educator trainers were well aware that many attending their workshops did so only because their supervisor had sent them. One trainer estimated that of twenty people at a training session, five didn't want to be there, two were keen and would "go out and do it," and the rest would go back and make a presentation or two before fading out. Another trainer thought that about half of those that management nominated could be brought around to actively participate in the training. At a training session I attended, trainers teased the "nominees" on account of their blank faces when they were asked, as part of the introductory exercise, why they were there.

Some nominees do take up the cause. Lebohang Kekana, a team leader in a back office of Finco was sent to a peer educator training course by his manager. Before the training, he did not think HIV/AIDS had anything to do with him and hadn't wanted to attend. He'd confided his reluctance to a woman whom he'd got to know during the course. At the end of the course, she had quietly revealed to him that she was HIV-positive. Kekana had felt acutely embarrassed about the things he had said and decided to continue as a peer educator. It also dawned on him that several members of his extended family had died of AIDS not of the various reasons that had been suggested at the time. By the time I interviewed him, he was energetically coordinating a network of twenty peer educators across his building.

Peer educators personally gained little from their activity. At best, there was some time allocated for their activities and a token stipend. Autostar gave a R50 (approximately $5) voucher each month for peer educators who formally reported on their activity. Elsewhere, tangible rewards, if any, took the form of T-shirts, occasional social events, training, and access to information on HIV/AIDS. But this does not mean that there are not benefits to being a peer educator. Some employees saw peer education as a step toward a career in HIV/AIDS counseling or management. Often these individuals were forced to abandon their studies because of financial reasons before they entered the employment market. Mpho Mbovane had studied for an HR degree for a year at collage before "problems at home" meant that she had to find a job. Working on the assembly line of Autostar was something she did to earn a living. She saw her work as a peer educator as a step toward her career ambition of becoming a full-time HIV/AIDS counselor.

But despite a range of motivations, peer educators were acting, in the words of one, "for the love of people." Occasionally this came across as patronizing, but for the vast majority of peer educators, their actions drew on direct experiences. Almost 83 percent of the surveyed peer educators said they knew somebody with HIV or who had died of AIDS. This rose to almost 98 percent among those with the lowest incomes of less then R2,000 ($200) a month. As one peer educator explained, "There were seven of us at home, but I've lost two sisters to AIDS. It's affecting everybody's family now."

When I asked in the survey of six hundred peer educators what they believed was the most important contribution they could make in response to HIV/AIDS, of the 1,380 responses given (the question was open-ended and respondents were asked to suggest three contributions), there were only 10 on supporting the company or adding value to its activities. Not one of the 75 people I interviewed raised the need to protect their company's economic viability as a motivation for being a peer educator, though it was clear that they were aware of the business argument for peer education. Late in the interview schedule, I asked peer educators what they would do if management closed down their program. The response was defiant outrage, and they drew on economic arguments to illustrate why their company would be foolhardy to end their programs. This was nearly always the first time in the interview that arguments based on the value of peer education given the economic implications of AIDS for the company were made. Clearly, economic arguments for peer education were understood; however, they did not constitute a primary personal motivation, as the love of people did, but were instrumentally invoked in an appropriate situation. Peer educators were not aware that these economic arguments might not be as compelling as they thought (see Chapter 2). Also striking was that, with only one exception (a white, male manager), none said they would acquiesce to such a management decision. Rather, they expressed incredulity, disappointment, and mounted counterarguments as they vowed to continue. "I'd be disappointed, but I'd go on like a peer educator and help other people," said a Finco peer educator in a typical response, "I'm not doing it for them [management]. They can't stop me meeting people; they can't stop people coming to me for advice. I'd just carry on." While Manuel at Autostar explained that:

> I'll be very upset. And I'll approach management myself and ask them, "Why?" And if they don't give me a good reason I'll give them a piece of my mind. But what I would do is I'll carry on. I'll still have my campaigns. I'll talk to people slyly while I'm working. I'll go in the canteen and I'll still be canvassing. And I won't stop doing it because I have a passion. I think it's more of a personal issue. You know I've lost a loved one and I wouldn't want to see other people losing their loved ones.

Peer educators' concern for people, not companies, is also reflected in the way they got involved in peer education: The most common way of becoming a peer educator was through volunteering. Fifty percent of the surveyed peer educators said this was the best way to describe how they became involved. The second most common way was being elected by coworkers (21.5 percent). In practice, an elected peer educator may well be the person who volunteers, or at least agrees, to stand for election. Along with self-starters (at 4 percent) who began peer educator activity on their own, and those recruited through networks (6.5 percent), 82 percent of all peer educators took up their role either on their own initiative or that of coworkers (Table 3 in Appendix 1).

Not surprisingly, few of the peer educators surveyed had become so as a result of nomination from supervisors or managers (8 percent) or being sent on peer educator training (10 percent)—which was sometimes the way in which a nomination was communicated. Rachel Baloyi, a Call Centre Agent in Finco, explains how she was "asked" to become a peer educator because she "talked a lot."

> Baloyi: I was chosen by my senior manager because at the time that this [peer educator] program was introduced each department had to have a representative.... The Call Centre didn't have anyone representing them, and Mr. Roberts [the company HIV/AIDS manager] from Corporate Office was complaining about that. So, I was like chosen [laughs]... Not forced. Ah, not really given a choice. I was told, um, no, did they tell me? Let me rethink that.
>
> Dickinson: It was an offer you couldn't refuse?
>
> Baloyi: I guess yes, yes. [Laughs] When my Manager came to me she said: "You know what? I really want you to go to this program. The Call Centre doesn't have a representative [peer educator]. And I know you talk a lot, so I'm sure that you'll be able to influence the staff and come back and communicate whatever needs to be done by the Bank for this particular program."

In fact, nominating an employee for peer educator training because he or she talks a lot may be a good idea. Thomas Valente and Rebecca Davis (1999) argue that peer educators should be selected on measured interpersonal contact with other target group members. However, most HIV/AIDS managers used no pretraining selection criteria to determine whom would be trained as peer educators. Only 29 percent of peer educators reported being evaluated prior to initial training, and this showed a downward trend from around 40 percent for peer educators recruited in 2000 or earlier to fewer than 20 percent for those recruited in 2004 and 2005. Typically, with companies ramping up their peer educator programs, they accepted any volunteers willing to come forward. Similarly, managers who had received instructions that their section needed a peer educator might pressgang employees. Those who were inappropriately selected usually dropped out.

The turnover of peer educators was a major concern for many of the company HIV/AIDS managers interviewed. One company received a shock when, on running a second national HIV/AIDS campaign, it discovered a turnover of some 30 percent of its peer educators in two years. However, while this is a genuine issue, there are also long-timers within the ranks of peer educators. Nineteen percent of peer educators surveyed in 2005 had become peer educators in 2000 or before, and another 15 percent in 2001, indicating that it is possible to sustain activity over a number of years.

Different Purpose, Shared Interests: Training and Opportunity

As we saw in Chapter 2, companies need to respond to—and be seen as responding to—AIDS. Largely independently of corporate concerns, employees were also responding to the epidemic. What binds company and peer educator together is training and the opportunity to influence. In short, peer educators became part of company HIV/AIDS programs because they receive training on HIV/AIDS and because it opens up space for them to respond to the epidemic.

The training companies provided, sometimes in-house but usually contracted out to specialized service providers, was for many peer educators a vital source of information on HIV/AIDS. Nearly all peer educators had been to an initial training program and most had received some follow-up or refresher training. The peer educators rated the training highly because of the information provided and the communication and presentation skills conveyed. These gave them the confidence they needed to be peer educators. Those peer educators who had also attended NGO or government-run community-based training were adamant that company training was far superior. In the company training sessions I observed, motivated trainers encouraged participation and provided clear explanations to participants. However, the typical training program was only between two and five days, and thus restricted in what it could achieve. All the more so if participants had limited literacy and little access to information after training as was often the case (except for Finco with its predominantly white-collar workforce). However, while training can be improved, the bottom line is that peer educators found it very valuable and were often hungry for more.

After their training sessions, peer educators returned to a workplace environment in which realities on the ground did not always reflect company policies and exhortations about the need to respond to HIV/AIDS. This was all the more apparent in high-stress areas of the companies, such as the production lines in the auto companies or underground in Mineco—where the pressure to produce gave educators little opportunity to give formal presentations. As one peer educator in Mineco put it, "In the pit [underground] there isn't time for nothing [except production]."

Nevertheless, even within these high-stress environments, certain jobs provide space for peer education. Typically, these involved positions in which the individual was expected to move around and talk to different employees and had discretion in work routine. These include quality inspectors on the auto companies' assembly lines, frontline (checkout) supervisors in Bestbuyco, assistant branch managers in Finco, and Health & Safety officers in Mineco. Peer educators in these positions could conduct peer education activity "on the sly"—disguised from production managers or supervisors who did not know the actual content of their conversations. Beyond these facilitating positions, peer educators had to grasp whatever opportunity was available. In Mineco some peer educators used the time spent waiting at the "stations" to be brought back to the surface after the shift has been completed.

Supervisors and line managers were critical in determining the outcome of peer education. Many supervisors were supportive of peer education work. Nevertheless, reflecting the local nature of this issue, peer educators told me that some supervisors made presenting difficult, only giving them slots at short notice if there was nothing else that needed to be discussed at team meetings, and constantly looking at their watches when the peer educators were presenting. That managers did not stop supervisors from intimidating peer educators in this way suggests that companies are not fully behind such efforts. While senior management might publicly emphasize the need to educate about HIV/AIDS, peer educators clearly felt they depended on supervisors' goodwill to grant them the opportunity to talk about HIV/AIDS.

Profiles

If peer education is a labor of love, provides few material rewards, is based on limited training, and is often unsupported, who becomes a workplace peer educator? Given the idea of peer education, it is often suggested that peer educators should be representative of the workforce at large. Critical categories in this regard include race, gender, and occupational (skill) level. If we compare the survey of 600 peer educators in the five companies against the profile of the companies' workforce as recorded in Employment Equity Reports that all South African companies with more than fifty employees are required to complete, we see that in terms of race and gender, peer educators were *not* representative of the workforce, but were skewed toward women, particularly African women (Table 4, Appendix 1). Men of all race groups were underrepresented, least among African men (by 13 percent), most among white men (by 81 percent). African women were dramatically overrepresented (by 104 percent), and colored women also overrepresented but to a much lesser extent (17 percent). Indian women were marginally underrepresented (three percent) as peer educators; white women more so (29 percent).

The overrepresentation of Africans as peer educators can be attributed, at least in part, to the greater impact of AIDS on Africans than other races (see Chapter 1). While women in South Africa have higher HIV prevalence rates than men (HSRC 2005), this difference is smaller than the overrepresentation of women among peer educators. This overrepresentation of women would be better explained by a gendered pattern of concern and responsibility within society generally and the AIDS epidemic in particular.

In terms of occupational status there were few peer educators at managerial levels (Table 5, Appendix 1). Managerial positions accounted for only 7.4 percent of the five companies' total workforce, and few of these managers were willing to become peer educators. This was because they rarely faced the disease firsthand, given their social distance from the sections of the population most affected by AIDS. Most peer educators were therefore working class, had not been educated beyond high school, and were in low-income occupations with over 80 percent earning a gross wage of under R7,000 (approximately $700) per month, and 47 percent under R4,000 (approximately $400) per month.

Seventy-eight percent of peer educators were trade union members, while 30 percent were or had been shop stewards and 42.5 percent Health & Safety representatives. This extensive involvement in forms of "workplace citizenship" suggests that employees who are generally concerned with the well-being of others are more likely to become peer educators. A high percentage of peer educators were religiously active, with 79 percent reporting attending religious services at least twice a month. This is not surprising in a country where 83.5 percent of the population considers themselves to be religious—which generally means Christian (Statistics South Africa 2004). However, the role of faith for peer educators clearly extended beyond church attendance. Many of the peer educators whom I interviewed stressed the importance of religious beliefs to their peer education. The meetings of the Mineco peer educator group studied in 2006 always began and ended with prayer.

We should recognize that there is no such thing as a standard peer educator. As will be clear throughout this book, they come in all shapes, beliefs, and colors. Nevertheless, what we can say is that the typical workplace peer educator is an African, a woman, has limited education, is working class, is a union member, has a strong Christian faith, and is involved in helping others.

What Do Peer Educators Actually Do?

The short answer to this question is, "a lot," though this varies tremendously among individuals. Most peer educators were doing what was asked of them: conducting formal talks with coworkers, talking informally with individuals, and conducting HIV/AIDS–related activities in their communities. But peer educator activity diverged significantly over and above these expectations. They engaged in a range of roles at work and home that no job description adequately captured. Their activity beyond the workplace was extensive but only rarely focused on the goal of promoting the company as a good corporate citizen. Finally, running through their work, like fine threads joining it together, was the informal activity that peer educators conducted far more extensively, and often at a greater level of intensity, than was expected.

Formal Talks

According to most experts who promote peer education, peer educators' core function is to act as conduits who regurgitate the information provided—using their linguistic and sociocultural access—to peers (though it would not be put so bluntly). Indeed, most peer educators run formal education sessions. Of the six hundred peer educators surveyed, 90 percent gave formal talks at work—mostly to small groups. Two-thirds reported that they presented weekly or monthly. The majority (55 percent) of peer educators gave these talks to twenty or fewer peers and another 21 percent to between twenty-one and forty coworkers. Many peer educators relied on lesson plans provided by HIV/AIDS managers or occupational nurses. This material varied from purely factual accounts of HIV/AIDS and other health issues to highly creative exercises designed to stimulate participation and encourage people to think about the implications of HIV/AIDS for themselves. Irrespective of the pedagogical value of these "oven ready" lessons, however, those relying exclusively on this menu would eventually run out of topics. That's why most successful peer educators developed much more fluid and independent approaches to formal talks. Typically, they used question-and-answer sessions to identify topics of interest to their peers and then addressed these issues in future talks.

In interviews, a number of peer educators pointed out that a key benefit of giving formal education sessions was that it gave them a high profile within the workplace. Many peer educators reported being approached by coworkers with questions after a formal education session in which only a few questions were raised. "After the meetings people are buzzing me," Kekana in Finco recounted. "There may be no questions in the meetings, but as soon as I've got back to my desk the calls come in." Data from the questionnaire provides support for this argument. Peer educators who gave formal talks reported an average of nine informal discussions with other company employees per month compared with less than six for those who did not give formal talks.

Informal Activity

While formal activity is, of course, important to peer education, the real action between peer educators and their coworkers and community members takes place informally. A group of workers will, for example, be having a discussion and the peer educator will take advantage of the topic to steer the conversation to HIV/AIDS. Alternatively, an event will provide an opening for the peer educator to strike the right tone and create a "teachable moment." Nadia Reddy, a peer educator in Finco, explained how she both creates and capitalizes on teachable moments.

> If I read something and I find it's of value to the staff, I would make mention. So if I read an article...I would say, "Guys, have any of you read the paper yesterday with regards to this particular article about this HIV issue?" Or any other issue of interest that I find is of relevance, and maybe one or two people will have and then, the next thing, we're discussing it and then people give their input...And then the ball is rolling because now everybody coming in is contributing to it [the discussion]...and [if] they want to know more, then we bring the article in [the next day] and then we start reading it and talking about it.

Informal activity often takes more intimate forms, including providing advice, support, and practical help. Though such activity may sometimes have been set up in advance, it is characteristically different from formal presentations in its responsive (rather than scripted), confidential, and individualized format. That workplace peer educators were engaged in such informal activity was not a surprise, but the extent of this was not realized prior to the research. On average, 86 percent of peer educators reported informal interactions with other employees, 63 percent with other people at work (who were not company employees),[1] and 89 percent with people

1. The category of "other people at work (who are not company employees)" was added to the questionnaire when it emerged, during piloting, that peer educators in the retail company were talking to customers about HIV/AIDS. It was hoped to establish the scale of such interactions with customers in the retail company and also, possibly, the financial institution (since many

outside of work. Excluding a small number of claims to speak to very large numbers of people informally,[2] peer educators reported a monthly average of nine informal interactions with other employees, eight more people at work who are not company employees, and a further nine with people outside of work; a total monthly average of twenty-six informal interactions. More in-depth research of informal activity among the group of peer educators in Mineco, in which the peer educators kept diaries of their activities, found levels of informal activity closer to the medians of the larger study, with a total monthly average of fourteen informal interactions per month or approximately one every other day.

At Mineco, these informal interactions took place with an average of just over two peers, though most commonly it was with one. Nevertheless, informal activity occasionally involved fairly large groups of up to twelve people. On average, informal sessions took just under fifteen minutes with sessions being as short as one minute and as long as one hour.

In their efforts to normalize the epidemic, peer educators at Mineco recorded that they raised a wide range of topics focusing on prevention of infection and support for those infected or affected in these informal interactions. They often discussed more than one issue in a single interaction, reflecting how, typically, conversation flows from one topic to another (Table 6, Appendix 1).

Activity in the Community

All five companies linked their peer educator program to community activity. Some companies set targets for this activity, either in the form of

employees of both companies have extensive dealings with the public within the work environment). In fact peer educators in *all* the companies reported high levels of such interactions. During in-depth interviews it was established that such figures included not only customers but also subcontracted workers, employees of outsourced functions, visitors, and, in the retail company, outside merchandisers. Thus, this category is a valid indication of informal work conducted by peer educators, though further research would be required to establish exactly who falls into this category and in what proportions.

2. It was established that this related to making speeches at funerals or other gatherings. While such activity is extremely important and should not be ignored, for the purposes of clarity any claim to speak informally to more than sixty people per month was excluded.

visits to community-based HIV/AIDS projects such as hospices or child care centers or, in the case of one company, educational events in public places, such as taxi (public transport minibus) ranks. Others simply encouraged community activity, but effectively allowed this to be driven by peer educators.

Despite these variations in organization, workplace peer educators conducted community-based activity irrespective of the peer educator/community activity model their company adopted and at a greater level of activity than was expected in "job descriptions." As discussed above, most workplace peer educators were engaged in informal activity with people outside of work. Mineco's peer educators kept diaries that recorded where each interaction took place. The majority of these (57 percent) took place outside of work (Table 7, Appendix 1). Just under half of workplace peer educators were involved in community-based HIV/AIDS projects, which often had little—if anything—to do with projects that the company had formally adopted.

Peer educators conducted a wide range of AIDS-related activities in their communities. These included discussions within families; providing home-based care for neighbors dying of AIDS; advice to local youth; "hijacking" conversations in taxis to counter myths and misinformation; offering condoms to friends when on a "girls' night out" (i.e., a social event for a group of women friends with the possibility of attracting male attention); and giving talks to church groups, youth groups, and schools. Only the latter, along with the formalized company visit to AIDS-related institutions, really fit into the job description of a workplace peer educator. The other activities reflected a more deeply embedded process of community membership.

Workplace peer educators operate across company and community. Given their motivations for becoming peer educators, this engagement straddling work and community is not surprising. While AIDS managers running company peer educator programs sometimes believe they have, Pygmalion-like, created peer educators, many employees are peer educators not because the company asks them but because the company provides space and opportunity for them to respond to the epidemic. It is helpful, therefore, to understand that these peer educators treat their work-based activities as a component, rather than as the center, of their work to combat AIDS.

Roles

Some managers tried to monitor and evaluate peer education programs by collecting and analyzing a range of statistics that "sliced and diced" their activity. Such an exercise in dissection missed much of the texture and variety of peer educator activity. Those who become peer educators were, by definition, asked to act as lay educators. In addition they were often asked to take on other roles such as filling condom dispensers or organizing World AIDS Day events. Beyond these practical tasks, as Shaun Pulse at Bestbuyco explained, the roles, or "hats," that peer educators needed to wear and the rapidity with which these needed to be changed could be daunting.

> You have to see that a person is being treated in a [correct] way; whether it is counseling, playing doctor, playing nurse, playing mother, playing father. That kind of thing. Because sometimes someone who's got a family or friend who is HIV-positive, he needs to speak to somebody. So, then you have to take up the role of say a priest, by consoling that person. Then you get a person who lost someone to AIDS and then you have to play the role of a mother by consoling that person by saying "OK, right, you must cry." So, there's many hats in the role of peer educator that you need to wear because the one minute you are an educator [and] the next minute you need to play a consoling [role].

Peer education in practice is not just about ticking off the number of talks given, the number of visits to AIDS orphanages, or the number of conversations about AIDS in the course of the day. Rather there are processes and patterns that, while made up of a string of discrete interactions, amount to more than the sum total of a completed Monitoring & Evaluation form.

Consider, for example, what it means to initiate a discussion about safe, or safer, sex—a critical component in preventing HIV infection. The peer educator must openly discuss what this entails and encourage its practice. This is not easy because every individual will interpret and deal with the three key recommendations—abstinence, being faithful, and using condoms (ABC)—differently, while putting them into practice is often hampered by different belief systems and norms. Realistically, maintaining abstinence may require encouraging masturbation, a deeply taboo activity in some communities. Remaining faithful may require couples to use pornography, games, and sex toys to prevent monogamy becoming monotony. How do you facilitate such a conversation between husband and wife? Similarly, condoms are, for many people, not something they are comfortable with or able to easily use and—as we shall see in Chapters 4 and 5—initiating a discussion about condom use can open a Pandora's box of problems for one or the other partner involved in the relationship.

Moreover, if peer educators were to help their coworkers and community members talk about an uncomfortable topic, they themselves needed first to become comfortable. Peer educators, however, are embedded within the often sexually conservative and/or hypocritical values of their communities. As Manuel at Autostar explained, "I was scared to talk about it [sex]. [But the company training] was very useful, and it was very [pause] like [pause] um, how can I say [pause] educational, *ja* educational…it's very enjoyable to talk about it…I had known about it, obviously I had known about sex, it's just that I got more information on things [about which] I thought [there] was a limit."

Good facilitation at training sessions encouraged talk about sex within a supportive group of other peer educators. When peer educators laughed together they could more easily move collectively into previously taboo areas. The trainers at Finco used an exercise in which participants assessed the infection risk of different sexual practices. At one session, after they evaluated anal and oral sex, with and without condoms, the session erupted into laughter when the facilitator asked them to assess "vaginal sex with a condom" and a female peer educator loudly heckled her answer of "Lovely!"

Taking the same messages out into the general workforce was more difficult, and peer educators sometimes faced a hostile reception from coworkers. They had to be careful not to make implications that could cause offense while at the same time getting their message across. Manuel explained that she needed to tread carefully when addressing members of her work team who paid for sex outside of their marriages in local *shebeens* (drinking places):

> I would make it a joke. Like I'll say, "You know, guys that are married, I don't think girls should be going around looking for excitement from [other] men. They have excitement [their husbands] at home and you know you can get some for [your wife] in adult [sex] shops to show how you can

> make your sex life exciting after fifteen, twenty years." I'll make it up so that they'll accept it. If I tell them not to go to the *shebeen,* they'll ask me "Who the hell do you think you are?"

Even though peer educators became "sex talkers," they constantly drew into the center of their work the importance of the family and the need to actively address personal relationships between men and women. (Outside of Finco none of the peer educators I interviewed identified themselves as being gay or lesbian. Most peer educators were well aware, from their training sessions, of the dangers of male gay sex in regard to HIV transmission, but in their day-to-day experience they appeared to deal only with heterosexual relationships.) Such an approach called for a holistic understanding of a range of problems, not only HIV/AIDS, that they encountered among people at work and in their communities.

Just over half of peer educators reported that some discussions with coworkers were emotionally stressful. This was greater than the percentage of 40 percent that reported that coworkers had disclosed that they were HIV-positive. Disclosure is likely to be emotionally difficult. Lena Mosia in Bestbuyco explained, "Being a peer educator is stressful. When you come face to face with somebody opening up to you [that they are HIV-positive] you have to keep it to yourself. You have to be a rubbish bin for whatever they cough out."

In addition to learning that a coworker is HIV-positive, peer educators may learn that a coworker's relatives have been diagnosed positive or are dying of AIDS or they may be told about sexual abuse, rape, or family violence—which is a widespread problem in South Africa. Such revelations contribute to their emotional labor (Hochschild 1983).

Although peer educators were empathic when dealing with their coworkers' revelations, this did not stop them from exhibiting a will of steel when it came to the stigmatization of those with HIV/AIDS. As part of the workforce, peer educators were in a strong position to challenge stigmatization. To do so in a way that confronts coworkers with whom they must remain in close contact required courage and deft action. Phumzile Sithole, a peer educator in Bestbuyco, discovered that one of her coworkers had been gossiping about the status of an employee whose husband had died. She knew she had to intervene and asked the woman why she was gossiping and also if she knew her own HIV/AIDS status. The woman did not. She left the woman to form her own conclusions about her own ignorance but threatened to take her to the store manager if she continued her malicious gossip. Sithole's actions signaled to other employees that their fellow workers' HIV status was not a good topic for *skinder* (gossip) and that such gossip would be open to public censure.

Another way that peer educators made it clear that stigmatizing those with the disease was no longer acceptable was by deliberately and openly befriending those who were HIV-positive. A number of colleagues who were HIV-positive confided in Juliet Hennings, a frontline (checkout) supervisor in one of Bestbuyco's supermarkets. One had been considering quitting his job to be nearer his stepmother for support. She had persuaded him otherwise, telling him that: "In this store there might be [some] people who don't support him, but I will be here for him always... he doesn't get that much support from his stepmother, so I spoke to him and asked him if maybe it's not better for him to stay."

When I asked Hennings why she had done this, she said that she saw this colleague as a "brother" and made a point of chatting to him every day at work. Hennings also befriended another peer who was known to be HIV-positive: "So you know, I decided from that day on[wards] that she's my friend... [and] now since that day she's my friend."

In their role of "stigma busters," peer educators are far more than conveyer belts for—or translators of—information. If their actions are to be successful they must, by example and by intervention, stake out a public position on the shop floor in order to reverse the moral standing of AIDS within their own workplaces.

A Response from Below

Describing roles that peer educators take on—such as sex talkers, family builders, and stigma busters—moves us away from an abstract evaluation and highlights how they are embedded within context, cultures, and emotions that are often far from the institutional imagination of the company. Important as this is, it still does not do justice to the larger project that peer educators are undertaking and which the following chapters attempt to capture. This is, in part, because this larger project appears, on the surface, to be much less dramatic, and certainly much less quantifiable, than peer educator activity measured by type, by location, or even by categorized roles.

Embedded within communities at work and at home, almost every act undertaken by peer educators can, when viewed through a wider lens, be seen as part of an ongoing struggle to mitigate the impact of the disease, to normalize AIDS, and to engage in the construction of meaning around the epidemic. This latter task is paramount. It is the starting point that has too often been overlooked. Experienced from below, AIDS remains contested in the social space of peer educators and their peers.

4

Backstage Social Divisions

A half dozen or so peer educators are holding their monthly meeting in Robert Mokwena's office in the mining hostel where well over a thousand men live far from their homes. Mokwena has had an office for only a couple of years, though he's been a peer educator for six. He was promoted to a clerk after twenty years working underground. He is short but powerfully built; underground his job was to shovel loose rock that the mechanical grabs were too clumsy to scoop after blasting. A table is stacked high with brightly colored government leaflets on HIV/AIDS and other sexually transmitted diseases in a range of languages next to several large boxes of condoms. The walls are plastered with posters, photos, and newspaper clippings about AIDS.

The peer educators have come in from their various jobs on the mine. Those who work underground have supportive supervisors that approve their attendance. Nelly Tlouane has to keep nipping out of the meeting to check on her office just down the corridor; there is nobody able to cover for her today. Everybody, except myself, is African and, apart from Nelly, all are men. They are all ethnically Batswana[1] and, although for my benefit they speak in English, when the discussion gets animated they break into Setswana in which they are more comfortable. Most can speak several African languages as well as Fanagolo—the hybrid language of instruction used on the mines. Less than half the active peer educators were able to make it to today's meeting, but even if they all had been able to attend, the profile of the group would be the same.

The meeting starts, as it will end, with Isaac Taung, who works in a maintenance team but is a *moruti* (preacher) on Sundays, leading them in prayer. There are several items of business, but not infrequently the agenda gets sidetracked into discussions around AIDS, where the problems lie, and what they should be doing about it. That's when the discussions heat up. There is, as in almost every meeting, criticism of the government's handling of the epidemic. Saul Makoko is explaining that the government isn't doing enough to push prevention because it argues that it is not AIDS that kills but poverty. "Does poverty say 'don't use a condom?'" he asks rhetorically. But Tlouane doesn't agree. "The poor concentrate on having sex because they don't have enough to eat!" she counters—making an eating motion with her hand as she speaks. Peter Mopedi, a big man who operates a winch underground, attempts a compromise, "poor women who have to work as a prostitute can't refuse [to have unprotected sex]." Nevertheless, Tlouane is not mollified, "it's one [and the same thing]" she stubbornly maintains about poverty and unprotected sex. The matter is clearly unresolved, but another topic is already melding into the discussion. "What about rich people, they can also be infected," Charles Mothibi, a store man, throws out. He tells an apocryphal story about a man with the three *C*s: cell-phone,

1. Within the Sotho group of languages (Sesotho, Sepedi, and Setwana) a largely standard set of word prefixes denote different noun classes. The prefix *ba* refers to people in the plural; hence *Batswana* refers to a group of ethnic Tswana. In the singular, the prefix is *mo.* Robert Mokwena's surname refers, in a literal translation, to him being a person of the *kwena* (crocodile) clan that forms a major subgrouping of the Batswana. Though to confirm if this is actually the case, we would need to know not Robert's surname but his clan name. While not appearing on any formal documentation, every African in South Africa knows to which clan (to which membership is passed down the male line) and ethnic group they belong. The prefix *se* indicates a group of nouns that includes language—hence the language of the Batswana is Setswana. Finally the prefix *bo* can be used to indicate a location, hence Botswana the state that borders South Africa's North West Province where most South African Batswana live. In Sesotho, the prefix *le* is used to make the name of the Basotho state, Lesotho.

cash, and car. Enough for him to tempt a woman. "When can I pick you up?" and they arrange to meet. He lies to his wife and uses cash to put petrol in the car. "He gets infected; she [the wife] gets infected."

Mokwena, always wanting to focus on what can be done, asks the group, "How can we as peer educators empower women?" Makoko counters, consistent with his line that it's not poverty that determines condom use, that it's a problem of machismo culture; *ke monna* (I am man). He draws on the Jacob Zuma rape trial and how his wives are in no position to negotiate safe sex with him (after he'd had sex with an HIV-positive woman).[2] The group now launches into a discussion as whether it's best to empower women or change male attitudes.

Suddenly, Taung, who has said nothing since his opening prayer, asks everybody, "Why do nurses and doctors get HIV/AIDS?" The point brings everybody to a halt—doctors and nurses are educated, are not poor, and must know about HIV and AIDS. There is no satisfactory answer on hand. Mothibi breaks the silence by making the point that anybody can be infected and starts to list them: "Teachers, doctors..." Tlouane jumps in enthusiastically and adds to the list, "Managers!" On this they agree wholeheartedly—managers can also be infected (and by this, they mean not just managers but whites). Mokwena sums up this point of consensus because we are now well over time and the meeting needs to be brought to an end. "It cuts across [everybody]; it's just that we're still in denial."

These overlapping discussions about HIV infection looped endlessly within and through the peer educator meetings that I attended. What is driving the epidemic? And what, if the epidemic is to be checked, should they be doing with whom? If they were moving to consensus on these questions, it was a very slow process. But that is not surprising; some of their debates closely mirrored the confused discourse of experts who, despite prodigious AIDS research, have yet to produce a unified model of how and why the AIDS epidemic is unfolding with such aggression in South Africa. But I suggest the peer educators' discussion is valuable. I hope this, not untypical, vignette highlights three points.

2. In December 2005 Jacob Zuma, a polygamist and then the country's deputy president, was charged with the rape of a family friend in Johannesburg. He was found not guilty but admitted to having unprotected sex with a women he knew to be HIV-positive—despite being the chair of the South African National AIDS Council.

First, that in many respects the peer educators in Mokwena's office were very similar: all Africans from the same ethnic group, all workers, most were men, all were Christian, and all had received some formal training on HIV/AIDS. The second point is that they disagreed with each other over why people get infected and what they should be doing about it. The third is that the problems they were grappling with are complex, interlinked, and stoutly defended from different subscribed perspectives.

The ability to grasp these points depends partly on perspective. From the viewpoint point of, say, a white, university-educated, English-speaking manager running a mining company's HIV/AIDS program, a group of African, polyglot workers who volunteer as peer educators seem—on the face of it—to represent the majority of employees the program wants to reach. However, from the point of view of those same peer educators, the difference between themselves and their peers, and, indeed, among the peer educators themselves, has a tremendous influence over the work they will do largely out of management's sight.

Both views have validity. Compared to management, peer educators do have an advantage in communicating with workers about HIV and AIDS. When they operate they are functioning on one side of, rather than across, the industrial divide within South African companies and its extension outside workplaces as social divisions between white/rich and black/poor communities. This allows peer educators to circumvent an initial set of communication barriers, between distinctly dissimilar individuals. However, what this chapter explores is how quickly differences and tensions emerge among seemingly similar individuals. This phenomenon, and its implications for peer educators, is illustrated using gender, race, and belief in traditional and spiritual healing. These three important facets configuring individuals' identity determine, in part, the degree of similarity between peers. They do not, of course, form the sum total of any individual's identity. Additional facets of identity are potentially endless and attempting to describe them all would produce a very long chapter. The three examples of gender, race and belief in traditional healing illustrates, rather than comprehensively charts, how different identities structure backstage social spaces and what this means in the era of AIDS. The next two sections draw on Erving Goffman's dramatic conceptualization of social interaction to build an analytical framework that will assist us in understanding the work of HIV/AIDS peer educators.

Conceptualizing Social Space: Front- and Backstage Presentation

The use of peer educators acknowledges the differences between people that influence communication. The nature of interaction between people demarcates social spaces and the norms or rules that operate within them. Goffman's *The Presentation of Self in Everyday Life* (1958) outlines a dramaturgical conception of social interaction to supplement four existing perspectives: technical, political, structural, and cultural. This perspective differentiates between public, front-stage and private, backstage spaces.

Front- and backstage spaces are socially constructed understandings of a situation with different characters and roles. *Front-stage spaces* are the site of public performances or encounters between individuals or teams of actors and an audience. As with a staged play, the actors seek to convince the audience of the credibility of what they are watching—something that requires intimate cooperation between the cast or team members to project the appropriate image. The audience also constitutes a team with its own image to project because they are simultaneously aware of their own credibility being assessed as a performance itself. The important thing is to carry off performances convincingly and to maintain consensual understandings of the social situation for actors and audience. If achieved, social order is maintained, with actors and audience reproducing social relationships between them and the credibility of individual actors within teams sustained.

In contrast to front-stage space, there is only one team present in private, *backstage space,* and there is no need for staged performances. As Goffman (1958, 69–70) outlined, frank preparations for front-stage performances can be made in these private spaces: "illusions and impressions are openly constructed...Here the team can run thought its performances." Moreover, in backstage spaces "the performer can relax; he can drop his front, forgo speaking his lines, and step out of character." Backstage, Goffman argues, performances are not necessary; one can be oneself, not an actor.

Thus, for example, a family will put on a public performance when entertaining a (nonintimate) visitor to the home that is likely to be very different in content and style to what takes place in the absence of an outsider. Homes, if large enough, may be physically divided into front-stage space—a reception or best room were public performances are staged—and the backstage spaces such as the kitchen or family living room when only "team members" spend time and where a different, less scripted mode of interaction takes place. But, in Goffman's conception of social space, front- and backstages are not physically determined. Thus, a manager's office may be the setting for front-stage performances, such as instructing a subordinate. Here the manager, supported by the stage props his office provides, will ensure a desired definition of the situation, including their managerial prerogative, is maintained. Yet, with only a minor change in stage props, such as putting one's feet up on the desk, the same office becomes an intimate backstage space where the manager may share uncensored criticism of the way the company is being run with another manager.

Although much of Goffman's work focuses on front-stage performances (1958, 1961, 1966), he is aware of constraints on just how far one can truly move out of public character in backstage spaces. Thus, he notes, in a chapter of *The Presentation of Self in Everyday Life* (1958) on backstage space, that members of a team need, even when backstage, to sustain the impression that he or she is reliable and will, when an audience is present, perform well front stage. Additionally, morale needs to be maintained backstage—limiting the extent to which criticism can be expressed—if the team is to be able to sustain effective front-stage performances. Both these points are pertinent to the central focus of this chapter: the recognition of back stage social space as complex and structured terrain for peer educators to operate within rather than straightforward, honest and relaxed social spheres. A third point made by Goffman about backstage limits provides a more direct entry to this idea. Constraints on behavior also occur when members of a backstage team are not the same. Thus, if the team, "[c]ontains representatives of fundamental social divisions, such as different age-grades, different ethnic groups, etc., then some discretionary limits will prevail on freedom of backstage activity. Here no doubt, the most important division is the sexual one, for there seems to be no society in which members of the two sexes, however closely related, do not sustain some appearances before each other" (1958, 79).

This chapter explores backstage divisions concerning HIV/AIDS, starting with gender. Before this, however, we link some of the key aspects of peer educator activity—formal talks and informal discussions, described in the previous chapter—to Goffman's conception of social space to establish the value of dramaturgical theory in understanding the work of peer education.

Peer Education, Front-Stage Encounters, and Backstage Advantages

Although the need for peer educators is often rationalized in terms of language barriers and educational differences, the idea of a manager educating workers about HIV/AIDS is additionally inappropriate because whenever a manager encounters workers a front-stage performance comes into being. However genuine intentions might be, it will not be possible, irrespective of prop changes such as invoking AIDS as a national crisis rather than company concern, for either side to engage frankly about HIV and AIDS. Communication will be curtailed by the power differential inherent in the relationship. It does not take long for employees to learn that when interacting with management they must maintain a performance as a competent and capable worker. To do so includes guarding information about health that might compromise this performance. Such performances may need to be maintained even in encounters with company medical practitioners because, despite their professional status, they are part of management. As a peer educator in one of the auto companies explained, workers feared that managers, keen to maintain production, would use information on their health to remove them from the workforce.

> Most of the people they don't trust the medical department. They don't trust even the [medical] sisters...[T]hey think that at medical department...they want to eliminate those who have this [HIV] and send them home....They don't trust anyone...Not actually about HIV/AIDS only. Some have been taken from their department because they are diabetic. They [management] have now taken them to a labor pool [i.e. on standby to fill in when other workers are absent]...They are waiting there, they are going to float in the plant....They've been diagnosed at the medical department that they've got the diabetes. [But] they are always present at work, they did not complain about their job, and they are always doing their job in a right way. So, why on earth are their managers choosing

> them? Why on earth are they the first people to be taken out from their job?

Thus, there may be tangible concerns on the part of employees that underlie the need for carefully guarded performance during encounters with management. Any spoiling of an image as a competent and capable worker may have negative consequences. In the highly charged atmosphere that surrounds AIDS even taking too much interest in the topic can be (mis)interpreted as indicating that the questioner is HIV-positive, or at least at risk. Given the possible consequences, managers, far from being people who can be confided in, are to be feared. One peer educator from a retail company vividly demonstrated this point in an interview with her own improvised stage props. Reaching over and grabbing some of my papers, she raised her hand as though holding a pen over an imaginary disciplinary letter. "They don't listen! They just reprimand! He [the manager] has a pen and paper, he's going to reprimand you! [Her hand lunges down as though about to sign the letter.] Just reprimand! [Again, she lunges forward with the pen.] Just reprimand! [A final lunge.] While you are trying to explain your problem. [She exaggeratedly signs the disciplinary letter and pushes it across the table toward me.]"

Because the relationship between management and workers invokes front-stage performances, workplace peer education is a better way of communicating about HIV/AIDS. As a peer educator in Finco put it, "There is an open-door policy in this company [for employees to approach managers], but peer educators can be trusted." Peer education offers a more effective communication channel on HIV/AIDS because relationships of power present in front-stage encounters between management and workers are sidestepped and the need of the audience to perform is less prominent.

Peer educators giving formal talks on HIV/AIDS (as described in Chapter 3) represents a first step in this direction, but it is limited. Rather than a manager standing up to deliver messages on HIV/AIDS to workers, a worker volunteers to do so. This confers advantages, but the context retains many aspects of a front-stage encounter and its disadvantages.

One problem is that the peer educator is seen as acting on management's behalf because, for example, they may be given time to speak during the shift meeting while the supervisor stands by, tacitly demonstrating that this is managerially approved activity. There is some irony here. A frequent problem for peer educators attempting to conduct formal talks is *not* being given time to talk to coworkers because of production pressures, or, when permission to speak is given, this is constrained by the supervisor's evident desire to keep the session short and start production. Yet, such talks may be viewed by workers as management's attempt to advance their own agenda. If so, such talks will be passively endured or actively subverted by difficult questions and undermining stage whispers.

Even if peer educators can demonstrate independence from management, formal talks may invoke other familiar front-stage encounters such as the teacher instructing a class or the preacher delivering a sermon to a congregation. These associations with other front-stage encounters with deeper psychological grooves affect both the audience's interpretation and the peer educator's own performance. For many South African workers, encounters following these familiar patterns are likely, reflecting their experiences of schooling, to suggest that there is information that they must learn, without necessarily understanding its relation to their own lives. Alternatively, reflecting their experiences of organized religion, that there is a set of values to which they should publicly subscribe but about which they may feel ambiguous in their daily lives.

Formal talks can be done well or badly. At its worst, a peer educator may deliver information they do not understand, while the audience feigns appreciation; and the module is ticked off as "done" by the HIV/AIDS program coordinator. At its best, well-understood information is presented clearly, and the audience is engaged and asks questions. Nevertheless, even in this latter situation, individuals within the audience may hold back on what they ask given the presence of coworkers. Formal talks can also be replicated away from the workplace wherever performances between actors and an audience are staged. These can include church services, formal speeches at funerals or other social events, talks to youth groups, meeting of clubs, unions, political parties, and so on. But even when staged away from the front line of industrial and class divide, pressure for both sides to maintain appearances—the peer educator as competent authority, the audience as competent recipients of information—may hinder communication within this setting. This is not to dismiss the value of peer educators' formal talks, but to highlight that this form of activity is likely to remain framed as a front-stage encounter despite the change of actor from manger, or AIDS expert, to peer educator.

Only with informal peer educator activity are the constraints of front-stage encounters shaken off. Backstage spaces, where only one team is present, include the family watching TV in their living room, employees sitting together in the work canteen, friends drinking in a *shabeen,* members of a church congregation chatting after the service, banter in the changing room, traveling to or from work, preparing food during a night vigil, and so on. The idea that backstage space is one in which people are able to relax and drop pretenses should mean that communication within them should be easy and effective. The advantage of similarity and familiarity lies at the heart of peer education. Peer educators should, it is assumed, make rapid headway in these backstage spaces. Introducing appropriate information on HIV/AIDS should facilitate open discussions leading to a clear understanding of the disease and a consensus around how best, as a group or team, to respond individually and collectively. The following examination of backstage space in terms of gender, race, and belief in traditional healing, illustrate why this is rarely the case.

Gender Relationships and the Family: Intimacy by Proxy

In a heterosexually transmitted epidemic, relationships between men and women are central to the transmission of the HIV virus. These relationships, which contain the potential to transmit disease, also anchor families, which are regarded as the most intimate of all social spaces. The bond between the couple is seen as one of the closest of all relationships and that between parents and children as one of guidance, protection, and care. It is to these relationships that we most readily resort to the idea of love—the prioritization of another over the self—as explaining what holds together individuals of different genders, in the case of (heterosexual) couples, and ages, in the case of parents and children. While we recognize these as idealizations that cannot live up to all we hope for, they remain powerful projections; considerable effort is made to support the intimate privileges of these relationships and concern expressed when they fail.

Such relationships should provide myriad centers of resistance to the spread of HIV/AIDS, with regular sexual partners—whether in a marriage or not—seeking to protect each other from infection, and with parents preparing children for a world in which HIV and AIDS is ever present. Yet in the experience of most peer educators, this is far from what happened within families. Often, rather than protecting family members from AIDS, the emphasis within families was to keep members ignorant about AIDS.

This was especially so when the disease was close to home. Thus, a number of peer educators explained how after company training on HIV/AIDS they had come to realize that family members had in fact died of AIDS but that this had been denied and disguised. As Ntokozo Ndlovo, a peer educator in the financial institution explained, "I had one of my cousins [who died of AIDS], all the signs were there. My mother is a nursing sister [professional nurse]... my mother knew what was wrong, but she kept on saying it was something else, not this [HIV/AIDS]." Public denial of AIDS is widespread, and this silence extends into the most intimate of family spaces. Tlouane in the mining company recorded in her diary how, during a visit to a sick teacher whom she knew, she discovered that the teacher was attempting to hide her HIV-positive status from her daughter.

> I understood that Edna [the teacher] was not well for some time. I then went to check her at her place. She then told me that the doctor said its "gripe." When I [had to] leave, her daughter, Mpuse, volunteered to take me half way [accompany her part of the way back home; a common politeness in African cultures]. On the way, she told me that she saw ART [antiretroviral drugs] in her mother's bedroom when she was busy cleaning it, but her mother never told her about that. Mpuse said Edna was hiding the treatment, saying the doctor said she had gripe. She was so upset because her father passed away in 2002, and she is the only child.

Tlouane also recorded a more dramatic betrayal of family relationships in which a husband had been hiding his HIV-positive status from his wife. In a diary entry, entitled "Playing innocent but dangerous within the family," Tlouane recorded her visit to a hospital where Bongi, the husband of Mando, had been admitted.

> Bongi was a man aged forty-one [who] lived with his family for ten years. He was a hard worker, and also treated his family with honor and respect. The amazing thing was that he never told his wife, friends, nor his family

> that he was HIV-positive. He took the treatment and even the diet secretly. As time went by he became tempted, no longer taking treatment as usual as he thought he was 100 percent fit. The sickness struck him like lightning [and] he ended up being admitted in hospital diagnosed [as] a long-term HIV patient who failed to stick to the treatment...
>
> His wife, Mando, [had] only [just] realized that he was HIV-positive. Her husband felt so ashamed and asked for forgiveness. Bongi also said to his wife that he was aware that he acted so humble and innocently to his whole family while dangerous within them.

Commenting on this account of how Bongi had maintained a deceit within the intimate sphere of the couple and family, Tlouane pointed to the gap between expected family relationships and what had happened. "Bongi was not supposed to hide his HIV status from his wife or family especially. Because they are the first ones who are expected to support him."

Any explanation of why a man hides his HIV-positive status from his wife or a mother's from her daughter underlines the extent to which HIV and AIDS remain stigmatized. Appreciating this is critical in understanding how someone might "play innocent but dangerous within the family." But this only shows one side of a coin; there remains the need to understand why the supposed intimate relationships of family frequently fold so completely in the face of HIV and AIDS.

One explanation focuses on aberrations from the family ideal: adultery, married men using sex workers, rape, child sexual abuse, sugar daddies, and so on. Answers incorporating deviations from idealized relationships are easy to construct. They feed off a number of social narratives: moral breakdown in South African society, which can be projected from a Christian standpoint or a traditionalist world view; the detrimental effects of poverty on peoples' ability to control their lives, and the subordination of women within South African society. There is frequently juggling among proponents of particular explanations as to the relative weight of these factors and often consensus building around particular social pathologies to which all can agree. For example, the sex worker who is forced to accept risky sex from a married man because she needs the money and cannot turn down his demand for sex without a condom—a scenario that neatly incorporates moral, economic, and gender perspectives. Such deviations from an idealized set of family relationships are responsible for HIV transmission. However, this pathologizing approach to the problem all too easily sets up a cast of villains and innocents that is emotionally satisfying but distracting. The more mendacious the plot, the further it becomes removed from problems that lie at the heart of a "normal" family (Baylies and Bujra 2000) and the belief that (normal) families constitute an intimate backstage social space.

Eilsa Sobo's (1995) research among poor African-American women stresses how they employ interlocked narratives to convince themselves that they are in a faithful relationship. The first is a Monogamy Narrative, in which their partner is seen as being faithful to them despite other women's men being unfaithful; the second is the Wisdom Narrative, in which they regard themselves as astute judges of their partners, which has enabled them to select a partner who will be faithful. The use of condoms within a relationship negates both these narratives: "Because condoms are associated with infidelity and deceptive behaviour, using them implies that partners do not truly care for one another" (137). The rupture of these narratives in the face of undeniable evidence to the contrary, such as being tested positive for HIV despite themselves being faithful, leads, in Sobo's view, to a third narrative, Betrayal, in which it is retrospectively determined that their partner must never have really loved them.

What Sobo describes is not an intimate backstage space that a couple share together. Rather, the relationship is one in which individuals separately construct "intimacy," which is confirmed not with their partner but by symbols—such as not using condoms. This is intimacy by proxy, rather than being truly oneself with another.

This understanding of how intimacy is achieved through the symbolic abandonment of condoms without direct communication between partners was one that South African peer educators are familiar with. In explaining why she thought people continued to be infected with HIV, Rachel Baloyi in Finco explained, drawing on her own experiences as well as more broad generalizations, that part of the problem was,

> The way we conduct our relationships. Unfortunately, we [start a] relationship and we come to a point where we feel comfortable and you think you know somebody...Maybe [we're] not communicating enough in a relationship, because I feel if we are going to be in a relationship and decide that we're not going to use condoms we need some commitment from both parties. And it's probably because people don't even think of sitting down and

> discussing about such things.... *Ja,* people being comfortable, you know, you reach that stage. "I've been going out with him for six months... I know him." And you feel comfortable and you think it's the right time, without even discussing it with him, you know? And it's something that you wake up one day and guess what? We forgot to use one [a condom]... why should we use it the next day? And it becomes a pattern.

In Mineco, Karabo Semenya, made a similar observation, also drawing on her own experience.

> From my personal point of view, when you are going out with a person, at first you use a condom, and you use a condom, and you use a condom, and then once you get used to the person and everything [clicks her fingers] just happens so quickly and you just forget the condoms, you just do whatever. And you think, because I was with this person for this long period, I think we trust each other now, not to play around... It just happens. Like you have to do something, and it just happens... So, if like um, for example, let me talk about me. I used to go with my boyfriends. And like, there were times when you would think, "Oh, you are stranded and you have to do something," [laughs briefly] and there are no condoms around, but it just happens. [But with your boyfriend,] you come to trust him. You give your life to him. You think that, "Okay. This is the person I want to be with. Why should I not trust him?"

A key point made in these two accounts is that intimacy within a couple is achieved in silence with discontinuing condom use. Doubts are overcome, not through discussion and agreement, but through one-sided narratives that use symbols rather than communication for verification. This form of intimacy between two people, far from reducing risk through open talk about the dangers that unprotected sex might bring, introduces risk because unprotected sex becomes the foundation of the couple's intimacy.

Given this, attempts to talk openly within close relationships about the risk of HIV infection may well break implicit understandings on which backstage family order is based, including acceptance of unequal power between men and women. Janet Bujra (2006, 5) argues that "[t]he micro-politics of sexuality reflects a strategic conjuncture of power struggles at more macro levels.... AIDS emerges as a terrible threat to existing patterns of sexual behaviour and expression of sexuality, it is also a threat to power relations because the rules no longer apply."

Bujra's point here is to demonstrate how sexual behavior for couples is determined by a broader set of gender-biased rules governing what is acceptable. Because these rules are not effective in protecting against HIV infection, both men and women are threatened at a biological level, but a response in which women question the status quo, starting with the micropolitics of their own sexual relationships, threatens the wider social rules of gender relationships. Tlouane's report on a women's meeting at her church touches on how women are constrained in what they can initiate with their husbands.

> We as Christian Women's League decided to spend the day at the church to share ideas and information about HIV/AIDS. The league's chairperson, Sibongile... made us aware of the [actions] of our husbands, especially [those] who have extra [marital] affairs. She said that married [women] are the most at risk.... What Sibongile was saying is true, because a women cannot tell the husband all of a sudden that he must use a condom because he can turn things and say you slept around.

Here, even when the dangers within intimate relationships is publicly, and collectively, recognized, doing something about it drops back from the public, to the private, and the man can retaliate, invoking public norms in which the idea of a women sleeping around brings shame and sanctions. However, we need to take care before reverting to the idea of relationships in which women lack agency because of wider, socially constructed, rules. Tlouane, in an interview, talked about an incident in which she had first asked, and then confronted, a group of Xhosa male colleagues over the value of circumcision. In most, but not all, African ethnic groups in South Africa, ritualized circumcision is regarded as an important right of passage into manhood. Generally this is prepared for over a period of weeks or months at initiation schools in which boys are isolated from the rest of their community before the process culminates in circumcision.

> I don't know the reason why do they attend circumcision school. That's why I wanted to know from them. There are always the Xhosa's... they do this circumcision stuff... So I wanted to know from them, "Why?"... Some

said, "If you aren't from the circumcision school, they don't allow you to marry. Because you are not a real man." ... and then I disagree.

I said to them "Most of you are from the school. That school, neh? What are you doing now? You left your wives at home [referring to Xhosas from the Eastern Cape]. You are not supporting [them]. You don't respect your wife. You've got *nyatsis* [girlfriends] here. So, what is the use of that circumcision school? You are not real men." ... I told them straight, "What's the use of going there because you don't respect your wives, neh ... You don't give them money. You are not a real man. "*Eh-eh* [No], you don't support your family. A real man supports his family.... There's no good relationship between yourself and the wife. Because there's no commitment. There's no honesty. There's no whatever. You lack so many things. But you are from circumcision school."

Here the power of a socially assumed set of values—that circumcision confers manhood—is challenged. Tlouane, who had "chased away" the father of her daughter because he didn't support their child, points to the need for men to provide for wives and also to the lack of honesty within their relationships. Working in the company's HR department, she frequently witnessed the breakdown of these social relationships, with abandoned wives arriving at her office to complain that remittances from migrant husbands had ceased. Like Tlouane, a number of women peer educators had, despite social constraints, engaged the micropolitics of their own relationships. Baloyi in Finco explained how confronted with incontrovertible proof that her husband had been unfaithful without using protection (a child outside of their marriage), she had forced the use of condoms.

You know. I was married and I chose not to use any contraceptives so that I can use a condom with my husband because I have seen that he is capable of being unfaithful. And it was a choice, in a marriage, I had to make. And I did it.... And you know, it's not something that he denied. When I confronted him about it, he said, "Yes, there were no condoms for the day." Not even to say that something went wrong with the condom. There weren't condoms.... So, that's when I said I'm putting a stop to this.

But while these circumstances, in which her partner was caught acting recklessly, enabled her to introduce condoms into the relationship, she recognized that for others similar action would not be easy. "How do you just come one day in the house and say 'Love, I want us to use condoms' if there aren't any signs [of him being unfaithful]? If he asks you why, what will be your defense?" When I asked Baloyi if she though any man could be trusted in a relationship, she responded at first softly and then with increasing emphasis: "No. Much as no woman can be trusted. We tend to push everything onto men, but you still get unfaithful women. Unfortunately, we [women] are too clever. When we cheat, we do it right! [Laughter] Especially now [with HIV/AIDS]. It's everyone for himself. Everyone for himself and God for us. So, if you're going to say, 'I trust you with my life,' guess what? You'll be down six feet!"

She concluded this point by asserting that, in responding to AIDS, "The battle will be in marriage." But what this battle consists of can take two distinct forms. One, that Baloyi and some other peer educators took, was to win the "war of risk" by separating from their partner-cum-potential-death-sentence. Among the 598 peer educators who reported on their marital status in the 2005 survey, 11.4 percent of women were divorced (Table 8 in Appendix 1), compared to 3.5 percent of women (15 years and over) nationally (Statistics South Africa 2004). In being able to take such decisive action, female peer educators probably represent a more empowered group, both because of their self-selection and correlated leadership qualities and, at least in part, because of training that not infrequently stressed the importance of looking after oneself.

Peer education training often reinforced individual responsibility, sometimes quite starkly. In an observed training exercise, peer educators were told to imagine they were on a sinking ship with only one lifeboat that could not save everyone. First, participants were required to make a short speech to justify why they should have one of the limited places, and then they cast three votes, in secret, for who should get in the lifeboat. In fact, the votes were never counted; instead, the organizers asked who had voted for themselves. The few who admitted to doing so were praised; those who hadn't were chastised: "You have to look after yourself first because you can't trust other people without trusting yourself. You can help the community when you know how to help yourselves. It's important to look after ourselves." This message was focused specifically on the risk of being infected with HIV in a relationship, but at a deeper level clearly encouraged individual agency.

The limitations on what people, women especially, could do in relationships was however widely recognized. Reflecting on the lifeboat exercise, a nursing sister who coordinated a regional grouping of peer educators in Finco explained how peer educators might recognize their own situation as ones that put them at risk, but that confronting this would not be easy:

> When I did the [lifeboat] exercise, I thought "Shit! I'd like to be on the boat," but I never put myself on the boat. And that's wrong. We're wanting women to be empowered, but we are not showing them how disempowered they allow themselves to be.... It also made me realize it's OK to make choices for myself. In my interests. OK. I'm sorry Tommy, you're not going on the boat, but actually I want to be there... And it was a good penny drop [realization] for a lot of women.... They [the peer educators] got it. They got it. A lot of them got it loud and clear. But a lot of them I could see they could never change. Because they are caught in their whole way of life, whether it's for religious or cultural reasons. But they could never change it. Or they would have to wise up on how they would change it if they can't do it bulldozing [i.e. forcefully].

Some peer educators had left partners because the "penny had dropped" and because they had the courage and resources to follow through. In a couple of cases, this was attributed in part to their peer educator training. Others, like Tlouane, had left their partners before AIDS was a threat but for similar reasons of male unreliability that they had been unable to rectify within their relationships. For Nicol Manuel in Autostar, the lesson about needing to take no nonsense from men in a relationship had been learned from her mother, who had demanded that her husband leave because he was a *joller* (someone who enjoyed partying). "He used to go out and enjoy himself, he used to drink and he used to come back and fight." Although Nicol had a boyfriend, she pointed out that, "One thing that my mother taught me is that as a lady, an independent woman, you don't need to have a man in your life really because at the end of the day, if you're going to stick a man's nonsense, it can cause you to maybe lose your life." This point had been tragically underlined shortly before I interviewed Nicol.

> I count that [her mother separating from her father] as a blessing. It was hard for us growing up with a single parent, but at the end of the day it paid

> out because...on the eleventh of July [three weeks before the interview], my birthday, I spent half my day, from about two o'clock to six o'clock at the hospital with my father. I had to go and give him a bath and change him and feed him because he had thrush all over his throat and everything...he was really bad, and the nurses wanted my mother's consent to take blood tests and, obviously, he was [HIV] positive [and died a few days later]...
>
> So, as I was saying, I believe...that it was a blessing in disguise that he had to go because obviously if my mother stuck his nonsense, she'd have been infected...you know, um, he was the man. He could have done what he wanted to do and then still come back home, and my mother was, like, in a situation where she had to play the wife's role there, you know, wives have to sleep with their husbands...So, I believe that he would have definitely infected my mother and I would also have to be burying my mother, so I'm happy in a way, that she stood up for what was right.

But this ability to take control of their lives, and protect themselves from HIV infection, by doing without partners was not open to the majority. Louise Rasool, a female peer educator in Bestbuyco, explained how the women approached her for advice because their male partners were beating them or having affairs. She concluded that the most important thing she could do was help them stay HIV-negative even though they would most likely remain in an abusive relationship. "It's not easy to have him arrested or leave him because it happens to a lot of women and people have lived and stayed with men that are abusive for years and years and years. So you can't just tell somebody to leave her husband or go and have him arrested, you have to try and get better solutions that will suit her."

These better solutions, of smarting up to the danger of HIV infections within risky relationships, are explored in Chapter 5. For the moment, and in summary, peer educators sought generally not to undermine these relationships, but to support those within them; even when, as frequently was the case, there was little if any prospect for direct communication around sex and the risk of HIV infection as the result of one, or both, partners being unfaithful.

The central point of this section has been to establish that the social space of the family, and the couple in particular, is not a relaxed backstage social space in which communication between peers, albeit of different genders, is frank, relaxed, and straightforward. This is not a surprise; Goffman flagged gender as an exception to the backstage dropping of performances. Within the context of AIDS, however, it takes on added significance. Putting on performances in a relationship is likely to put you six feet under.

That performances are maintained in the backstage space of relationships is in part because of the privileges that, as Bujra points out, wider social values afford to men within their relationships. Speaking frankly about these would openly expose gender inequality and undermine them. Not surprisingly there is resistance to this from men and, given potential sanctions, reluctance on the part of women to challenge them. But women also maintain performances and, as Sobo outlines, play themselves into these roles.

Getting yourself out of these performances—of intimate sex without intimate knowledge—is not easy. As grassroots leaders a number of peer educators had taken direct personal action: closing down the show through separation or divorce. Peer educators recognized that this was not possible for many women, but that the threat of HIV infection required that something be done without the relationship itself being directly challenged. Neither of these responses fundamentally changes the sexual partnerships of backstage space nor the supposed intimacy of families that often remains a no-go zone for frank talk about HIV and AIDS.

Race: Similarity Undermining Credibility

In contrast to gender divisions that permeate most backstage spaces, race in South Africa still approximates to homogeneous backstage spaces. Frontstage industrial relations encounters are between different races, as well as classes. This picture is complicated by South Africa's four racial categories: African, colored, Indian, and white (see Chapter 1). Upward mobility of blacks (Africans, coloreds, and Indians), accelerating under post-apartheid affirmative action legislation, means that this situation is far from static, but racial division across the industrial divide remains. In the five companies researched during 2005, whites dominate management positions, while blacks, particularly Africans, constitute the bulk of lower-skilled workers (Table 9 in Appendix 1).

Depending on companies' location, the absence of significant numbers of coloreds and Indians in the workplace can simplify this situation to a stark contrast between white managers and African workers; this was the case in Mineco, which was included in the 2005 research and was also the company researched in 2006. Over 93 percent of Mineco's top and senior management was white, as was 85 percent of middle management. Africans made up 97 percent of semi-skilled, and 98 percent of unskilled workers (Table 10 in Appendix 1).

The salience afforded to race within South Africa powerfully projects similarity within, and difference between, racial categories. Despite the importance of "subsidiary" identities such as ethnicity, race provides an apparently clear-cut advantage for peer educators seeking to change behavior. White peer educators should be recruited to work with their white peers, while African peer educators should work with other Africans. However, there was not a proportional racial balance between company employees and peer educators. In the five researched companies, 82 percent of employees were black (African, Indian, or colored), but among peer educators the percentage was 92 percent. Whites composed 18 percent of employees, but only 8 percent of peer educators (Table 11 in Appendix 1). In Mineco, with its simpler and starker racial divisions, Africans made up 87 percent of employees but 93 percent of peer educators; whites 13 percent of employees but only 6 percent of peer educators (Table 12 in Appendix 1).

Thus, blacks are overrepresented, and whites, although not absent, are underrepresented (and few in number) as peer educators. In the mining company, with few coloreds and Indian employees, a simpler picture emerged in which Africans are overrepresented as peer educators, by 7.4 percent, and whites underrepresented, by 56 percent. What this should mean is that whites with a lower number of peer educators are subject to less peer communication on HIV and AIDS, but that Africans are better catered for with racially similar peer educators. At a statistical level this is true. But to see this double imbalance—in the racial structuring of the workplace and in the racial profile of peer educators—as unproblematic for African peer educators working with their African peers is mistaken. This section examines how the skewed racial composition of peer educators creates barriers to African peer educators within their racially homogeneous backstages spaces.

Data demonstrating an objective underrepresentation of white peer educators confirms what peer educators already knew from their own experiences. In a meeting of peer educators at Autocircle, the racial composition could not be overlooked: all twenty-five peer educators were African, as were the company's peer educator coordinator and the nursing sister attending the meeting. During a discussion on the need to have peer educators drawn from all levels of the company, one of the peer educators commented in open session that, "The peer education program is too black, it says hourly [paid workers]." In meetings of the Mineco group, again exclusively African in composition, this acknowledgment of a racial division of peer education was thinly coded as the "us and them issue" to which discussions not infrequently circled back.

Sometimes perceptions trumped objective evaluation of whites' role in company peer education programs. Thus, at one of Mineco's operations, a young African woman complained bitterly that there were no white peer educators. Yet that same day I interviewed a white man who had been an active peer educator at the site for six years. Nevertheless, despite sometimes overstated perceptions, the reality of a racial division of concern within companies around AIDS was evident. In Bestbuyco, Abraham Kgaba, an African who had been a peer educator for three years, talked about the lack of interest whites showed in their activity.

> In the [HIV/AIDS] talks that I have given I only saw one white person. And it hurts me a lot. Because even in the [company HIV/AIDS] booklet itself there's a questionnaire where it says, "Do we think that HIV is for blacks or for whites?" The majority in the talks are blacks and we only see one white. They [whites] don't want to attend because they believe it is [our problem].
>
> I've complained about it, but you don't even get the support of the [white] GM [store's general manager]. We've now got a new GM, it's almost a year and a half [that he's been at the store], he's never asked me as a Peer Educator what problems do I have, how can he assist me... It's the same [with, also white] Human Resource [management]. They have never asked us [what we are doing], they don't even attend. Not even to come and monitor what we do.

In Finco, Sibongile Muthwa, an African woman, explained how she felt when selected to attend training to become a peer educator as the only black person in her branch. "I was very uncomfortable when they nominated me [to be a peer educator] when I was in Richmond [branch]... [A]t that time I was the only black person there. And at the time of nomination I thought I was nominated because of my color and my [pause] and there's a stigma [pause] you know, with HIV [pause] black people." Nevertheless, she had attended the training and, as a result, had her own concerns about the racial profile of the disease addressed. "After attending the course, I didn't want to look at it [HIV/AIDS] as a color disease. I didn't want to see it as a black or a white person's disease. I looked at it as a disease out there and it affects everyone. No matter the color."

However, when Muthwa got back from training it was clear to her that, while the branch needed to have a peer educator, because of instructions from Head Office, they didn't want peer education. "Within the workplace people still feel that it's a black disease. It's your problem. You're black. You need to deal with it. [Attitudes] are still there. I requested that they give me a slot to give a talk [to colleagues], but it was very difficult for them to give me [time]. It was like, 'Who do you want to speak to here? Everyone is safe.'"

Where unions were racially mixed, a similar understanding of the epidemic was evident. Thus, in response to my questioning as to why white shop stewards were not peer educators, a union official of one mixed-race white-collar union in Mineco explained that problems around HIV/AIDS among the membership were confined to the few Africans members of the union. In a matter-of-fact way, he went on to observe that the union's one African shop steward dealt with any AIDS issues. Moreover, he added that white shop stewards steered clear of peer education because it would, they felt, mean interacting with Africans.

The view that AIDS is a problem for Africans and not for whites is not without basis. There are stark differences in HIV prevalence levels between races, with Africans statistically far more likely to be infected than whites (see Chapter 1). But, irrespective of this, a racially skewed response in the workplace creates a number of problems. Whites' disinterest over AIDS threatens to re-racialize South African workplaces at the very time that attempts, albeit often sluggish, are being made to overcome apartheid divisions. Additionally, since the trajectory of the epidemic is still unknown, the possibility that HIV will bridge groups and equalize racial prevalence levels cannot be discounted. Such a possibility will be more likely if whites continue to maintain psychological distance from the epidemic as an African problem, which an absence of white peer educators facilitates. As one member of Autocircle's all-African peer educator meeting noted, "A group like this feeds the view that it [HIV/AIDS] is a black problem."

Less obvious, but critical to understanding the contested nature of backstage social space around HIV/AIDS, is the impact that this racialized response to the epidemic has on the ability of African peer educators to bring about behavioral change among their African peers. Within South Africa's black population there continues to circulate folk theories that HIV is a biological weapon whites use to control the black population. A lack of concern on the part of whites about AIDS serves to support such theories. So, too, does a history of white attempts to limit black fertility in South Africa (Schneider and Fassin 2002; Stadler 2003; Webb 1997) and the Truth and Reconciliation Commission's revelations that an apartheid security program led by Dr. Wouter Basson investigated the use of biological weapons that would target blacks (Niehaus and Jonsson 2005; Washington 2007). In hearings of the Truth and Reconciliation Commission, it was established that while the front companies used by Basson developed a wide range of chemical and biological weapons, these did not include HIV. In 2002, Basson went on trial for seventy-six charges including murder and fraud. The trial collapsed, but in 2005 the Constitution Court ruled that a retrial could proceed. To date this has not happened.

Genocide-linked beliefs around AIDS are not confined to South Africa. In a study of 520 black American adults, 27 percent "endorsed the view that HIV is an artificially created virus designed by the federal government to exterminate the black population" (Klonoff and Landrine 1999). A study by Bogart and Thornburn (2005) of five hundred African Americans found belief in AIDS as a form of genocide against blacks to be held by 15 percent of respondents. Sobo (1995) describes a range of conspiracy theories present in African-American and Latino communities in the United States in which AIDS is seen to be a form of germ warfare waged against blacks. The U.S. equivalent to Basson's germ warfare program is the Tuskegee Syphilis Study (in which treatment was withheld from poor black participants) that discredits white scientists by linking them to the oppression of blacks. Such theories, which resonate with personal experience of racism, provide a psychological defense mechanism against the collective stigma that racially concentrated HIV prevalence creates.

In South Africa, such theories are located within the context of the apartheid regime's war against the liberation movement, white control of scientific knowledge, racial voting patterns, and majority rule following the 1994 elections. They also counter Western medical explanations of the disease and prevention messages based on this understanding. Much of this is concisely captured in a diary entry by Moses Direko, a peer educator in Mineco, when explaining why he thought peers had incorrect information on HIV/AIDS. "Most of the people they ask me about HIV and AIDS. They ask, 'Where does this come from? Because before there was no HIV and AIDS.' [They say,] 'This disease comes from those white people. They put injection into us black people because we get more babies every year. When we vote, black people pass [win] because we are many.'"

Dr. Basson not infrequently makes an appearance in these theories around the origins of AIDS. Mokwena also at Mineco recorded the comments of an African teacher during a discussion on a court case in Libya where a number of health professionals were on trial accused of infecting children with HIV. "Pule [the teacher] said, 'The nurses and other health workers are puppets of evil doers.' 'How?' [I asked her] 'Doctor Basson,' [she replied] 'infected soldiers with HIV and gave them money to sleep with black women, because they [whites] want to kill us and be able to win the elections.'"

Explanations as to how a white minority might want to use AIDS to control the majority black population can be expanded onto a global scale—with the racial dimension scaled up so that AIDS is viewed as a weapon of more powerful (white) countries to dominate developing (black) countries. Kgaba, in Bestbuyco, explained that prior to seeing people die of AIDS, he had assumed that it was something thought up to prevent Africans from having more children. "I always had the impression of America specifically not wanting Africa to grow. [So] I took the abbreviation of AIDS as an American Invention to Discourage Sex." He then went on to note that many people may continue to think like this because death certificates in South Africa do not record the cause of death as AIDS. Sam Mangala, a peer educator in Mineco, suggested that the nature of the disease supported the idea that it was a deliberate plan to control developing countries.

> HIV/AIDS is killing... [so] how are we going to stand on our own as a nation? Because we need to grow and when we grow we need our offspring... to take us forward and to compete with other nations... And another question

> is that, I understand, yes, the virus keeps on changing... [but] that's where our people become doubtful of this changing. So, isn't this a biological [war] issue? A biological disease that's been created by some scientists who are now trying to rule the world? ... Isn't this type of virus coming along with the intellectual status [knowledge] of various [developed] nations? Because here it looks like a chess [game] to manipulate other countries, you know, because the more you've got knowledge of controlling that virus, the more power[ful] you become and then the nation with lesser knowledge of controlling that type of disease will remain subjugated to the one who has got more knowledge.

These accounts of how white scientists and doctors are using AIDS to control the African population, by reducing the birth rate through the use of condoms or by killing Africans though the use of AIDS as a biological weapon, utilize a range of explanations of how HIV is transmitted. In the teacher's account, there is a combination of injecting the virus and sexual transmission. Other accounts dislocated this white-induced disease from sex, with white doctors simply injecting the virus into their black patients, "Some people believe that white South Africans are injecting the virus purposefully. And they are not consulting white doctors when they are sick." In other versions, the Western medical explanation of how condoms prevent the virus being sexually transmitted is turned on its head: condoms are the mechanism that transmits HIV as the virus is deliberately put into them. A common detail of this explanation of how whites infect blacks with HIV-laced condoms is that if you pour hot water into a condom, you can see worms that are responsible for infection.

The details of alternative transmission mechanisms form technical elaborations to the core, racial, hypothesis at the heart of these genocidal explanations of HIV/AIDS. These elaborations buttress the central argument because, in themselves, they can often be verified: if you put hot water into a condom you can (just) make out the alleged worms (i.e., dissolving lubricant). However, the real power of these explanations lies not in how subsidiary hypothesis support the core argument, but the extent to which this core idea resonates with audiences. In this respect, racialized explanations of AIDS often find fertile ground given South Africa's apartheid past and legacy.

A peer educator in the mining company detailed in his diary how a white doctor at a private hospital conducted an HIV test on his daughter without consent from him or his wife. Having remonstrated with a nurse that this was unprofessional conduct, he suggested that they not tell his wife that they had conducted an HIV test without permission. Unfortunately, the doctor took it upon himself to ring and apologize, but then compounded the situation when he gave the child's negative test result—no doubt assuming this would calm the situation—over the telephone. The peer educator's wife had exploded in anger, hung up, and refused to collect the medicines that the doctor had prescribed for their daughter's actual complaint saying, "It is true that doctors can infect people with HIV." Talking about this incident later, the peer educator explained that, "She's not accusing all the white doctors, [but] because of some of his attitude and the way he handled things she become very angry and very bitter.... It boils to something. Bad memories come from the past."

Thus, historic inequalities as well as current behavior support racial AIDS theories. Within workforces in which whites continue to dominate higher positions, inequality and behavior meld, and it is an easy step to see why company AIDS programs are viewed as a managerial cover to hide true actions. As a result AIDS program protagonists, in the form of peer educators, are viewed with skepticism. Mokwena in the mining company explained,

> The attitude or the actions of the whites in the company makes people believe that those perceptions [of whites using AIDS to kill blacks] are correct. [And] what we [peer educators] believe and what we are saying is wrong. [They say] "They [management] have brainwashed you; you are one of them. You want us to believe [you] but why don't you have white peer educators in your group?" So, in fact now it's very difficult for us as peer educators to convince them.

In this situation, the racial homogeneity of peer educators, far from being an advantage in communicating with peers, becomes a disadvantage. That there are no white peer educators, or at least no white peer educators visible to the majority of employees and their families, raises questions in an environment where racial division and inequality remains salient. Racial similarity between peers, given a configuration of meaning around AIDS that draws on race and the conflict between races, can, paradoxically, discredit peer educators.

Racial explanations of HIV/AIDS do not constitute a unified entity. Rather, they circulate in a range of contradictory theories: that AIDS is a fiction propagated to prevent the African population multiplying, that it is germ warfare waged by whites on blacks and/or to dominate developing countries, that whites do not see themselves at risk of infection and do not care that blacks die, and that HIV/AIDS programs are to implement management's agenda. Nevertheless, any one of these theories may, in itself, be well constructed with a range of buttressing arguments and observations.

That different racial understandings of HIV/AIDS may be contradictory is probably of little practical importance and certainly unlikely to win many arguments. More important is the platform that racism, both as a historical legacy and as continued practices, provides for these arguments. For Africans who have experienced generations of discrimination and continue to live and work in segregated environments, any theory rooted in this understanding has a dramatic head start to the racially neutral explanations of Western science.

Racially rooted theories derive their power not only from explicit recognition of the racism that pervades the lives of many South Africans. Because they provide an alternative explanation of HIV/AIDS to Western medical science, they can be used to defend and justify actions that are desirable but threatened by the recommendations of biomedical doctors and AIDS specialists. At a broad level, as Paul Farmer (1990) argues, conspiracy theories provide a rhetorical defense for people with little power. To the extent that AIDS, a sexually transmitted disease, is portrayed as a disease of blacks and Africans in particular then racial explanations of whites deliberately infecting blacks provides a defense of African identity. When it is believed that infection results from the use of condom, then racial theories have the additional advantage of justifying more pleasurable and intimate unprotected sex (Bogart and Thornburn 2005). Similarly, when racial theories incorporate medical personnel directly introducing infection, avoiding injections by white doctors is an easier prevention strategy to follow than abstinence, being faithful, or using condoms.

For men at least, there is the further attraction that subscription to some form of racial explanation of HIV/AIDS maintains their privileged gender position. As described in the previous section, gender roles and power can remain unchallenged if the problem lies not in sexual behavior and gender relationships but in the malevolence of whites. Here we see how two domains of identity—gender and race—can interlock to create a more entrenched set of beliefs. In this case, the belief that AIDS is a disease inflicted on blacks by whites not only provides a defense of the dignity of blacks but also continues gender privileges along with a license to have unprotected sex.

African Traditional and Spiritual Healing: Competing Cosmologies

Belief in African traditional and spiritual healing marks differences and tensions within backstage social spaces that, from the outside, are often invisible. This section explores traditional and spiritual healing and its alternative messages to Western medical science around HIV/AIDS. In doing so, we further add to the picture of how backstage social space is divided and difficult terrain for peer educators to operate within.

Belief in traditional and spiritual healing presents across social space differently from either gender or race. On the side of, largely white, management there are few believers in African traditional healers. This is a result of different cultural beliefs (though this does not mean that whites do not put faith in other alternative or complementary healing), but it is also emphasized by Africans' realization—whichever side of the industrial divide they might be on—that belief in traditional and spiritual healing is not acceptable when whites are present. As a result, Africans entering into white-dominated management structures keep any views on healing to themselves. This further obscures management's collective understanding of healing practices. To Africans, however, traditional and spiritual healing is visible because, rooted in their own communities, they know who is involved and how it operates. But this knowledge does not mean that there is uniformity of belief. Far from it: Within the African population, intense, often complex differences exist between peers on this issue.

African Traditional and Spiritual Healing

African traditional healing refers to indigenous practices linked to an African cosmology, while *spiritual healing* refers here to the practices of African churches that, additionally, draw on an introduced Christian cosmology. This section links traditional and spiritual healing and treats them, in regard to peer education in backstage social space, as essentially similar. Many practitioners in either healing form regard themselves as different from each other; indeed, some see themselves locked in conflict with each other. But, I argue here that it is the locking together of their cosmologies, albeit it sometimes conflictual, along with similar processes of diagnosis (or divination) and, often, treatment, that allows us to treat them as similar phenomena.

The extent of belief in African traditional healing is unclear. In its 2005 questionnaire of 16,000 South Africans over the age of fifteen the Human Sciences Research Council (HSRC) asked where they usually went for healthcare. Only around 1 percent said that they went to traditional healers. By contrast, the Department of Health (2003b) estimates, it is not clear how, that there are 200,000 traditional healers in South Africa. Clearly one—or both—figures are misleading. If they are both accurate, each traditional healer would have an average practice size of just 2.3 patients, yet observations of township-based traditional healers not infrequently reveal a steady stream of clients coming for consultations. One problem with the HSRC survey is that it did not allow for medical pluralism with both traditional and Western or allopathic medicine consulted. Additionally, the use of nursing sisters to administer the HSRC's questionnaire no doubt influenced responses since the use of traditional healers is not something that Africans will readily admit to when dealing with someone that forms part of the Western medical establishment. (The same survey reported that over 80 percent of African's claimed not to drink any alcohol, a finding that can only be described as incredulous. By contrast, whites, responding to the same question, appeared to be more truthful, but also knew how to "correctly" respond; just under 40 percent claimed to be abstainers, while over 50 percent gave responses that put them in the low-risk drinkers' category.) The World Health Organization (2002) estimates that up to 80 percent of Africa's population makes use of traditional healers; for many people it is the only health system available to them. South Africa, with its greater level of economic development and relatively large non-African population, almost certainly comes in under this level: though what it is is impossible to know.

Traditional healing represents indigenous knowledge. Such knowledge is often far from welcome in colonized and divided societies because it provides an alternative power source. Within a colonized society, indigenous knowledge systems are typically suppressed, but do not disappear (Mamdani 1996). Within divided societies alternative world views coexist but rarely come into open conflict (Scott 1990). As Max Gluckman (1956) points out, increased tensions are likely to promote traditional responses to stress. Far from disappearing, it may be that—though it is impossible to verify—under the twin strains of mass unemployment and AIDS, for which official responses are at best weak, that the use of traditional healing in South Africa is increasing.

Not infrequently, interviews with African workers reveals that they have some, often strong, beliefs in traditional healing. But typically these are not immediately forthcoming, indeed they initially may be explicitly denied only to be later reintroduced and expanded on, sometimes in depth, when the researcher is able to indicate familiarity with and acceptance of such practices. Thus, for example, when interviewing a shop steward who was not a peer educator but had attended a number of course on HIV/AIDS, it emerged, as the interview progressed, that he had been a traditional healer for nine years. He had, among the workforce from which he drew most of his patients, five who had come to him because they were HIV-positive (though he had his own parallel diagnosis to that of HIV), and a sixth was due to come for an initial consultation the next day. Depending on the patient's condition, his treatment might take up to two years, and he needed the help of the company clinic's (antiretroviral) medicine, but unlike Western medicine he claimed to be able to completely cure his clients of their "HIV."

Appreciating how practitioners and users understand how these healing practices work requires placing them within a traditional African cosmology that operates very different logical systems to that of scientific inquiry. To place this in perspective, we should note that few, if any, people anywhere in the world rely purely on scientific understandings in regard to their own health; they also draw on a range of nonscientific practices, such as prayer or positive attitude. However, given the composition of peer educators and their peers, the focus here is on alternative beliefs among Africans, which draws on traditional African healing practices.

African culture covers a wide span of ideas, values, and beliefs. Some, such as *ubuntu,* the philosophy that "a person is a person because of other people," are much more acceptable within contemporary South Africa than others. David Hammond-Tooke (1989) identifies South African traditional healers, in line with writers describing traditional healers in other parts of Africa (e.g., Evans-Pritchard 1977), as part of the traditional African "world view" that includes a belief in ancestors, witches, and the polluting nature of certain objects and practices. These elements of the traditional African worldview constitute—as do all worldviews—an attempt to "make intellectual sense of the world and of life, so that in the broadest sense it involves theories of explanation" (Hammond-Tooke 1989, 33). Operating within this traditional worldview, African healers are often divided into diviners, who, though a range of rituals, such as "throwing the bones," (see Chapter 1) establish the underlying cause of a person's problem, and herbalists who specialize in treatment. In practice, apart from a small number of specialized herbalists, most traditional healers combine divination and treatment. Treatment includes rituals to allow the patient to communicate with disgruntled ancestors, holding appropriate cultural events that may have been neglected, protection against witchcraft, emotional empathy and support, and a range of herbal treatments to purify or protect individuals and property.

Healers, while constituting a distinct element of the traditional African worldview, are linked with its other elements. Thus, Hammond-Tooke (1989, 121) explains that traditional healers are often, "Highly respected, indeed an indispensable, member of traditional society, whose activities are closely linked to the benevolent ancestors and whose role is quite specifically [but not exclusively] that of combating the forces of evil [emanating from witches] that constantly threaten the lives and well-being of his patient."

This articulation is now rooted within modern settings. Workers in manufacturing companies report that (always other) workers employ *muti* (usually a mixture of plant and animal substances) to gain favor with superiors so as to be promoted or to doctor their machines so that others cannot operate it with the same proficiency. In response, workers procure their own *muti* from traditional or spiritual healers that will counter any negative impact on themselves. This belief in measures and countermeasures means that, viewed from within, traditional healing, even when making specific claims, is impossible to prove or disprove (Evans-Pritchard 1977).

Alongside traditional African beliefs are more recently introduced religions, notably Christianity. As essentially rival cosmologies, they are competitors over the construction of meaning. However, the relationship between traditional beliefs and Christianity is, in practice, complex. Although some churches take a strong oppositional position to traditional beliefs, individual church members may practice traditional beliefs in (concealed) defiance of church practice or with tacit acceptance on the part of other churches that this is not incompatible with membership. But there are also a large number of African churches that openly synchronize traditional and Christian beliefs and operate their own, parallel healing practices. In a simplified scheme, traditional African cosmology consists of the following: the ancestors, who are supportive when paid sufficient respect in terms of traditional rituals, slaughtering animals, and libations of beer; witches representing evil; and traditional healers who can help communicate with ancestors, counter the power of witches, and restore individual and community health. When synchronized with Christianity, supreme representations of good and evil (God and Satan) and prophets are added. Simplified, this cosmology links God to church prophets who are engaged in constant warfare with witches who operate under Satan. Traditional healers may, in secret, also be witches—since God and Satan can be at work in everybody. Ancestors continue to remain important and, indeed, may be your best bet in ascertaining whether a traditional healer, or even a church prophet, is really what they say they are and not also a witch.

Although members of these churches may see themselves as locked in a battle with evil, prophets combat witches in much the same way as traditional healers do. Divination processes are often different in form: typically traditional healers "throw the bones" while prophets use trance states, but both rely heavily on ancestral help. Treatment often follows similar ritualistic lines, though prophets emphasize simpler substances, such as water, ash, and tea, that have been blessed, while traditional healers use a vast array of plant, animal, and sometimes synthetic substances in their treatment mixtures. Since the real enemy of both traditional healers and prophets are witches (who may or may not be operating on behalf of Satan), then, although they may view each other as opponents, it is also possible for a person to openly combine both positions. Thus, since traditional and Christian cosmologies are synchronized around common beliefs and similar methods—something that applies to AIDS as well as other problems—we consider them as similar phenomena in regard to backstage beliefs and HIV/AIDS.

A second introduced belief that traditional beliefs engage with—though very differently—is Western medical science. In contrast to the more malleable beliefs of the Christian churches with the possibility of synchronization, Western medicine has refused to contemplate any role for traditional healing. Thus, the South African Medical Council successfully lobbied government for the closure of nonallopathic medical colleges in the 1960s (World Health Organization [WHO] 2001), and traditional healing is, aside from some weak voluntary associations, unregulated and without any systematic referral between the two systems. Indeed, traditional healers complain that when they do refer to clinics or doctors for problems they perceive to be beyond their competency, patients are frequently instructed not to return to them.

Essentially then, traditional healing and Western medicine represent rival healing systems in which the latter dominates publicly through an alliance with the state and employers, but the former privately retains considerable sway within large sections of the population. Despite being driven underground, traditional healing retains its influence because it is rooted within a wider cosmology that colonial institutions have not been able to dismantle. Thus, the term "traditional" in regard to an African worldview should not be seen as synonymous with "past" but as encapsulating a still-active worldview that can claim—for the African population—deeper and more legitimate roots than Western medicine offers. In addition to this cultural base, traditional healing can be superior to Western medicine in that traditional healers are more accessible to many South Africans and—unlike the majority of Western doctors—live within African communities and therefore understand the problems that Africans face.

Any examination of peer educator activity in backstage social space in regard to traditional healing and HIV/AIDS needs to consider not only the suppression of traditional healing, which creates on one side of South Africa's industrial and social divide an inability to see these practices, but also sharp differences among Africans on the other side of this divide. Although reliable data on these differences is lacking, many African do *not* believe in traditional healing. Where these nonbelieving individuals are located in management structures or other white-dominated groups, such professed beliefs need to be treated with caution; however, the rejection of traditional healing is also present among Africans who work and live alongside the majority of Africans. This rejection comes, most commonly, from religious beliefs where denominations take a strong line against traditional healing, but it can also come from atheism or any other philosophical structure that provides an alternative worldview to a traditional African cosmology. Thus, for example, one occupational nurse whom I interviewed explained how she had stopped using traditional healers herself because when studying psychology during her training she had realized that "prophets and healers are just another belief" and that the divination process of healers could be replicated by clever guesswork and suggestion. More generally, African nurses tend to express skepticism about the value of African traditional healing because they are allied to Western medicine through training and employment and because they see the problems (such as renal failure) caused by traditional treatments. Nevertheless, this rejection is usually specific to the efficacy of traditional healing, rather than a wholesale rejection of African cosmology. Few Africans would go so far as to deny the importance of ancestors and the value of holding traditional cultural events that honor their memory, even if they do not believe in their ability to actively influence the living. These individuals who understand traditional healing but do not believe in its efficacy could be viewed as a potential bridging group between traditional healing and Western medicine.

Yet despite the presence of these bridging groups, who understand but do not believe in traditional healing, this African worldview is often all but invisible to those outside African communities. In Mineco, an African clerk explained how he regularly accepted sick notes from medical doctors knowing full well that this was just a necessary cover on the part of the employees for sick leave to be approved since they were in fact consulting traditional healers. The ease with which sick notes can be bought from doctors facilitates this (and represents an additional health cost that provides an economic rent to the Western medical establishment based on their legislatively entrenched monopoly position). But peer educators, forming part of African society, both see and need to respond to traditional healing when it conflicts with their attempts to educate people on HIV/AIDS and bring about behavioral change. Here Nosimo Mpengu, a peer educator in an Eastern Cape supermarket who strongly disapproved of traditional healing, describes how she responded when visiting an HIV-positive friend in another town who was taking traditional medicine.

> When I visit her, she was alone in the bedroom. Then I said to her, "Undress" and she did undress. And then I take cold water, because I could see she was sweating and very hot, and I tried to sponge her so that she [her temperature] can come down. Then I look on the table, I could see what medicines she's drinking, and then I said to her, "Listen here my friend, I'm going to call your doctor [though she didn't]. This [traditional] medicine, Xhosa medicine, you're drinking, it's not going to help you. What you must do? You must throw it away. Because these medicines, you don't know who made it, you don't know what it was made of, but you're drinking it and I know the way you are sick, you are not eating properly. So, this medicine is going to give you diarrhea, you are going to have a running stomach all the way. [Many traditional treatments involve inducing diarrhea, vomiting, or enemas (colonic irrigation) designed to assist purification by removing pollution from the body.] Then you won't be strong so that you can go for your [antiretroviral] treatment again." [I don't know if she took my advice,] but she did pass away.

More publicly, Mpengu went on to describe how she had confronted a colleague in the supermarket's canteen who was advertising a traditional healer who claimed to be able to cure HIV/AIDS.

> There was a lady in our work. At lunchtime she used to give the people the address [of a traditional healer] where they must go when they've got this [HIV]. I said to her, I stand up and said, "This won't help." I'm telling you, she said she knows that there's somebody who's giving this medicine for HIV. Then I said "There is no such [thing], we've never heard of such thing in our [peer educator] training. Never." She did shut up, but the people did write [down] the address.

Such private and public confrontations illustrate peer educators' ability to see, through their physical and sociocultural access, this alternative health system that is all but invisible to managers and health experts. In this case, however, it is far from clear whether Mpengu's approach achieved a change of heart among those she addressed.

Division over the merits of traditional responses to HIV/AIDS is also present within families, and this setting proved no easier for peer educators to win over those who prefer traditional explanations of the disease. Thabo Seloba, a peer educator in Mineco whose father and grandfather had been full-time traditional healers, explained how he was unable to persuade an aunt of the efficacy of antiretroviral drugs. The aunt, despite having tested HIV-positive, was blaming her illness on her sister who she believed, on the advice of her *sangoma* (traditional healer), had bewitched her. That a third sister had died only a few months earlier, refusing to take antiretroviral drugs despite an HIV-positive test result, did not convince her otherwise and was, rather, used to strengthen the bewitchment explanation. At the request of the accused sister, the peer educator visited the sick aunt with his wife, but their attempts to convince her of the value of antiretroviral drugs failed. The sick aunt—who was unaware that her visitors had already been told that she was positive—told them that the doctors had said there was nothing wrong with her and that she would continue with the medication that her *sangoma* provided to counter the bewitchment. Two weeks after the visit, the aunt died, and Seloba noted how, "It is not easy to change peoples' beliefs, particularly when *sangomas* are involved."

In Mineco peer educators frequently discussed traditional beliefs on HIV/AIDS among the workforce. Those who conducted induction talks for employees returning from leave included a short awareness session on HIV/AIDS. This provided a rough gauge on employees' beliefs around AIDS. They estimated that around 30 percent of the company's employees—many of them migrant workers from rural areas of the Eastern Cape—believed traditional healers' explanations of HIV/AIDS. This estimate was admittedly crude; on good days, when they felt they were making progress, it could drop to 20 percent. Numerical certainty aside, peer educators viewed traditional healers' explanations of HIV/AIDS as important. Indeed it was suggested that peer educators could use belief in traditional healing as a lightning rod to identify peers who needed to be targeted.

Explaining HIV/AIDS through Traditional and Spiritual Healing

Traditional healing provides two main alternative explanations to Western medicine regarding HIV/AIDS: (1) that AIDS results from bewitchment and (2) that AIDS is not a new disease, but the current epidemic is a manifestation of a breakdown in social order and the abandoning of practices that previously kept these older diseases in check.

A belief that AIDS emanates from witchcraft frees a person from the stigma that is attached to the disease and/or the relatively unattractive implications of accepting the Western-medical explanation: a lifetime on medication and the need to always have protected sex. Rather than having to accept how the disease was acquired and face its implications, citing witchcraft as the cause allows the person to portray themselves as the victim of malevolent deeds perpetrated against them. As is often the case with witchcraft, specific accusations around AIDS frequently mesh with existing social tensions and conflicts over material resources. Hence, the accused person is often a family member or neighbor. Seloba, the peer educator who was unable to dissuade his aunt that she was bewitched, reported three deaths from AIDS in his extended family over the three and a half months of the diary project. The second of these, in which an older (half) brother died, also involved a witchcraft accusation. In this case the accusation was leveled against the brother's former wife who had returned to help care for him when sick. The particular accusation in this case was one of *sejeso.* Sejeso entails a witch introducing a small animal into the person's stomach, usually through doctored food, that eats the person away from the inside. Personal accounts of people who claim they were cured of *sejeso* by a traditional healer report, however, less dramatic objects being discovered when induced to vomit under the guidance of a traditional healer, such as a piece of food regarded as being too big to have been swallowed whole. It is conjectured that this was the introduced animal still in the process of reconstituting itself after having been introduced and having been caught before it could do more serious harm. But, irrespective of quibbles over agency, symptoms of *sejeso* fit those of AIDS reasonably well. In this case, the accusation against the woman linked into the prior history of tensions leading to the couple's separation, and her return shortly before his death was interpreted as her coming back to "finish him off." At stake was the house that they had previously lived in, which was now open to conflicting claims between the deceased wife and other family members who were making the witchcraft accusations.

The tense nature of backstage social space in regard to AIDS is well illustrated by what the peer educator was able to say in his speech at his brother's funeral. The extended family, with its web of intimate ties, did not provide an environment in which the truth could be openly spoken.

Rather, there were tensions over how the death was to be understood and explained. Any public statement on this required a degree of consensus unless there was to be open family conflict (which would, in traditional belief, anger the ancestors). In this regard, family members held a spectrum of belief over the cause of death, and each one had different implications. When speaking, Seloba needed to make a choice, constrained by consideration of family unity. The options were (1) that his brother had died from AIDS, (2) that he had died of TB (which was on the death certificate signed by a medical practitioner), or (3) that he had been bewitched. The easiest, fourth, option was to avoid any of these choices and remain silent over the cause of death as is so often the case in funerals where AIDS is involved.

Graveside silences are a cause of frustration for AIDS campaigners—especially because funerals are significant communal gatherings within African society. These silences, however, as this account illustrates are not induced only by shame or by considerations for the deceased. Rather shame and respect, along with other considerations, feed into different, opposing views, over what has happened. Silence may be the only way to avert open conflict within families. In this case, Seloba, despite intense discussions with other relatives, was unable to get agreement to say that his brother had died of AIDS. He was able to avoid silence, however; the family agreed he could say that his brother had died of TB. It was a partial victory, and he used the opportunity as best he could, encouraging everybody to test for TB and to take treatment if they were infected.

The second explanation of AIDS that traditional African beliefs provide is that AIDS is not new but a new name for older afflictions that result from failures to correctly follow traditional practices. These cited practices vary in detail but focus on sexual transmission from somebody who has not been cleansed of polluting influences; for example, the failure to ritually clean a woman or man after the death of their spouse and/or to have sex with them before cleansing can be completed—often regarded as being a complete year. In Setswana culture, for example, failure to comply with these traditional processes results, in the event of a woman's not being purified (*ho nwa dipitseng,* literally; to drink from the pots [of ritually cleansing herbal mixtures]) after the death of her husband, in *boswagadi* with symptoms similar to AIDS. Related diseases that may also be confused with AIDS within this traditional perspective results from a failure to correctly purify a woman after an abortion, miscarriage, still-born child, or infant death.

These explanations of "AIDS" as traditional diseases that have become rampant because of widespread failure to follow traditional practices are usually put forward as intellectual explanations for the AIDS epidemic. In contrast to the desperate hopes of sick people that witchcraft is the source of their problems, this explanation is promoted in a measured way by believers in traditional practices as well as traditional healers who seek a coherent overview of the epidemic rather than individual explanations of sickness.

The two explanations do, however, overlap. Within an African worldview, people who neglect their ancestors by failing to conduct appropriate ceremonies are more vulnerable to witchcraft because their ancestors are less closely protecting them. It is important to note here that believers in traditional African cosmology are mounting an intellectual counterattack against rival forms of Christianity that offer a worldview more closely aligned with Western medical practice. Thus, for example, traditional African wife inheritance (practiced by some ethnic groups), in which a man takes over his brother's widow, is often critically cited as a cause of HIV transmission by AIDS campaigners. This is, of course, a position that resonates with most contemporary Christian teachings that frown on such practices. In contrast, believers in a traditional African cosmology argue that the problem is not traditional practices but rather the breakdown of these practices as a result, in part, of Christian proselytizing.

Thus, proponents of traditional beliefs are able to put forward explanations of HIV/AIDS that not only provide comfort but also a coherent intellectual structure mobilized in contradiction to the publicly dominant scientific canon and, often, against predominantly Western forms of Christianity. Not surprisingly, the presence of these rival cosmologies often divides backstage social space; within families, there are often sharp divisions as well as synchronization between traditional, Western-science, and Christianity. Peer educators have to work in these spaces, and the difficulties that they encounter are not hard to see. As the next section outlines, tackling these difficulties begins by recognizing that peer educators are themselves embedded within this divided backstage space.

Peer Educators as Backstage Team Members

It is tempting, for those running HIV/AIDS programs, to believe that peer educators unambiguously champion information on HIV/AIDS that is based on scientific knowledge. Given this, we might expect peer educators to offer alternatives to the belief that bewitchment or the failure to observe tradition causes AIDS. Certainly, this was the publicly articulated modus operandi of the peer educator group at the Mineco operation, with peers' adherence to traditional beliefs regarded as a barometer of the conditions that they operated within. However, below this public stance there was a more complex set of understandings.

There were some peer educators who, like Mpengu, the peer educator who confronted her coworkers in her canteen, simply had no dealings with traditional healers. They believed that such healers could achieve nothing and needed to be sidelined. Any shift on the part of peers toward this position was progress. Here Tlouane, in the mining company outlines, in private, a very similar view to that publicly articulated in group meetings.

Dickinson: Do you think traditional healers educate people in the right way or the wrong way? …

Tlouane: [Interrupting] No. In the wrong way!

Dickinson: …about HIV/AIDS?

Tlouane: In the wrong way. In the wrong way… Because everyday I'm giving people induction [sessions, during which she gave an awareness talk on HIV/AIDS]… So, I'm so happy because today [in the induction session] they tell me that "Nelly, there's no cure really for HIV. This treatment [of] traditional healers, they can make you better, but after that, you'll become sick again."

Other peer educators conceded that healers could usefully contribute to the response to AIDS, but only if they acted in support of Western medicine. After explaining how many traditional healers made their patients worse by prescribing treatments that involved "making your stomach run," Florence Diseko, also in Mineco, explained what a traditional healer should do if a patient came to them with symptoms of AIDS without having first consulted a medical doctor.

> Our traditional healers, they are just looking for money. The problem is there. That is why they don't ask you [the patient's relatives], "Is this person from the doctor or not?" If it's a professional one [traditional healer], . . . he will say, "I will ask you [the patient's relatives] to take this poor man or lady to the doctor first. Then you must come and tell me what the doctor say." [So that the healer can support any treatment prescribed by the doctor.] The professional ones [will]. But most of them they are not [professional].

Some healers are working, at least partly, along these lines. For example, they ask to see patients' HIV-test results and even CD4 counts (immune system strength) to complement their own diagnosis and treatment process. However, Diseko's suggestion, similar to that most medical practitioners and champions of antiretroviral drugs such as the Treatment Action Campaign offers what amounts to a "partnership" between two healing systems based on the surrender of one to the other. While there is a strong desire on the part of many traditional healers for public legitimacy, this cannot, in their perspective, come at the cost of abandoning any claim to knowledge or power.

Some peer educators recognized the need to offer more meaningful roles to traditional healers. Despite skepticism about the value of traditional healing, they tried to educate traditional healers on HIV/AIDS and appropriate treatments so that they could operate in a complementary fashion alongside Western medicine. However, such endeavors could be frustrating. The fragmented structure of healers, with no regulation or agreed standards in place, meant that even when peer educators established good relationships with some healers, there were others who would claim, in competing for clients, they could cure AIDS and undermine these efforts.

Seeing peer educators as either hostile or cautiously willing to accommodate traditional and spiritual healers conceptualizes them as being apart from their own social spaces. In thinking about how I would structure this book, I considered a chapter that would focus on peer educators' own beliefs, as distinct from their peers. I realized that this would be a mistake. As peers, rather than as professional, socially distant educators, they reflect the values of their peers. This is no more clearly illustrated than over the issue of healing. Just as in the wider African population, there are opponents and supporters of traditional healing among peer educators. Thus, in the case of the peer educator group in the mining operation, beneath the public articulation that belief in traditional and spiritual healing was a marker of peers' failure to properly understand HIV and AIDS, there was a less visible plurality of beliefs that not infrequently included traditional and spiritual healers as a component of maintaining physical and psychological health.

Jacob Senabe, at Mineco, is a good example of how peer educators may hold a range of beliefs around questions of health. As a lay preacher, shop steward, peer educator, and father he would appear as an ideal person to engage with his peers around HIV/AIDS. Trained by the company on the basics of prevention and treatment of HIV/AIDS and other sexually transmitted diseases, a superficial evaluation would assume that he would consistently put forward a Western medical perspective. But in additional to these "acceptable" identities, Senabe held other beliefs that were woven into his understanding of the world.

Some time back his late father had visited him in his dreams telling him that he was getting cold. This was interpreted by Senabe as meaning that he should erect a tombstone for his father. Once this was done, the dreams ceased. After a close lightning strike, he had on the advice of family members visited a *sangoma,* since this was a sign of witchcraft aimed at his household. His most recent trip to a *sangoma* had been triggered when the wheel of his car came off shortly after he had seen a cat near his car. The *sangoma* had identified a relative who was attempting to kill him. At the time he had believed the *sangoma,* but when the interview took place, he had revised his view and put the accident down to the wheel nuts not being strong enough. He now thought that what the *sangoma* had told him was "nonsense." This shifting illustrates the fluidity of explanations that individuals can choose to prioritize—an issue we examine in Chapter 6.

Although Senabe generally used a medical doctor when ill, this was partly because the company medical aid scheme helped pay for prescribed medicines, and he would forfeit funds if he did not spend his annual medical allowance credited to his scheme's account. In an interview, Senabe explained that he believed Western doctors were "stronger" than traditional healers when it came to AIDS, but that traditional healers were sometimes stronger on other problems. As an example, he explained how he had been cured of "burning urine" (probably a sexually transmitted disease) by drinking *muti* that a *sangoma* prescribed. Several of his friends had reported similar success for the same problem. Finally, it emerged outside of the interview that he had, along with another peer educator, taken an HIV-positive colleague to a nearby village for treatment by a spiritual healer. He, and the other peer educator, reported that this healer had a strong track record regarding HIV/AIDS. The other peer educator had a friend whose HIV-positive test had, he reported, been reversed after treatment. They liked the insistence of this particular healer that people had to go to the hospital and bring their HIV test results back to him before he would treat them.

Senabe did not view these beliefs and actions as incompatible with the medical explanation of HIV/AIDS that he had been given in his peer educator training, nor with his role as a peer educator. But they do illustrate how much more complex his beliefs on health and healing are than what we might expect from a peer educator who may be seen as a mere delivery mechanism for information. Of the eight most active peer educators I interviewed from the mining group, five of them consulted traditional or spiritual healers for health or family concerns. When asked why they did not raise their views in the peer educator meetings, where at times they would have been in the majority, they said that they believed such views were not acceptable to others. To some extent this was an open secret, for at least some of the peer educators who expressed public hostility to traditional healers had a fairly accurate idea which of their fellow peer educators privately dissented from this publicly expressed view.

This should not be a surprise. If peer educators are peers, we should expect them to represent the full range of social beliefs. Indeed, it would be a disadvantage if this was not the case. Nevertheless, this group of peer educators demonstrates that, even within backstage social space—with all the peer educators Africans and at roughly similar occupational levels in the company—the issue of traditional and spiritual healing is disputed, divisive, and, at times, disguised.

Traditional and Spiritual Healing and HIV/AIDS in Backstage Space: Summary

Although it may not be visible to those in charge of company HIV/AIDS programs, different beliefs around traditional and spiritual healing and its efficacy in regards to AIDS create tensions in the backstage social settings that African peer educators operate within. That many people give credibility to explanations of HIV and AIDS and treatment that traditional spiritual healers put forward complicates the roles of peer educators seeking to provide information and influence behavioral change.

South Africans turn to these alternative explanations of HIV/AIDS for a number of reasons. These include limited access to Western medicine in general, and antiretroviral drugs in particular; the shoddy way health practitioners often treat patients; the stigma attached to AIDS (but not to falling victim of witchcraft); and that understandings of AIDS plays into domestic and community power struggles over status and resources. If this was all, it could be thought that increased access to antiretroviral drugs and greater openness around the disease should see beliefs around the power of traditional and spiritual healers over AIDS diminish and peoples' behavior change in line with this.

What this view fails to consider, however, is that alternative healing response to HIV/AIDS is more than the choice of individuals, but a confrontation between competing cosmologies. And in this regard AIDS is but one battleground on which traditional and spiritual beliefs compete with science, medicine, and monotheistic Christianity over the construction of meaning. Even if those championing modern medicine against other health systems were to win outright over AIDS, this would be victory in only one battle; the war would continue.

What is perhaps most striking about this battle is the parity between the competing cosmologies of medical science and traditional and spiritual healing over HIV/AIDS. Never mind the failure to get Western medicine's best shot—antiretroviral drugs—to people. Even when this is achieved, its promise is distinctly limited; a lifetime on treatment, with the dangers of side effects and resistance, and eternal condoms. On the other side is a hydra of traditional and spiritual practitioners able to promise hope and better the claims of Western medicine. Operating in the shadows, this hydra cannot be comprehensively confronted or disproved. But most important, until Western medicine demonstrates an unambiguously better solution to the problem of AIDS, the power of traditional and spiritual healing around AIDS lies not in its specific responses to the disease but in its embeddedness within a wider cosmology, deeply rooted within African society.

What is happening over AIDS and traditional and spiritual healing is not only an individual process of decision making but, rather, a conflict of cosmologies that cuts across the African population. The divisions among peer educators themselves illustrates this. Given the arguments made, this should not be surprising. But it does provide us with a clear understanding of why, when peer really means peer, we need to think of peer education as most effective not as a vertical communication aid but as horizontal communication in which peer educators are active agents of change.

As vertical conduits for experts, peer educators are unlikely to faithfully reproduce messages given their own immersion in traditional and spiritual healing. If we bothered to find out what peer educators really think, we would know this, but instead we send out messengers that hold beliefs that are not fully compatible with the messages we wish them to transmit. Some will attempt to do what we ask, though how effective given the wider conflict that they are stepping into is questionable. Others will give mixed messages—though these will not be reported back. And others will try to resolve for themselves the different, conflicting information that they now possess.

If, on the other hand, peer educators operate as active agents engaging in horizontal communication, the question of AIDS and traditional and spiritual healing becomes a process in which Africans are able to reconfigure their own cosmology. Not as the defeat of the old by the new, tradition by science, but rather by establishing, in the era of AIDS, what traditions remain of value and what needs to be adapted and changed.

Conclusion: Backstage Social Order and Changing Belief

Peer educators, drawn from the ranks of employees, sidestep the communication barriers of industrial and social divides and the front-stage performances that are enacted at these frontiers. But, that should not prevent us from seeing the differences that lie behind these divisions and the difficulties that these present to peer education. Indeed, once away from more obvious divisions between workers and management, and its wider embodiment in class difference, it is clear that there are many differences among peers. Such an examination calls into question overconfident assumptions on the automatic effectiveness of peer educator similarity. These opinions may have more to do with a homogenizing view of the "other" than with careful evaluation of what constitutes peer status.

Reacting against this, we may overcompensate with ever-narrower categorization of peers. But the identities of gender, race, and healing beliefs used to illustrate this chapter cannot be organized into subgroupings of peers that will constitute homogeneous subcommunities. While it is theoretically possible to define peer identity in ever-more detail, there are not, in reality, corresponding closer circumscribed social spaces. In other words, identity permutations are myriad and analytically separable, but the social spaces individuals inhabit are more constrained in type and are internally heterogeneous. They are shared. Thus, for example, in desiring similarity between peer educators and their peers we could consider the categories of race, ethnicity, gender, religion, age, occupational level, sexuality, marital status, traditional beliefs, urban or rural background, and so on. Taken to extremes we might seek to recruit as a peer educator an African, Zulu, woman, Catholic, in her twenties, manual laborer, heterosexual, married with children and living with her partner, who believes in the importance of traditional customs, and comes from a rural background, but is now living in a township. Such individuals exist, but they do not work or live in communities of identical individuals. While peer educators are able to sidestep the primary lines of divisions in South African society, they are not able to avoid subsidiary divisions. Peer educators inevitably work with peers who are different from themselves.

Gender, race, and healing beliefs do not fully account, by any means, for the lines of conflicts that peer educators encounter around HIV/AIDS in backstage spaces. Far from being a relaxed, frank, and open environment, backstage spaces, despite their insulation from the main lines of organized social conflict, are sites of tightly constructed, complex social order. There are divisions specific to particular backstage spaces, such as belief in African traditional and spiritual healing; divisions found in nearly all backstage spaces, such as gender; and identities that correspond to primary social divisions but which can divide backstage space over the issue of HIV/AIDS, such as race. Peer educators enter this space with concerns about HIV/AIDS that has implication for this social order. Their messages, however well-intentioned and humanistic, cannot remain neutral but inevitably stir up opposition.

If we take this on board, then the bluntness of peer education exclusively designed and supported as a vertical communication strategy to bring about behavioral change is obvious. Yet, it is also obvious that without peer education (or a similar process of lay involvement) operating in backstage spaces, we will not make the slightest impact on beliefs. In Chapter 5 we look at how peer educators operating backstage attempt to bring about individual behavioral change within this dense set of interlocking and defended beliefs.

5

Slipping Out of Order

Beyond World AIDS Day

There is a sharp contrast between the work of peer educators and institutional responses to HIV/AIDS. Although peer educators welcome corporate initiatives around AIDS, they are aware that these responses often fall short of what is needed. Mokwena in Mineco made the point by contrasting the missionary-zeal of peer education to annual displays of corporate concern on World AIDS Day. "I'm not only doing my job [as a peer educator] at the company, [but also] at the family, at the church, wherever I go I'm a peer educator. I will take that knowledge with me and everything I know about HIV/AIDS...[By contrast,] toward the first of December [World AIDS Day] a lot of companies will buy expensive T-shirts and this and that to celebrate the day. But during the year they are doing *nothing!* Nothing! Nothing! Nothing! Nothing!"

If peer educators are to move beyond annual displays of corporate concern about AIDS, they need an essential trait: passion. This is the consensus of those peer educator coordinators and peer educators who were asked about what makes a good peer educator. The one quality almost universally cited was a passion for people that would enable peer educators to reach out to others however difficult that might be. Without passion, a company might be able to recruit peer educators but these educators would not be taking their mission wherever they went.

A peer educator coordinator in Finco, herself a peer educator, explained how she selected potential peer educators. Her selection process demonstrates an understanding that peer educators have to go beyond the rote delivery of messages. When interviewing potential peer educators, she would probe their responses to her question "Why do you want to become a peer educator?" until she had a clear grasp of their motivations. She would then sum it up "in a nice sweet way" to check that she had read them correctly. At this point, she said, it was clear that, "Some wanted to be there for the wrong reasons, they just wanted to build their CVs, but you have to have that passion [to be a peer educator], not just stand up in front of people." She then went on to test their commitment by asking what they would do if their manager said "no" to a request for a peer education activity because the unit was busy. The incorrect response was "put their boss's needs first and accept the refusal." The answer that she was looking for was that they would "persuade their manager of the importance of HIV/AIDS and get his or her commitment to peer educator activity." She also asked potential recruits whether they would do HIV/AIDS related work on a Sunday. The wrong answer was "no, that's my time" because it begged the question, "Where's the passion?"

But even with this passion for people, peer educators were well aware of the uphill struggle that they faced in getting people to change their behavior. I asked all peer educators why, given the amount of information available, they thought people were still being infected with HIV. A common response was that people were "ignorant." The peer educators did not mean that people were ignorant of HIV and AIDS, but, rather, that they chose to ignore the available information. Nicol Manuel in Autostar explained, "There's so much information that's getting circulated, and wherever you go now, even on the street pole ads... they're not advertising the transport, they're advertising about HIV/AIDS. They're not advertising holidays, they're advertising HIV/AIDS. People, there's so much that they need to learn but they're just not taking it in. They're blocking out the information that they should get... there is so much of information out there."

Asked what might change this situation so that people would take heed of available information, peer educators often said that they could make information available, but they could not go further. On several occasions they repeated the axiom, "You can bring a horse to water, but you can't make it drink." Some peer educators left it at that. Others described a range of ideas and lay theories they were practicing and developing, usually individually and in isolation from each other, that would help them get people to change their behavior. This chapter describes these lay theories and practices and illustrates that effective peer education often requires not only the sidestepping of front-stage encounters, but the careful working of backstage spaces and a further step—that of slipping out of (backstage) order.

AIDS Facts and Behavioral Change

Continuing HIV infection amid a sea of information presents a challenge to peer educators (and everybody involved in AIDS prevention). Since surveys in South Africa indicate high levels of knowledge about HIV transmission and prevention (e.g., HSRC 2005), it seems all the more puzzling that people continue to be infected. Eilsa Sobo (1995, 26) suggests that people may memorize the information provided to them on HIV/AIDS but don't put it into practice because it is not presented in ways that are relevant to them. "In general people do have the facts on HIV—but because they are not presented in ways that are relevant they are disembodied... As a result, people often have done little more then memorize the 'AIDS facts' they are taught. Once memorized, this information is easily regurgitated in response to questions such as those posed on surveys meant to measure AIDS knowledge levels."

The term "AIDS facts" is pertinent. Most of the information that experts disseminate *is* factual. Indeed many experts are obsessed with ensuring that the facts are correct so that there can be no room for confusion or error on the part of the audience. A standard accusation of alternative, or dissident, views of the underlying science around HIV/AIDS and HIV prevention is that it causes confusion because people are presented with alternative accounts of what they should be doing, rather than with the facts. But apart from knowing how to "correctly" respond to research questionnaires, there is no guarantee that people hearing disembodied facts can or will act on them.

Indeed, disembodied AIDS facts can provide an avenue for displacement activity. In AIDS education sessions, a commonly debated point is whether HIV can be transmitted by mosquitoes should they feed first from an HIV-positive person. Though the answer is "no," this is not an easy question to answer convincingly. The more it is asked, the more it is seen as something that must be responded to correctly, even though this may take up considerable time. There can even be a sense of pride among those reporting the length of discussions around this topic (or other tricky transmission scenarios) because they see such discussions as proof that target audiences have been engaged. Such engagement is of course superficial, despite the intensity of debate generated, because it fails to engage with actual risky behavior. In all likelihood some of those disputing whether or not mosquitoes are potential HIV vectors are practicing unprotected sex with multiple partners. Public arguments over abstract facts easily divert attention from more difficult issues of private behavior.

But even when education campaigns avoid being sidetracked and retain a focus on priority messages, information provided through front-stage encounters (or the mass media) is not enough to bring about widespread behavioral change. Once *this fact* is accepted then the role of peer educators, operating away front-stage performances, takes on great significance. Given Sobo's concern that AIDS facts are often disembodied, do peer educators have the ability to not only convey correct facts but also help people incorporate this information and its implications in their daily lives?

Technical Specifications and Human Values

Condoms are an important component of HIV prevention. Putting a condom on may be relatively easy in comparison to other behavioral changes. Nevertheless, using condoms is an adjustment in personal behavior. As we've seen in previous chapters, if condoms are to be used, a number of considerations—ranging from the technical and factual to aspects of sexual practice that relate to human values rather than the physical properties of the prophylactic—must be addressed.

Condom education generally focuses on a four-point checklist of physical and technical steps.

1. Check that the expiration date has not passed.
2. Check that the packet is still intact and that the lubricant has not dried out.
3. Open the packet correctly so as to avoid damaging the condom. (Don't use your teeth!)
4. Ensure that you expel the air from the tip of the condom before rolling it down over the… demonstration dildo.

That the condom must be put on the man's erect penis, and not the dildo, is often coyly (and revealingly) addressed by a well-worn joke: An apocryphal team of health workers go to a remote village and use broomsticks (or bananas, depending on the version of the joke) to demonstrate condom use to the village women because they don't have dildos with them. On completing the workshop, the health workers leave the women with a supply of condoms. Returning to the village a year later the health workers find there has been a baby boom. Upon inquiring, they realize that the women had been dutifully replicating their training by putting the condoms on their brooms (or bananas) before having sex.

Most peer educators leave training sessions on condoms with little more than the four-point condom checklist and the broomstick/banana joke. As peer educators relay this information through workplace talks, their coworkers often ask questions that indicate that condom use is not always as simple as one, two, three, and four. Can, for example, a condom be used with a femidom (female condom)? Why do pharmacies charge for condoms while the government condoms are given away free? And what if either partner is allergic to latex? It is in discussions outside of formal presentations that it becomes clear how something like condom use, which is often conceived as a simple technical intervention, is complicated because their use is embedded within human behavior, emotions, and beliefs. The reality is that many peoples' sex lives are more complex than following the four steps for correct condom use. Mineco's Moses Direko recorded in his research diary a ten-minute conversation with a woman neighbor in which it was clear that the reported problem was not about how the condom was being put on, but the husband's approach to sex.

> She said she always uses free [government] condoms when she has sex with her husband to prevent pregnancy. Her problem is that her husband does not romance her [i.e., engage in foreplay] before sexual intercourse. He just sleeps with her using a condom. On her side she is still dry. She feels painful [and] sometimes the condom gets torn [presenting a risk of possible HIV infection as well as pregnancy]... My understanding is that it is good to use [a] condom, but her husband is wrong to have sex with her without to romance her first so that she can feel good. Then [they can] start intercourse [and the] condom won't get torn.

This is only one example of the many problems that arise around the issue of condom use reported to peer educators. Only some, more straightforward problems can be effectively addressed by reviewing the four points for correct usage. Direko, writing a month later about a discussion with a male neighbor, reported: "This man came to me and he say... 'you talk about condoms. Yes, we must use condoms. But I got a problem with woman. When I condomize with the woman I take so long time to get finished [orgasm]. That is my problem.'" Besides condoms delaying ejaculation, another concern was being unable to put one on in the first place because of weak erections that were further deflated as they attempted to "condomize," or use a condom.

While difficulties with condoms can stem from communication or physical difficulties around sex, condoms also present problems to those with a good sex life. When one reflects on the explicit four-step protocol for condomizing, one sees that this is nested within an unstated four-step protocol for how sex should take place: (1) engage in foreplay until the woman's vagina is wet and the man's penis hard; (2) put on the condom; (3) commence penetrative intercourse and continue until the man ejaculates; (4) stop. Sex often is like that, but a lot of people, given the opportunity, like to be more creative around one of the most pleasurable and intense of human experiences. Once you start to think about changing positions, of alternating penetration with another sexual activity, of having more than one orgasm, or simply taking breaks between periods of intercourse, then condoms become much more intrusive than a once off process that can, with practice, be smoothly integrated into "four-step sex." Why there is such silence about how people really have sex is illustrative. In large part, it no doubt stems from prudishness, which means that details of our actual sex lives are rarely shared. But it is hard not to see this also, in part, as based on unfounded assumptions about the poor, the primary target of most condom campaigns: that they don't have the imagination, desire, space, or time for a creative sex life.

If problems related to condoms required peer educators to try their hand as sex therapists, there were other situations in which no amount of sex talk was going to shore up inadequacies of the ABC prevention message: Abstain, Be faithful, Condomize. Implicitly and sometimes explicitly in campaigns promoting ABC, there is an assumption that condoms are the only option because the preferred options of abstinence or faithfulness cannot be maintained. Thus, for example, George W. Bush's acceptance that condoms formed part of an HIV prevention strategy, drawing on the Ugandan experience, nevertheless relegated them to a back-up role: " 'They've started what they call the A.B.C. approach to prevention of this deadly disease. That stands for: Abstain, be faithful in marriage, and, when appropriate, use condoms.' . . . He [Bush] was quick to add that 'in addition to other kinds of prevention, we need to tell our children that abstinence is the only certain way to avoid contracting H.I.V. . . . It works every time' " (Sanger and McNeil 2004).

Whatever the differences over the relative merits of different preventions methods, there are times when *none* is appropriate. Not infrequently, people approached peer educators for advice because they had to make complex choices about lovers and the risk of HIV infection. Although the stories varied, the general plot line is a change in sexual partners combined with a desire to limit condom use in a quest for intimacy, defined as demonstrating love through flesh-to-flesh sex, or to have children. Men and women expressed these same motivations. The churn surrounding peoples' relationships meant that at least one participant—who had approached the peer educator—was aware of the risk of HIV infection but was also weighing competing desires that necessitated unprotected sex. Thus for example, Mineco's Tlouane explained in her diary how her neighbor confided in her that "Her boyfriend had divorced his wife three years ago and since then they have been using condoms ever since. Now he wants her [to have] a child with him. And she is afraid because she doesn't know his [HIV] status. Since she met him, she was faithful to him [but she can't be sure about him]."

Such scenarios reinforce the point made in Chapter 4 that the family, despite being a backstage space, is far from an intimate forum for frank talk about HIV and AIDS. Despite their conversation about having a baby, the couple is unable to discuss the possibility that, given their previous sexual relationships, one or both of them might be HIV-positive. In understanding how peer educators operate when faced with such situations, it is important to note that problems that originate from backstage space have to be responded to in that same space. Any solution that the peer educator might suggest has to be implemented in the environment in which the problem was generated. Thus, in the example above, Tlouane's neighbor needed some way in which she could, realistically, find out her boyfriend's status, even though the problem that she brought to Tlouane was that she was unable to raise this with her boyfriend.

If this was not the case, peer educators could be integrated into models of vertical communication with their role confined to clarifying what experts had said in front-stage presentations (or in mass media messages) and what people were too embarrassed to ask about in public. While explaining confusing or complex messages is part of peer education, peer educators also have to think about how responses to this information can be implemented in hostile backstage spaces. Simply providing information may not address concerns around condoms and HIV transmission. Rather, addressing these concerns involves first finding out exactly what the problem is and, second, finding a solution that will work in backstage space.

Peer educators have to listen carefully to what is being said to them. The immediate concern presented, while genuine, may only be a surface manifestation of a problem rooted deep in backstage space. In the case cited above, the problem of burst condoms could have easily been interpreted by Direko as one of inferior quality, especially given that free government condoms were being used. There have been persistent rumors or myths as to the quality of government-issued condoms. In 2007 these perceptions were supported by the withdrawal of twenty-five million government-issued condoms over concerns about their quality. Alternatively, the peer educator could have assumed that the woman's sexual partner was not faithfully following the four-point protocol for condom use. But the real problem was that the women's vagina was still dry when intercourse took placed because there was no sexual foreplay. That problem stemmed from the nature of the relationship between man and wife as well as the husband's beliefs—that the woman was unable to question—about appropriate sexual behavior.

The problem of unequal gender relationships, and its implications for HIV transmission, is widely recognized (Abdool Karim 2005). Women's vulnerability to HIV infection is not only a result of their physiology but also stems from norms in which the man is seen as the breadwinner and head of the household while the woman is the caregiver—norms that may well be internalized by women. Such norms make it difficult, if not dangerous, for the woman to raise concerns about HIV infection, such as insisting on measures such as condom use to protect herself, even if she believes her partner is being unfaithful (Abdool Karim 2005; Abdool Karim et al. 1994; Gupta 2002; Klugman 2000; Newmann et al. 2000; Sprague 2008; Susser and Stein 2000).

Peer educators also have to carefully select what advice to give to peers. With the condom burst/lack of foreplay problem, simply repeating the correct procedure for condom use was hardly going to be of assistance. Even though this particular woman understood that condoms were bursting because "romancing" was not taking place, she made it clear that she was unable to raise the topic of sexual stimulation before intercourse with her husband. When I interviewed Direko and asked whether he could talk directly to the husband (who was a neighbor), he explained that this would only make things worse. "The *mosadi* [woman] says I must not talk to him, if she told him that she'd spoke to me he would hit her [*smack!* claps his hands together]... That man would hit her if he found out she'd been talking about sex. He will hit her. He drinks."

The solution Direko suggested was that the woman use female condoms that her company had started supplying free. (With a female condom, friction is generated between the head of the man's penis and the lubricated polyurethane-lined vaginal wall, while with a male condom it is generated between a latex-sheathed penis and relatively large surface area of the vagina that can quickly absorb the limited lubricant provided by a condom.) Enthusiasm for female condoms and their ability to bypass some of the problems that male condoms present within a male-dominated sexual partnership is not limited to peer educators but also shared by professionals (see, e.g., Susser and Stein 2000). The woman had taken up the peer educator's suggestion and had reported back that, despite the continued absence of romancing, sex was less painful and the femidom was remaining intact.

Behavioral Change in Backstage Space

Condom promotion campaigns may attempt, through the provision of guidelines, to ensure that condoms are used correctly and prophylactic performance optimized. But condom use depends on much more than technical information. Condom use is often loaded with meaning because condoms occupy a space larger than the couple having sex. Even bedrooms are, in a sense, populated by more than two people because the couple is part of a wider sexual network. One or both members of the couple may be having, has already had, or will be having sex with other partners. Physically, only two people may occupy this backstage space at any one time. But in the era of AIDS, the physical connections that make up sexual networks haunt even the most intimate of social spaces.

Beliefs about condoms that go beyond the technicalities of correct use extend the couple's backstage space even further. The multiple communities of belief that each member of the couple may individually or collectively subscribe to, or believe they should subscribe to, adds another layer of complexity. The physical extension of a couple's social space through sexual networks interacts with its extension through belief structures to make truly intricate situations. For example, if an unfaithful partner is to act responsibly, he or she will have to introduce condoms into a sexual relationship. This not only threatens to reveal his or her infidelity but also challenges the explicit or implicit assumptions within which that the relationship is located.

There are times when the provision of technical information is all that is required. Thus, peer educators need to have the correct technical information on condom use. The far more challenging task, however, is facilitating the social and emotional acceptability of condoms in backstage spaces. Given that behavioral change needs to take place within contested and often highly charged backstage social spaces, technical information is necessary but insufficient for behavioral change.

If this is true for condoms with their technical simplicity, then it is even truer for other aspects of behavioral change. The use of antiretroviral drugs by those infected with HIV presents a vast amount of technical information that users, and other members of their social spaces, need to know. This includes when treatment should be started, when drugs should be taken, the dangers of drug resistance, possible side effects, and diet and lifestyle changes that will support treatment. On occasion peer educators were called on to provide such technical information. The question of starting treatment came up most often; peers were not infrequently confused as to why, if they had been diagnosed as HIV-positive, they were not given tablets to start treatment. Current treatment protocols for HIV require that treatment begin—along with clinical symptoms of opportunistic infections—only once the CD4 count, a measure of the immune system's strength, has dropped to approximately 250 cells per cubic milliliter of blood (the figure varies among treatment protocols), from a normal level of somewhere between 500 and 1,500. Prior to this, while dietary and lifestyle improvements are recommended, medical intervention is limited to the regular monitoring of the patient's CD4 count.

This protocol is counterintuitive to many South Africans; if someone is sick, they should be treated. Moreover if the disease has been diagnosed in a Western medical setting, then appropriate Western medical treatment (i.e., pills) should be prescribed. If this was not done, the individual could not only be confused but, given the skepticism described in Chapter 4 around race and HIV/AIDS, might also doubt that the medical practitioner had the patient's interests at heart. Tlouane provided a straightforward account in her diary, recounting how she had satisfactorily explained delayed commencement of antiretroviral drug treatment to a woman with whom she attended church:

> We were [walking home] from the church when Fiona told me... that her son is HIV-positive and was receiving [a state disability] grant for his status. She also said that her son was not yet on ART [antiretroviral drug therapy]. I said to Fiona that maybe her son's CD4 count was more than 250. Because they don't just give ART to anyone who is HIV-positive unless his/her CD4 count is less than 250. If one's CD4 [count] is more than 250 you don't need ARV.

Kabelo Mothotse, who worked in one of Mineco's human resources offices, described an even more highly charged situation around the same question. Themba, a coworker whom he did not know well, had come into his office for assistance.

> Themba told me that he is on [sick] leave and he is sick, but the nurses at the hospital and at the clinic do not want to give him medicine because they want him to die, just like other people who died at the hospital while he was [previously] hospitalized. He wanted me to help him to get all his moneys [owed to him by the company] and go and die in peace at his home in the Eastern Cape.
>
> He told me that he tested [HIV] positive at the hospital, but the nurse refused to give him treatment after testing him. I asked him if we can go to the Sister [i.e., nurse] at the clinic [and] he agreed. After [talking]...to the nurse I realized that he is HIV-positive, but it was not yet his time to start ART. I think the nurses must speak the language of the patient to make sure that he understands. I and the nurse managed to convince him because we were speaking Xhosa.

A superficial reading of this interaction suggests that peer educators provide an auxiliary support role to Western health care systems. Their linguistic and sociocultural access allows them to clearly explain the technical information that needs to be conveyed. This ignores a more uncomfortable reading of this kind of interaction. A more profound analysis points out that the peer educator is not so much translating messages provided by Western medical science and its practitioners (the nurse could speak Xhosa) but covering for their failures to explain the procedures to which patients are subjected. Moreover, a superficial reading also misses the skepticism on the part of this individual who has grave misgivings about the intentions of the Western medical system. The peer educator was well aware of this. "I doubt these VCT [Voluntary Counseling and Testing] counselors [responsible for explaining the implications of an HIV-positive test]. They ignore illiterate people and label them as stubborn; they don't take time [to speak] in their language. Or they don't know the beliefs and cultures of these people."

Clarifying why treatment does not necessarily follow diagnosis is only one small detail within a wide range of issues that need to be worked through if HIV treatment is to be effective. People must accept that HIV exists, that one is at risk, that one needs to know their HIV-status. People need the courage to test; they then need to accept a positive result, to tell sexual partners and loved ones that they are positive, to take treatment, and to live openly with the disease. An individual can work out some of this on their own, but even steps that can be taken by an individual alone are overshadowed by further steps that would have to be made openly in back- and, possibly, front-stage space.

The Constraints of Backstage Space

Focusing on the scientific protocols of diagnosis and treatments blinds us to the multiple social interpretations of HIV and AIDS and their consequences for achieving behavioral change. A small number of HIV-positive individuals publically disclosed their status, becoming a Person Living Openly with HIV/AIDS or, as they are often known, a PWA, based on the shorter (and usually technically incorrect) title of Person with AIDS. A number of peer educators explained the high stakes involved when counseling HIV-positive workmates who were thinking about disclosing their status. One motivation for disclosing a positive status is to take part in company HIV/AIDS programs as a PWA. Given the limited number of people willing to disclose their HIV-positive status openly, the few people courageous enough to do so are often used to give a "face" to the epidemic and to serve as an example to others who are also infected but afraid of acknowledging this. Given their small numbers and clear value to HIV/AIDS programs, these positions not infrequently become institutionalized with the employee being effectively employed on a full-time basis as a PWA. Alternatively, an openly HIV-positive person may be brought into a company to provide the same function (Dickinson 2004b). Many infected with the disease seemed to have an easier time revealing their status on a public platform as a PWA during a company World AIDS Day or Voluntary Counseling and Testing (VCT) event than giving the same information to their immediate family. When this was the case, despite a desperate wish to have more openly positive people, peer educators and AIDS managers would council against disclosure as a PWA. They argued that if family and friends had not accepted somebody's HIV-positive status, that person would lack the necessary support should things not go smoothly in more public settings. Front-stage performances at AIDS events are relatively predictable, if sometimes dramatic, with the PWA playing the role of a brave survivor warning others not to become infected or, if already HIV-positive, to follow their example in acknowledging and dealing with the disease.

During a 2004 VCT event that I attended in Deco, the company we encountered in Chapter 2, around one hundred employees participated in the day-long session during which they were encouraged with a series of presentations to take a confidential HIV test for their HIV status. Toward the end of the day, the event organizer—Hillary Botha—said that she wanted to introduce an important person. Botha explained that this person had approached his manager last year wanting to resign because he had found out that he was HIV-positive and needed money (from his provident [pension] fund payout) for his wife and children. Fortunately, the manager had "put him on the right track," and he had not resigned. In fact, she exclaimed, "he's here today!" Extending her hand toward one of the ushers who had been guiding people to the testing rooms outside the hall, she revealed that the man she was talking about was no other than "Isaac, our usher for the day!" Although many employees attending knew that a PWA would be giving a talk, few if any had guessed that it would be one of the ushers. There was a collective intake of breath.

The show was only just beginning. Isaac, it turned out, was a marathon runner—giving the double message that healthy people could be infected with HIV and that infected people could be healthy. To ensure there was no doubt as to his bona fides, Botha pulled out a huge knot of marathon medals from a bag. While Isaac spoke, Botha unraveled the ribbons and they were passed around along with photos taken of him running in marathons over the years. The artifacts were treated carefully and with respect. Isaac's story was one of victory in which he likened his running achievements to his struggle with HIV. He was a "champion," and he gave the times of some of his best marathon runs to prove it. Being a champion meant that he was still working at Deco despite being infected with HIV. He had been on treatment now for nine months. His CD4 count (earlier inputs during the day had explained the CD4 count and its significance in regard to HIV/AIDS) had been 197 when he started, it was now 375. The assembly spontaneously applauded this triumph.

Such events can, as with this one, be electrifying and deeply moving. But the steps taken to heighten drama also emphasize the distance between quasi-professional PWAs, such as Issac, and the audience. With such distances, which in other company AIDS events is often even larger with the PWA not even an employee of the company, it is relatively easy for PWAs to give a frank account and for the audience to play their own role of considerate, tolerant, and appreciative strangers. Everybody is aware that when the event is over, the PWA will most likely never be encountered again.

Disclosure to one's spouse, lover, friend, relative, fellow church member, or coworker is much more difficult. After disclosure, perhaps set in the kitchen, bedroom, or table in the work canteen, there is no parting of ways. The consequences of what has been revealed will continue to reverberate every moment that follows. As noted by Laura Lein in the introduction to *The Ties That Bind* (Lein and Sussman 1983, 4), "Social networks are the source of demands and constraints on individuals, as well as supports and opportunities. Network members challenge beliefs as well as support them, make demands for services as well as provide them, and close off opportunities as well as open them. Through gossip, the threat of ostracism, and the withdrawal of support, social networks can punish unconventional behavior."

This has far-reaching implications not only for those who are HIV-positive but also for peer educators' attempts to change the behavior around all aspects of HIV/AIDS. Their peer status gets them away from the more obvious barriers to communication that experts, such as occupational health practitioners, face when attempting to convince rank-and-file employees to change their behaviors at, say, a World AIDS Day event. But what appear to be private or intimate spaces do not necessarily provide an open forum for talk on HIV/AIDS. Attitudes toward gender, fidelity, healing, religion, or racism, to name only a few, are likely to mobilize opposition to any message. Because there are competing theories of AIDS, opposition may be direct—with protagonists of different theories defending their own beliefs. But the implications for the relative privileges and status of those close to someone with HIV/AIDS may also produce censure and punishment along the lines that Lein suggests.

Being revealed as HIV-positive can result in "social death." One peer educator explained what happened when a coworker's HIV-positive status had become known because he was too sick to continue working. Taken to a backyard shack, he was told by his relatives that he was no longer part of the family. Even less dramatic openness than revealing oneself as HIV-positive, such as seeking to know the origins of AIDS or how to avoid infection, may result in difference, dispute, and censure by one's social network.

When I interviewed peer educators, I often discovered that coworkers and superiors practiced "secondary stigmatization," by which they assumed that the only reason a peer educator would take such an interest in the disease is because they were HIV-positive themselves. (Students voluntarily taking my elective course on "HIV/AIDS in the Workplace" as part of their MBA studies have reported similar secondary stigmatization by their peers.) Some wore this as a badge of honor, some laughed about it, and some accepted it in solidarity with their HIV-positive colleagues. There are a lot of courageous people among the ranks of peer educators who were able shrug off such gossip. Many workmates, neighbors, church congregation members, and extended family members, however, were not able to do this. For these people, the majority of the population, open discussion about HIV/AIDS might not only breach the unity of important personal and community relationships but also raise questions about their credibility and even their continuing membership in important social networks.

The Dangers of Front-Stage Performances in Backstage Space

Given the tensions that exist in personal and private spaces, if peer educators take a stand that is too aggressive they risk opening up divisions around HIV/AIDS. The case of one peer educator in Mineco illustrates this dilemma. According to the diary he kept, over a period of thirty days he gave eleven talks, of between fifteen and twenty minutes, to his nine coworkers in a mine maintenance team on various HIV/AIDS topics while they were waiting to be assigned work. In the same period, he recorded only three informal interactions, two at work and one in the community. There is then a one-month gap in reporting until, in the following month, there are three formal talks recorded in the first ten days.

By the second talk of this final month, his supervisor had grown weary of the topic: "He [the supervisor] said to the people that they must not listen to me because I am talking lies and then people get less interested in listening to me." When he began his third talk, the supervisor exploded: "The supervisor... said that it is wasting time. He also said he can't eat the sweet with the cover paper [i.e., wear a condom]. [He] said according to his [African] culture he cannot condomize because he wants to have ten children." Not surprisingly, no more activity took place in the remaining twenty days of the month.

In this case the peer educator pushed his captive audience too far. While he piles on information, which may well be correct, people feel that he is bombarding them with his "sermons." Rather than calibrating just how far he can go, he provokes an open confrontation with his work team. His supervisor rounds on him with counterpositions, which, while perhaps exaggerated because he is exasperated, ring true to the backstage beliefs identified in Chapter 4. If the peer educator wants to bring about behavioral change, this is not the way to proceed. Competing worldviews and social positions are not reshaped on the merits of arguments in which protagonists restate their positions. Moreover, those who want answers are effectively warned, by such confrontations, that the price of upsetting backstage order is high.

Goffman's dramatic conceptualization of front-stage social space envisages two sets of actors: while one team or individual may be putting on a show, the audience also has to show its social competence by correctly responding. While there is the danger that peer educators use inappropriate front-stage methods (e.g., formal talks) in backstage spaces, there is also the danger that audiences put up a show of appreciation to satisfy requirements for social consensus but masks their true beliefs and behaviors. Mokwena reported on an interaction with two Mineco security guards:

> One of the security officers approached me while I was busy filling the condom can [dispenser] with condoms. He told me about his experiences with sex workers. He told me that they sometimes come across sex workers during their patrols. This sex worker offered sex and he refused because she wanted him to have sex without a condom . . . I don't trust what this security officer told me. I think he was trying to impress his colleague and me that he is always having safer sex.

Backstage space needs to be worked in different ways than the replication of front-stage performances. If this is not done, then despite peer status the barriers associated with front-stage communication reappear; social interaction is configured into performers and audiences. If peer educators are perceived to be preachers, peers may tune out, become resentful, or put on their own subversive countershow.

Peer Education in Backstage Space

While backstage space is far from the benign, relaxed space that naïve proponents of peer education assume it to be, this does not mean that peer educators cannot work this space when circumstances permit. The following account shows how Mokwena worked the backstage space of a family who belonged to his church.

After Mokwena spoke about HIV/AIDS at his church (of which he was an "elder" or deacon), Jacob—a church "Brother"—approached Mokwena and asked him to assist him and his immediate family, which comprised his wife, her sister, their mother, and the couple's children. Mokwena found a family in crisis. The wife's sister had just disclosed that she was HIV-positive.

> The sister to [Brother Jacob's] wife disclosed to the family [that she's HIV-positive] and there was different feeling about her disclosure. You know [would they] be able to eat with her? And so they start, some were afraid even to come close to her. The sister, Brother Jacob's wife [had the most problems]. That was why he [Brother Jacob] was too much concerned so that's why he comes to me for advice. That she might catch HIV/AIDS from her sister. Or maybe the children eating with her [will be infected]. It was stuff like that. Sharing food with her. Maybe her children would be infected. Things like that.

In response to these tensions, the infected sister had taken to her sickbed—a step toward social death. Instead of lecturing the family, Mokwena used the authority of prayer, and his own position in the church, to bring about harmony.

> I didn't put it in the form of a talk; I called them for a prayer. And in my blessing I tried to educate them as part of my prayer. Trying to explain to them what was happening and why. How you can handle it and that she [the HIV-positive sister] need[s] them and they must love her and things like that. So I used that prayer, because I know that they are listening and

> they know that I'm speaking to the Heavenly Father and they'll realize that this is a serious thing and then they must accept me as a leader in the church also. What I'm saying can convince them to accept her.

This prayer, which Mokwena estimated lasted between twenty and twenty-five minutes, conveyed the message that the HIV-positive sister needs to be loved and accepted within the family. It was also laced with practical advice; for example, that the family could share a meal without risking HIV infection. As a member of the same church, Mokwena deliberately utilized shared backstage beliefs in the interests of both the infected women and the family as a whole. "I put my message across through a prayer... It's like a prayer and counseling all at the same [time]... Because I know that really here I'm not really directly speaking to the Heavenly Father. I'm just speaking to this Brother's family so that they can understand what is happening."

The immediate results were dramatic. "When I said 'Amen' every member of the family was happy and hugging her [the HIV-positive sister] with tears of joy and reassurances of their love... you can realize that now they understand. They can hug her and they can come closer. Then you see now that they feel guilty for what they've been doing."

Over the following months, the situation continued to get better. "She improved a lot. You can't believe that this is the person who was getting thinner and thinner.... I think, something that contributed to her end[ing] up in bed. It was because the family didn't accept her situation. [Then] she's regained her body [weight] and in a few days I found her sweeping the [house]." In a diary entry over two months after his prayer/counseling, Mokwena recorded in his diary that Brother Jacob "was very happy to tell me that she [his HIV-positive sister in law] is back [working] after taking ART [antiretroviral drugs]."

This example illustrates how Mokwena mobilized common church membership and the family's desire to attain domestic peace to help the sister avoid the encroaching social and physical death. But the domestic peace achieved was circumscribed: One absent character in this story—the partner of the infected sister—was not brought within the reordered and harmonized family. He was not present when the peer educator visited the family, and "they [were] feeling like if they found him they could kill him. They were angry with him because they think that he infected her [Mokwena laughs—because this is not necessarily what happened]."

The peer education process was successful also because it made use of "back channels" of communication for issues that could still not be openly articulated within the family. Thus, ongoing concerns on the part of Brother Jacob's sister about the implications of her sister's positive status were not openly raised but shared with Mokwena's wife. She in turn conveyed them to Mokwena, who would then council Brother Jacob. "Bra [Brother] Jacob's wife is doing a lot of talking to my wife. And . . . my wife will tell me that 'Oh, I'm worried about this and this and this and this and this.' And it becomes easier for me to counsel Bra [Jacob], to council him and to strengthen him so that he can be able to guide the family through that problem."

Brother Jacob's ability to guide his family was supported by his church's requirement that families hold a weekly meeting to discuss family issues. But it also depended on receiving information about his wife's concerns not directly from her but through a circuitous route that bypassed the supposedly intimate social space of marriage.[1]

Although this case ended well, it was clearly a favorable situation to be intervening with shared church membership, Mokwena's authority, available backchannels, institutionalized "family time," and an excluded scapegoat. If peer educators do not have such favorable conditions, they must seek other alternative routes for interventions to bring about behavioral change.

Slipping Out of Order: Space for Strategy and Change

Victor Turner, an anthropologist, introduced the idea of "liminality" into the study of society. Turner (1974) describes *liminality* as a position of freedom from social structures that allows individuals' beliefs and social position to be reorganized. The idea of liminality is now widely used to describe positions of relative independence from prevailing social norms. Conventional thinking around peer education sees the similarity

1. I am grateful to Gila Carter and Karen Birdsall for independently pointing out the significance of these back channel communications in this example of peer educator activity.

between peer educators and their peers as allowing open and frank discussion in backstage social space. However, given our understanding that backstage space is often hostile and difficult terrain when it comes to HIV/AIDS, then peer educators need liminal spaces to work with peers. Such spaces need to be free from the multiple explanations of HIV/AIDS and, moreover, from the implications and sanctions that accompany these views.

When working in backstage environments, peer educators are not in a position to set up collective processes of liminality. Such procedures are large scale and involve extensive ritualistic performances, such as those used within company HIV/AIDS programs, notably around mass Voluntary Counseling and Testing (VCT) campaigns (Dickinson 2004c). Peer educators might be part of such events, but they do not provide the level of individual attention to peers' particular situations. Nor are peer educator and peer able to occupy positions of liminality for long periods of time. Long-term liminality, such as being an artist or intellectual, is not an option for most people. Thus, peer educators need small-scale, temporary spaces free of backstage (as well as front-stage) social pressures. Such spaces will be transitory but within them peer educator and peer can attempt to find solutions to individual questions, fears, and challenges around HIV/AIDS that will be robust enough to operate once the return is made back into the order of everyday life.

The first task that a peer educator has to undertake to slip out of order and into a liminal space with a peer is to signal that he or she is available, willing, and trustworthy. After this, the right conditions that facilitate being out of order must be in place. Finally, preparation for the return to order needs to be made.

Signaling

Experts such as doctors and psychologists have institutionalized reputation and status symbols that publicize and accredit them as sources of advice and help—albeit often for a fee. By contrast, peer educators do not have this advantage and have to find other ways to let their peers know that they are available to give advice. This may be straightforward; for example, giving formal talks at work or in their churches identifies them as peer educators. Peer educators who give formal talks to their peers at the workplace have, on average, more informal interactions with their peers than those who do not. Making it clear that one is happy to be approached outside of formal presentations is an easy way to signal availability. Churches increasingly provide opportunities for intervention; however, they often impose limits on what can be openly expressed. Thus, Florence Diseko in Mineco explained that when talking to the congregation of her church, she would signal to young people that she was available to talk about sex and condoms. "I'm just saying [in the church] 'protected sex' and if maybe they want more about protected sex they can come to me. And I'm telling them [to] feel free to come to me and ask me, 'When you are talking about the protected sex. What do you mean?'" When young people came to her for advice, she would respond to their questions, and, if she considered them old enough, would talk about condoms, teach them how to put them on and how to persuade partners to use them, and even hand them out from a box she kept at home.

Informal interactions as a follow-up from more formal presentations, however, is only one way peer educators signal their availability to slip out of order. Analysis of self-recorded informal interactions between peer educators and peers in the mining company showed that formal talks, along with the signaling effect of peer educator "uniforms" (e.g., T-shirts, caps, badges) and opportunities opened by mass media, accounted for 22 percent of informal interactions. A much larger proportion, 59 percent, took place because the peer educator had an established reputation at work and/or in the community (Table 13 in Appendix 1). Of course, this reputation as a peer educator had to start at some specific point. However, the value of a long-built reputation is that it signals a range of qualities that encourages peers to approach the peer educator. As we shall see, knowing that somebody is a peer educator is one thing; being confident enough to approach them is another.

To operate in backstage space many peer educators had developed techniques to raise the issue of AIDS in as natural a way as possible; for example, drawing attention to media reports on the disease while being careful not to push the topic if peers did not pick up on these gambits. When it was clear that somebody needed help around HIV/AIDS, peer educators went out of their way to be available but were also adamant that it was necessary that the peer make the first move. Consider the comments of Busie

Dlamini, a peer educator in Finco, about a friend whom she knows to be HIV-positive but who is not yet able to confide in her.

> I have a case whereby one of my friends phoned, to find out if I was aware that [another] one of our friends has got this [HIV]. And because I'm a person who believes that I cannot say, "I can see that you are worrying about something" or, "Somebody has told me that you are worrying about something," I always prefer a person to wait until it comes from within themselves to talk to me.
>
> She [her HIV-positive friend] has been coming to me for advice on other general things. However, when that other friend mentioned this [HIV infection] and what has been going on I realized that OK maybe she's trying to reach out to me...So, I've been trying to be always there for her now. And just waiting for that moment...She hasn't chosen to tell me [yet], but I can see all the signs are there....I can see that she's trying to reach out in her own way, [but] I can't just say to her "Now, OK I know you're HIV-positive." Because it's not my place to do that. I prefer to wait for her to tell me.

Although Dlamini describes this as "waiting for her to tell me," it's also clear that she is going out of her way to make things as easy as possible by "trying to be always there for her." Or listen to Manuel in Autostar who, as we saw in Chapter 4, had recently lost her father to AIDS. After the funeral, her half-sister opened up to her:

> OK, so I haven't seen my [half] sister in like ages now, and she's just been down for the funeral [of their father]. The week that my father passed away she was here...and I noticed that there was something not right about her, and I decided, like, you know, to talk to her about HIV/AIDS....I weren't talking to her because I was trying to judge her. I was just trying to tell her that "Listen, you know, you are aware that your father died. He had AIDS." And she said "You know, I don't know." So, I said "Why is everybody in denial about this whole thing?" Because even his [their father's] sister was saying "No, it's not AIDS." So, I said to her that "All I want to do is just tell you about HIV/AIDS and how you get HIV/AIDS and so on." [Then] she said to me. "Denise, I have to tell you something." So, I said "What?" She said to me "That I'm also HIV-positive."

In these cases, peer educators directly signal to a specific individual that they are available to talk about HIV/AIDS. In other cases, signaling was done in public environments without necessarily targeting particular individuals. In the following example, Mineco's Seloba acts in a stigma-busting role during the preparation of food at a "night vigil" prior to the funeral of a relative. In his entry for events at the home of the deceased on the Saturday night he said:

> One of [my] cousins was complaining about skinny people coughing who are helping to prepare food at the funeral. She suspected that they are HIV positive and they can infect us. (There are people who slaughter cattle and sheep and prepare vegetables at all funerals because poor people cannot afford catering.) A lot of relative and friends were convinced [by her fears]. Then I come in. I used that opportunity to teach them that we only get HIV through unsafe sex, blood contact, and babies [born to HIV-positive mothers].

The following day, at the home of the deceased uncle Seloba added:

> My uncle's widow (her husband died last year) was among the friends and relatives at the [previous day's] funeral. She heard what I said to them about an issue raised by one of my cousins about people (HIV positive) handling food at funerals. She thought they were personally attacking her because they know that her late husband was taking ART at Taung Hospital...
>
> She was happy [with] the way I handled that matter. [She said] "I was relieved because my husband died of AIDS and I am also going to die of AIDS." I encouraged her [during a one-hour conversation that they had together] to attend funerals in the family and in the village and to do what other women do as part of our culture [i.e. prepare food together during the night vigil].

Here, Seloba's signaling in backstage space resulted from a spontaneous response to erroneous information and stigmatizing actions of extended family members. The peer educator's actions are educational, and he is aware that there is a wider audience listening both to his cousin's mistaken views about HIV transmission and to his own corrections. But as he finds out the next day, when his uncle's widow approaches him, the interaction had greater significance. His actions also signaled that he was somebody who could be safely approached to discuss this sensitive subject.

Signaling is necessary because when it comes to HIV/AIDS, it is far from clear who is safe to approach. If peer educators (like the rest of us) spend much of their lives in backstage environments, then they are, whether aware of it or not, constantly signaling their availability whenever HIV/AIDS is salient. This implication was not lost on Seloba, who thoughtfully concluded the diary entry about this funeral with the idea that, "I personally believe that a peer educator must speak to every person as if positive people are also listening."

This approach is quite different from conventional educational processes in which inputs are provided at set times, set places, and in set formats. Peer education is—at its best—a constant, careful process of standing firm within all social spaces. On one side of this balancing act is the danger of not doing enough—of letting opportunities pass because one is not brave or quick enough to challenge other viewpoints. On the other side is the danger of overimposing and alienating peers rather than making calibrated interventions that take advantage of opportunities and signal a willingness to go further with those who want to do so.

Out of Order

Slipping out of order can be done in different ways. It may have physical dimensions. For example, a female peer educator in one of the retail company's small-town stores explained that coworkers would ask to see her "privately" because they didn't want to be seen with her in the canteen. She accommodated their requests by clocking out and meeting them in a nearby park where, over a cool drink, she would listen to their HIV/AIDS related problems. Here, the act of clocking out demonstrates the need for peer educator and peer to remove themselves from public space. This social space could be the front-stage space of management-employee relations or the backstage space of the workers' canteen. While peer educators were well aware of the dangers of managerial discrimination, their own experiences of confronting workplace stigma usually involved gossip on the part of other workers, about which management was often unaware.

Although insulation from social pressures need not involve a change of location, there can be no slipping out of order if others can overhear or infer from seeing people together. In this regard, it was easier for some peer educators in certain positions to slip out of order with peers than others; for example, those in human resource functions or those with their own office (such as Abrams, the uniform clerk, cited in Chapter 1). But even without an office to which to retreat, a reason to be talking allows both peer and peer educator to slip out of order under the noses of coworkers and supervisors. As described in Chapter 3, quality-control checkers on car production lines, frontline (checkout) supervisors in the retail companies, and health and safety officials in the mining company are all expected to move around and speak to coworkers. This shields their peer education activities from management and the scrutiny of other workers.

Escaping backstage constraints requires that the moment of interaction between peer educator and peer be private, but also that this privacy be extended, if necessary, indefinitely into the future. The confidentiality of interactions is crucial to peer educators. This emphasis on maintaining confidentiality may appear as a characteristic of the human-rights narratives of civil society responses to HIV/AIDS. But peer educators have insisted on this with remarkable resolve. Whatever other people did in the workplace, peer educators insisted they could not gossip. Indeed, this self-imposed ban on gossip went beyond their HIV/AIDS work. To gossip about anything, even if it was entirely innocent, sent a signal that you might not hold more important confidences as a peer educator.

When a peer disclosed their HIV-positive status to a peer educator, the importance of maintaining confidentiality is obvious. Letting this slip out could have catastrophic consequences such as social death. But confidentiality was broader than this; peer educators would often refuse even to reveal whether they were having intimate discussions with peers. Thus, when I asked Abrams in Bestbuyco if the occupational health practitioner, at his store might also be counseling people about HIV/AIDS, the conversation went like this:

Abrams: I don't know.

Dickinson: They may?

Abrams: They may. Yes. Because you know it's very confidential. [Firmly] It's a very confidential story.

Dickinson: [Defensively] Yes. Sure.

Abrams: And I really hammer on that.

Dickinson: And you don't tell the Sister [that you are giving people advice]?

> Abrams: No. No. I tell you I'll go to my grave with a lot of secrets [Laughs].

This insistence on the need for confidentiality was mirrored by the often cautious way in which peers would approach them. Often, an initial approach would be about a "friend-of-a-friend." Peer educators would go along with this ruse, knowing that in subsequent interactions the peer would reveal that the so-called friend was the peer him- or herself, or his or her partner or child.

As they try to educate coworkers, friends, or community members, peer educators also understood that being overheard by those outside of the educator-peer dyad was not their only problem. The teachings of their own faith could undermine key responses to the epidemic. Karabo Semenya in Mineco, who belongs to the Roman Catholic Church, explains, for example, how and why she ignores its teachings on condoms:

> I think the minute the person said I am going to get married they said they are going to be faithful, but you never know what's going to happen next... If you want to protect yourself and your family, you have to make the right choices. So, sometimes, sometimes we have to skip the rules. Rules, rules are meant to be broken. You cannot just live with them forever... They [the Roman Catholic Church] don't really approve of condoms. They said you have to be faithful and stick to one partner in our faith. They think if you're using the condoms you are sinning or something. But if you know you are using them at least you know you are safe [from HIV infection]. Even if they preach about them, how bad they are, but you know, they are protecting you. So, that's what really counts... I'm taking that route.

A number of peer educators belonged to the Zion Christian Church (ZCC), which is the largest church in South Africa. Split into two factions, members identify themselves by wearing a badge that incorporates either a dove or a star. Over a million followers attend Easter services at its Moria headquarters in Limpopo Province. It synchronizes Christian and African traditional beliefs and emphasizes spiritual/faith healing. Members are required to abstain from alcohol, smoking, and eating pork; men and women are separated during services; promiscuity is condemned; and the church frowns on the use of condoms. One ZCC peer educator in Mineco described how he navigated around his church's disapproval of condoms: "[The] ZCC they're happy with condoms, because I don't come with condoms at the church. I just talk about HIV/AIDS [in church]...In the church, there are no condoms. But outside in my car, the condoms are there! So when we come outside [of church], anyone who's in need of the condom, I just distribute."

Peer educators, like Mokwena who had worked with Brother Jacob, often explained that peer educators needed to make an effort to put aside their own beliefs and work with the beliefs of the peer they were trying to assist: "The difference is that at work people come from different religions...But at church it's simple because this is a member of the church. So [you] just look at the gospel principles and the stuff like the commandments and things like that. [But] to someone who comes from outside the church, then it's different, you have to handle it differently."

Writing in his diary, Mokwena explained that he sought to "win a person with his/her own weapons [beliefs]" and that "I will never counsel a person before he tells me his belief. Because you will never help a person if you don't know his beliefs...It is not a sin to be different, we can agree to be different or to differ. I always accept and respect...because there is a solution for all problems in all beliefs...I don't concentrate on differences because difference will create barriers."

We need to carefully examine the choreography of attitudes and beliefs when educators slip out of order with peers. Successful peer educators seek to put aside their own beliefs around sex and to understand the worldviews and beliefs of those with whom they work. In this regard they reflect a public preoccupation in South Africa, since 1994, with accepting diversity. Peer educators also justified this attitude of tolerance in interviews with reference to their role as *workplace* peer educators who needed to assist everybody in the company. But such an approach is also pragmatic. Once they have encouraged a peer to slip out of order and share their concerns, it would hardly be helpful if they started proselytizing their own values. This would immediately re-create the tensions of rival belief systems that they were trying to escape.

Identifying a person's beliefs, however, does not mean that the peer would accept them at face value. There may be "a solution for all problems in all beliefs," but this may involve getting around, rather than complying with, the values an individual holds or, indeed, feels they should hold—something that we explore in the next section.

When peer educators invite those they counsel to slip out of order, they enter the most intimate of social spaces in which they can work. If the peer educator is able to set up the necessary conditions—speaking in private, maintaining confidentiality, and having only the interests of the peer at heart—then all need for performance ends. In such a space, it is possible for peers to talk truthfully and without fear.

Yet, even in this private and sheltered social space, peers may have incentive to lie if, for example, he or she thinks that there is advantage to be gained from influencing the behavior of the peer educator. Thus, Tlouane in Mineco recorded a string of interactions with a neighbor that took on a soap opera–like quality.

> I heard an abrupt noise from my neighbors at approximately 6:30 pm. It was…a lamentation of a woman, Beauty, that I decided to inspect the matter further so as to extend my helping hand. I found Beauty's clothes scattered all over the yard, with her face bruised from an earlier abusive act, and she was locked out. I then collected her clothes and informed her abusive lover that I would accommodate her [i.e. put her up for the night] as it was already late. The following day we had a heart-to-heart talk…[Beauty says she is HIV positive and that is why her lover, George, hit her and threw her out].

As the diary entries accumulate, we find out that, in addition to the alleged HIV-status, Beauty is infertile and George has another girlfriend with whom who he wants to have a baby. We also find out that Beauty has no option but to stay with George because she is not working and her father won't accept her back into the family. George appears in court charged with assaulting Beauty, and, at George's request, the police arrive at the house to (unsuccessfully) evict Beauty. Tlouane talks to both parties in the dispute, advising reconciliation, warning George against hitting Beauty again, offering food to Beauty so that she can take the antiretroviral drugs she says she's been prescribed. She also tries to find Beauty work.

Four weeks after the initial diary entry, the peer educator records little progress:

> I went to George's place to hear what was going on between them. Beauty was also present. George said to me that he does not love Beauty anymore and that he wants her to vacate his place. He said Beauty refuses to go, and he is going to install a burglar door so that she cannot sneak into the house. Beauty then said to him that she is going nowhere; he can do whatever he wants to do.

> The dispute is now deteriorated. As long as Beauty refuses to go I can write about them until year end. Because every day there is a scene. I will just see.

Six weeks after this last entry I interviewed Tlouane, and she enumerated the various issues raised by the dispute. By now, she doubted whether Beauty was HIV positive and suspected that the central problem between Beauty and George was really her infertility.

> [Maybe] Beauty was using the [HIV] status as an excuse that George cannot leave her because she is positive [i.e., because he infected her]. Because I didn't see the [HIV test] result. She just told me... So I don't want to [pause] go deeper. I don't know [pause]... Maybe [pause]... I mean into knowing what [status] really she is [sighs] well, I don't know maybe one day I will ask her to show me the [antiretroviral] treatment... I want to see it Nine/Nine [with my own eyes].

This soap opera of Beauty and George raises a number of important issues—how poverty shapes peoples' ability to respond to their situations, gender relationships and violence, the importance of fertility, and the fear of being alone. These issues need to be understood and addressed in responding to HIV/AIDS. But, if the peer educator's suspicions are correct, Beauty has not taken advantage of the opportunity to talk about her real problems. Instead she seems to use guilt over her, claimed, HIV status to manipulate those around her, including Tlouane.

Although some peers may forgo opportunities offered for honest talk, there are many who engage in honest discussions when they discover that a peer educator will slip out of order with them. As we saw in Chapter 3, peer educators hold informal discussions about a wide range of issues. Some of their informal discussions may simply clarify questions or concerns and thus seem innocuous. But there is little that is neutral or safe when it comes to discussing HIV/AIDS in the tightly contested terrain of backstage space.

Sweet Lies Concocted Out of Order

Once peer educators have convinced their peers to slip out of order, their next challenge is to figure out how concerns can be addressed once back in daily life. Critically, slipping out of order provides opportunities for peer educator and peer to strategize about what they can do about a situation. Although many stories I heard involved a woman trying to slyly overcome a variety of obstacles in backstage relationships such as resistance to the use of condoms, it was not uncommon for peer educators to strategize with men about how they could introduce condoms. Here, Mokwena explains: "They [married men] always say is 'It's not easy. If your wife knows that you would never wear a condom, why do you now [start wearing one]?' [Their wife will say,] 'It means you are using this condom in North West [Province, where the mine was situated]. So you want to bring it to me now. Why? Why? You are sleeping around. You [must] know that you are not clean. You are dirty.'"

In response, Mokwena had devised a number of ways in which men with different beliefs could bring condoms into their relationships. "The Zionist (Christians) believes that having sex during menstruation can cause harm to the man. I use that belief to convince them to use condoms while visiting their menstruating wives at the homelands [i.e., migrant workers returning to families in rural areas]. They now have a reason to take condoms with them. Because they were ashamed to take condoms [before] if people see them."

Mokwena understood quite clearly that he was using a ploy to enable ZCC members to use condoms despite the teaching of the church.

> They're working here for the whole month or two months, and he goes back home for only Saturday morning and Sunday morning. Sunday he must come back. Once a month he has to take the money home. And he wants to have sex with his wife. And it's natural. The body wants to do that. And then you are afraid that if you have sex with her when she is menstruating then I'll be defiling myself or things like that... Then I explain that "You can use the condom." I always encourage them to use it if they don't feel good having sex during menstruation.

Mokwena was careful not to get sidetracked by ancillary issues or goals. In this case, he was not trying to convince ZCC members that their church's teachings were wrong or to convert them to his own. His goal was simple—help them avoid being stigmatized by other church members for using condoms. He recognized that when working with different people, he would have to mobilize a different strategy. Thus when engaging with workers holding traditional African beliefs, who buy traditional herbal potions before returning home to their wives in rural areas, he took a different approach. Traditional healers make small batches of these potions, while variations are commercially available. They claim to cure a wide range of complaints, improve general health and appetite, and enhance sexual performance. Mokwena cleverly suggested that condoms could be used to prevent them polluting their wives as the herbal treatment purified their own bodies.

> They are taking [the herbal potions] to make them clean [from pollution, which might not be sexually related] and when they get to their wives then they are also more [sexually] powerful. They're pulling on four cylinders! [Laughs]. Because that's one of the things that the men likes. If you say, "Eat this [potion] then you will be very strong, sexually strong." They will puff [up] [expands his chest to demonstrate], they will come and buy your product! [Laughter]. And then those things help them to introduce the condom to their family because if you just come and say "I want us to use a condom today," then she will start suspecting. But if you say you are taking a medicine that's cleaning me, so "Can we use a condom?" It will be easier to negotiate.

In general, Mokwena's objective was simply to overcome cultural hostility to the use of condoms by providing "sweet lies." Assisting in such deception was justified on the grounds that having an excuse to use condoms was in everybody's best interests. "[In fact,] you are [being] honest [i.e., you don't want to risk infecting your wife because you've had unprotected sex with other partners]. That's [really] why you bring the condom. But if there is a reason and it goes with their religion and their beliefs it becomes easy [to introduce condoms]. It becomes a sweet lie."

Providing sweet lies was a not uncommon peer educator activity. Here, Nkosi Mantashe, an assembly worker in Autostar, explains how he suggests to other men how they can keep condoms available for casual sex if they had steady girlfriends who might (correctly) see condoms as a sign of infidelity.

> Most guys like to have steady girlfriends. [But] they are afraid to carry around the condoms with them in case the girlfriend finds them. So, now they go without condoms...[and] when they got that someone-special-for-now [a "spare" (secondary girlfriend) or an opportunity for casual sex] then

> they start looking [for a condom] but if they can't find it, they will do it without condoms . . . Because [girlfriends] they think that when you are carrying condoms, you are ready for someone.
>
> Well, you're trying to talk to them [about limiting their number of sexual partners] . . . But then [you also] try to give some tactics of course. The problem is that if you carry a condom around in your pocket, it will cause a problem, but there are some [AIDS awareness gift] key holders that you can put condoms in . . . you can carry that all the time, even in front of your girlfriend.

Mantashe then suggested that if condoms were kept loose in a box at home, ideally from the start of a relationship, then the condom kept in the key ring could be replaced without the girlfriend being any the wiser: "No, there is still a condom [in the key holder]." No peer educator that I interviewed thought that such deceit was ideal, but, as they put it, at least "they've had protected sex."

Slipping Back

Slipping out of order allows peer educators and peers to jointly assess backstage barriers to behavior change and to strategize about how to get around them before the slip back into order is taken. One such strategy—establishing one's HIV status—is often critical to knowing the extent of the problems faced. While the actual testing can be arranged in privacy, acting on the test result is likely to disrupt relationships in backstage spaces. Not surprisingly then, even going for a test requires courage. Thus, one peer educator at Minco described a twenty-minute interaction with a coworker who had a new girlfriend and wanted to stop using condoms so that they could have a child. "I spoke to my fellow colleague on VCT. I told him that knowing your status is knowing your future. He is afraid to test. I told him about confidentiality [of the test], but I failed to change his mind." Even though the peer educator's advice was not immediately taken, it did have an impact: The peer came back sometime later to inform the peer educator that he had tested for HIV and gave him a cool drink to thank him for his earlier advice.

Sharing a test result—positive or negative—with intimates is difficult. Tlouane in Mineco reported what happened when a coworker told her about her negative HIV test result during lunch break. Tlouane commended the woman for finding out her status; all straightforward and easy. The next day the peer continued the conversation, confiding that she told her husband the news but he refused to take an HIV test himself. The conversation then moved on to the more difficult issue of introducing condoms into the relationship.

This is not dissimilar to the earlier case in which a peer educator suggested femidoms to introduce lubrication and avoid condom bursts. Solutions need to be found to problems, yet it is generally symptoms and not causes that are being addressed. The introduction of femidoms, like the need to introduce condoms because the man refuses to get himself tested, fits a gendered narrative of men as the problem. All the more so if we assume that these men were being unfaithful to their wives. Undoubtedly, it's true that a much stronger solution than condoms or lubrication could be put forward. In the case of the surreptitious introduction of lubrication via femidoms this would mean that the women felt empowered enough to talk to her husband about her own sexual needs. Since we know that the man also drank and was violent, the ultimate act of empowerment would be to give him his marching orders and manage without his nonsense. Although this is the most complete solution, it's unlikely to happen and successful peer educators are constantly mindful of the restrictions that their peers typically face.

In Chapter 4 we learned how peer educators tried to find ways to help women who could do little to change their situations to protect themselves from HIV. Drawing on research conducted in the early 1990s in the KwaZulu/Natal Province of South Africa, Abdool Karim et al. (1994, 3) reported that "Women repeatedly expressed the need for clandestine methods that they could use and control which would serve the duel purpose of preventing pregnancy and protecting them from acquiring sexually transmitted disease." Typically, women peer educators also taught younger girls "skills" or "tricks" to delay intercourse or to insist on condoms. These included telling boyfriends that unprotected sex meant that they did not truly love them since it would be jeopardizing their future prospects if they were to get pregnant while still at school. If that didn't work, the final suggestion was to use a female condom and hope that the boyfriend would accept or perhaps not even notice its presence.

The idea that men would not notice a female condom seems unlikely—and no peer educator reported any feedback that this strategy had worked. At the time I was researching, female condoms had been made much more widely available, and they were being proposed by peer educators as a solution for a range of problems such as dryness, delayed ejaculation, and the refusal of men to wear male condoms. To some extent, this represents hopes on the part of peer educators that this new resource would solve a number of different problems that they were encountering. That they were probably overoptimistic in their assessment of just how much the female condom could achieve reflects the limited options available to peer educators. But, irrespective of efficacy, what we see is that, in response to identified needs, peer educators used an array of strategies, including tricks and lies, that they hoped would enable not only women but also men to introduce condoms and femidoms into backstage spaces hostile to their use.

Gender relations and gender inequality are important factors constraining behavior (Campbell and MacPhail 2002). Instead of focusing exclusively on these, however, we need to see the bigger picture in which a range of conflicting values in backstage space constrain all actors should they seek to change behavior and protect themselves or others from HIV/AIDS. Only for the fleeting moments when it is possible to slip out of order are peers free of these constraints. But slipping out of order, for all its liminal freedom, does not construct utopia. Rather, it grimly assesses what is possible to achieve—if necessary by stealth, tricks, or lies—within a fundamentally unchanged backstage order to which everybody must return.

Conclusion: Slipping Out of Order and Its Limitations

The knowledge that there are temporary spaces in which peer educators strategize with peers provides us with a better understanding of the possibilities and limitations of peer education. Peer educators have three available spaces for their work—front stage, backstage, and slipping for a while out of order into a temporary space free of social pressures. These spaces are available to anyone, not just to peer educators. An African Absenteeism Clerk who was also a union official at the mining company explains that he often shifts directly from recording employee absenteeism, a formal company function, into being a supportive confidant though there is no formal recognition for this role.

> I know the symptoms [of HIV/AIDS, so] I will know maybe there is a problem. Most of those that come [back to work] from the hospital, you can see this [HIV/AIDS] is that problem. Some disclose their status to me, they say they are HIV-positive... I'm not a peer educator, but most of them do trust me as a union rep... As I'm wearing two caps at the same time, when I talk to them in the office I talk to them as [an absenteeism clerk].... but if I see this guy has a real problem it is where I am using a union cap. I say, "Let's talk man-to-man. I want to know what your problem is so that I can help you." That is when people tell me that they are [HIV] positive.

Grasping the importance of these social spaces that can be worked helps us better understand that the line between peer educators who provide information and who counsel is blurred. Counseling roles have effectively begun before the peer educator even knows what information is needed. While there is an overlap between what peer educators and professional counselors do—establishing privacy, focusing on the needs of the individuals, and guaranteeing confidentiality—it is instructive to compare what these two different actors can and cannot do.

Peer educators are able work in backstage spaces where there are opportunities to provide information and influence behavior. Even though there are limits to their ability to change behavior within this space, they can, through carefully calibrated interventions, signal that they are willing to talk elsewhere without constraints. If their peers recognize these signals and take advantage of the opportunity, the peer educator is in a strong position—subject to their technical knowledge and access to resources—to strategize with the peer as to how they can best respond and bring about realistic change.

By contrast, professional counselors do not have access to backstage space but must formally signal their availability—often institutionalized in the form of referrals from other professionals. Creating a space free from any front- or backstage constraints is done much more explicitly by professional counselors than peer educators. This is perhaps typified by them having a dedicated, private room in which to talk to clients: a stepping, rather than a slipping, out of order. For peer educators the same conditions have to be created, in much more implicit (and less obvious) ways. Rather than a dedicated office, cracks in daily routines are utilized. Finally, while the professional counselor is likely to have a greater level of training and resources, they are less likely to understand the social conditions that influence clients' lives and thus to assess how their advice will, or will not, work within this environment.

While this comparison between professional counselors and peer educators is instructive, it is also useful to ask: What is the purpose of counseling, whether conducted by peer educator or professional? Is it to get the individual client or peer to align their behavior to some prescribed standard, or is it to see how the client or peer can best tailor their behavior to achieve necessary goals within frequently hostile backstage environment? Since much of the work of peer educators falls into the latter category, we can perhaps now more clearly see what horizontal communication processes, raised in Chapter 1, entail and how they differ from vertical communication strategies. In the latter, expert messages are pushed down, and peer educators are expected to assist their peers in both understanding these messages which, it is assumed, will then be put into practice. The reality of peer educator work—front stage, backstage, and out of order—illustrates that they are engaged in a process of adapting available responses and solutions to meet the specific needs of individuals within their daily lives.

This little-understood distinction means that peer educators continue to be seen as a conduit for prepared messages. This, in turn, means peer educators may get little support as they embark on the actual process of working around backstage constraints. Training is often largely a matter of getting peer educators to understand the messages that experts want them to transmit. Trainers do not generally encourage peer educators to share their own experiences with each other. Rarely are peer educators helped to understand how they can better work in backstage spaces, signal to peers, or engineer the complex act of slipping out of order. Nor are they helped to develop strategies that can bring about realistic behavioral changes when they and their peers return to backstage order. The result of this omission is that peer educators are often isolated from each other and have to work out theories and practices on their own. If the complexities of peer education are understood, then appropriate training and necessary resources as well as opportunities for peer educator–peer educator interaction can be provided. This is not a difficult task.

But it is not a silver bullet. Peer educators' work would be improved by greater networking and skills-sharing based on a model of horizontal communication with their peers as well as with each other, but even with such improvements, their modus operandi does not challenge competing explanations of AIDS. Many people find the messages of peer educators awkward, painful, unwelcome, frightening, or objectionable. Moreover, they have, in the form of alternative backstage values and beliefs, many psychological bolt holes that they can use to escape the implication of peer education. Chapter 6 looks at this fundamental challenge to the work of peer educators in changing beliefs and behaviors.

6

To Speak with One Voice

People Hear What They Want to Hear

While peer educators strive to change the behavior of their peers, some also recognize the limits of strategies restricted to working with individuals. To put it simply, there are too many avenues of escape for those who prefer, for one reason or another, not to listen to the messages of peer educators, irrespective of its vernacular delivery or sociocultural proximity. In response some peer educators encourage all social actors to "speak with one voice" and to close down these psychological escape routes. One of the main targets of their efforts are the South African unions that have, to date, been reactive in their response to HIV/AIDS. Other targets are churches and traditional healers.

Convincing unions, churches, and traditional healers to speak with one voice about the epidemic is critical because contradictory explanations about AIDS and what to do about it make peer educators' efforts difficult if not impossible. As Louise Rasool in Bestbuyco put it, "It's easy to forget [what we're saying] if you don't want to see the truth."

The long incubation period of the virus, which de-links HIV infection from AIDS symptoms, fosters this amnesia and denial. As Semenya in Mineco explains, the uncertainty around the cause of deaths further complicates the link between cause and effect that is essential to understanding HIV and AIDS.

> [We need to] tell people about HIV/AIDS, everybody has the choice, they can make... It's either you make the right choice or the wrong choice.... [But] some people they'll say, "I don't really believe HIV is there."... Even if you explain the numbers [of infection and deaths] they want to see the person who is dying of AIDS... But they are not very sure. Because the family will not disclose... You just heard that that person has died of AIDS, but you are not sure about that... You cannot be sure. In fact, it's a rumor. You just hear that "Oh! That person has died of AIDS." But you're not sure about that.

If most AIDS deaths are maybe-AIDS-but-we-cannot-be-sure deaths, then even those standing at the graveside may not be certain as to what is killing so many young adults. The living are free to pick and choose explanations, as Robert Mokwena in Mineco explains when he describes interacting with a colleague who recently joined the local Zion Christian Church (ZCC) and is teetering on the edge of realizing that he may be HIV-positive:

> I used to work in the same department with this man. He is now a supervisor. I did not know that he was sick. He told us that he was diagnosed with pneumonia. He is a man of big stature, but he was like a person who has full-blown AIDS. I struggled to recognize him. One of the peer educators [who previously] suffered from pneumonia helped to advise this man. He [the supervisor] was worried that people are suspecting that he is HIV-positive.
>
> He joined the ZCC. They are giving him [blessed] coffee and tea to drink and told him about people who want to kill him [i.e., witchcraft]. This man was on his way to Moria ZCC headquarters because he has a new religion. We tried our best to convince him that his [pneumonia] treatment must come first....
>
> I think we must do something to convince church leaders that HIV/AIDS is a killer. People are going to spiritual healers to hear what they want to hear.

In discussing how peer educators have reflected on the limits of their work, we see why and how they have expanded their targets to include working with unions, churches, and traditional healers to do what the country's leadership has yet failed to do: build a strategic response to the epidemic.

They Just Sign the Paper

During 2006, Kabelo Mothotse, a peer educator in Mineco went to the Eastern Cape for a month to resolve some outstanding benefit payments. His primary task was to identify dependents of deceased mineworkers and assess how money owed them should be allocated. During the course of this work, Mothotse found that some workers who had been medically boarded (found too ill to continue working) by the company were simply being cut loose or abandoned once they left employment. Without easy access to medical facilities, they were failing to keep up HIV and TB treatment that they received while employed. In other cases HIV-positive employees were medically boarded without any prescribed treatment. Mothotse told me about the conditions that were hidden from view in a remote part of the Eastern Cape.

> We were investigating a death benefit case. We found a sick [HIV-positive] woman. She was hungry and angry. Her late husband was working for the company. She told us that "I hate Middleburg [where Mineco operations were located], my husband brought me AIDS from Middleburg. I hate Middleburg." The late husband was medically boarded before he died. And he was not on ART [antiretroviral therapy] and his wife also [was not on ART]. . . . These people are dying like dogs. They are staying in the mountains far away from doctors and other health workers. It is not easy to reach them. I was not angry because the woman was angry, hungry, and dying of AIDS. I am angry because Mineco is not doing enough. We are dumping our sick people after serving our company for many years. . . . I want my leaders to see these people.

Although Mothotse's anger was directed at the company, he recognized that it wasn't only high-level executives who were at fault. The company's HR managers, medical practitioners, and union representatives were also not doing enough. All of them sat on the medical boarding committees that were allowing HIV-positive people to leave the company without either starting treatment or making sure it would continue. Mothotse's discovery far from the mine's operations brought home the fact that key leadership groups in the company had failed to deal with the disease despite the policies and procedures put in place to do so.

When HIV-positive employees quietly leave companies via this "sick route," there is often a conspiracy of silence, which doctors, managers, unionists, and the sick employees themselves tacitly maintain so as not to confront the ill individual's HIV-positive status. In such cases, an opportunistic infection, such as TB, and not HIV/AIDS is the documented cause of disability. The Department of Labour's *Code of Good Practice on Key Aspects of HIV/AIDS and Employment* (2000, Section 11.3) states that "the employer should ensure that as far as possible, the employee's right to confidentiality regarding his or her HIV status is maintained during any incapacity proceedings." Sick route misrepresentation is not confined to Mineco (Dickinson 2003). Each party may have different reasons for going along with the collective fiction, including fear, respect, and convenience. Nonetheless, their decision to take the path of least resistance has far-reaching implications. Describing another case that he had investigated during his visit to the Eastern Cape, Mothotse told how another employee had been diagnosed as HIV-positive but had refused to start antiretroviral drug treatment. After his wife died, he had impregnated a seventeen-year-old girl (herself an orphan) before he himself had died. Both the girl and her baby were now sick. While this child was to be included as a beneficiary of the employee's pension payout, along with the children he had had with his wife, the peer educator noted bitterly that this would only be the case "if she's still alive [by the time payment was processed]. Because she was very sick [when he had visited]."

In Mothotse's view, "It is his [the employee's] fault. *But I blame the* [HIV-test] *counselors.* Someone who counseled him, they could have convinced him [to take antiretroviral drugs]. Just look what he has done, he got a seventeen-year-old [pregnant], he impregnated her. There is another life that is HIV positive." Nonetheless he added:

> I think all of us [are responsible]. Because the unions are involved when somebody is medically boarded. And they can see the doctor's report. And the doctor is there. He will tell them that, because of this and this, the person

> cannot do his job any more. So he must go home. And they're going to give him medical board. The unions are there to see the record and demand, make sure that if this person goes home he falls in good hands. But, they just sign the paper. And then the person is on his own. Like this man. In his records, the file shows that he was HIV positive and he refused to take the treatment.

We do not know precisely why this man refused treatment. What we do know is that he may have been influenced by alternative explanations of the epidemic. His decision to impregnate a young girl may have been shaped by the myth that sex with a virgin will cure him of the disease (Leclerc-Madlala 2002; Meel 2003).

This story illustrates how an individual can easily slip through the system—and the hands of the medical boarding committee designed to protect both the interests of the company and employees—that has been put in place to treat HIV-positive employees. This expanding tragedy also points to a wider failure on the part of all those who came into contact with this individual to speak with one voice. Critical front-stage players at all levels did not challenge this man's actions—actions that were almost certainly encouraged if not promoted by other voices from within backstage social space.

Responding to Apathy and Opposition

Peer educators see the direct impact of the failure of institutional systems of care and protection that appear weak, indifferent, and incompetent when it comes to HIV and AIDS. Trapped between conflicting explanations of AIDS and flawed institutionalized responses are the individuals who, fearful of the consequences, take what appears to be the path of least resistance only to find a degrading, painful, and often lonely death. Peer educators see all this with different degrees of clarity. Knowing what to do about it is a different matter. Most, peer educators limit their focus to individuals they know or work with and tend not to strategize about how to confront institutional weaknesses in their company HIV/AIDS responses or beyond. Yet, even these peer educators discover that they must learn how to negotiate with higher-ups in their companies if they are to do their individual work successfully.

Consider, for example, one peer educator's journey in Finco. She'd attended a company HIV/AIDS training session where she had been asked to start giving talks on HIV/AIDS. The supervisors in her area, however, refused to release workers for the sessions that she had set up because they were under pressure to meet "hectic" production targets. She then met with the HR manager, who was supportive and set up a meeting with the management team, which agreed to approve her activity. With this official support, and now considerably smarter about how to get things done in her workplace, she organized a meeting with the supervisors and brought them on board. Only once this had been achieved was she able to get reasonable attendance at the training sessions.

Getting a platform to speak to peers is simply a first step. The logic of peer education leads from the shop floor, to the company, and finally to the larger society. This attention to a broader picture leads to the inevitable question of why so many other social actors fail to respond wholeheartedly to the epidemic. Nobody is "for" a deadly virus.

At the risk of oversimplification, we can identify four categories of social actors and a gap between what they are doing and what they would be doing if there was truly a united front against AIDS. First, there are professions, such as health care, that should be unambiguously in the front line of any response but, in practice, not infrequently fall short of providing what could be expected of caring professions. Certainly the (Western) medical establishment has dragged its feet, given their limitations in the face of HIV/AIDS, in reaching out to other potential allies of a united front. Second, there are organizations such as unions, government, and academia that should be central to any response given their mandates but that (as we shall see below in the case of unions) have not been aggressive in dealing with the HIV/AIDS crisis. (Others have discussed the South African government [Fourie 2006; Nattrass 2004] and academia [Cairns, Dickinson, and Orr 2006]). Third, there are organizations, such as companies, that should be supportive but, as we saw in Chapter 2, prioritize competing demands. Fourth, and finally, there are organizations, such as the churches and traditional healers, that have the potential to be part of the solution, or part of the problem, but have not meaningfully joined in a united front against AIDS. All of these organizations and institutions can play major roles in dealing with HIV/AIDS. The role that is perhaps most overlooked is how they can help to close psychological escape routes in backstage spaces. These are the open fire doors through which HIV and AIDS are currently raging and that, if closed, would help contain the epidemic.

One Voice, Backstage

Mokwena reflected in his diary how changing beliefs about HIV/AIDS requires action by a range of social actors. "Culture and beliefs are playing a big role here. I think cultural leaders must be work shopped on [brought together to discuss] HIV/AIDS. Because the chiefs, headmen, sangomas and herbalists [both types of traditional healers], and spiritual healers are the only people who can manage to convince their people to change their beliefs or attitudes. Priests and pastors also need workshops."

Peer educators recognize that they operate within a tangled weave of conflicting opinions about the meaning of HIV/AIDS. They thus understand that all those whom their coworkers, family, friends, and community members find credible must speak with one voice about the meaning of and solutions to HIV/AIDS. For peer educators, credible leaders can be helpful only if they go beyond pro forma expressions of concerns about the AIDS epidemic, obligatory representation on committees, and passing resolutions at organizational conferences.

Rather, peer educators want leaders to mobilize by genuinely and consistently attempting to drive discourse around HIV/AIDS down into their organizations so that these discourses occur at the lowest levels of operation. In other words, genuine social leadership on this issue means more than giving front-stage performances; it means working to penetrate messages through the networks and structures of their organizations into backstage space. If leaders can't do this, they are revealed as "talking heads" without real links into constituencies.

When judged by this more demanding leadership criteria, it is clear that not all social leaders are speaking with one voice—or speaking at all—in backstage spaces. This is evident when we explore the case of South Africa's unions.

"We Only See Them in Meetings:" Unions and HIV/AIDS

In Chapter 3, we learned that peer educators are overrepresented in lower-skilled occupational categories, which are more heavily unionized: over 77 percent of peer educators were union members, and just over 30 percent were or had been a trade union representative. In short, workplace peer educators can be seen as essentially a working-class movement.

Given this common working-class background, one might assume that cooperation between peer educators and unions would be extensive. In interviews peer educators identified a number of ways in which unions did, indeed, assist in their activity. Through collective action, unions have—at least in some companies—successfully demanded that employers provide antiretroviral drugs and other AIDS-related benefits. When asked, peer educators often identified individual shop stewards who were themselves peer educators or could be relied on to support peer education. Peer educators also valued union officials' speaking about HIV/AIDS in meetings or lending support to workplace AIDS programs, such as voluntary counseling and testing campaigns.

However, when I asked peer educators what the union was doing about HIV/AIDS in their companies, I frequently drew a blank: They didn't know because they hadn't seen any union activity in this area. This despite the fact that most peer educators are union members with many holding office in the union. Some said their union might be doing something about HIV/AIDS, but they were unaware of it. In Mineco, unions provided more structured support, though peer educators felt that the unions could be doing more. Beyond this, what emerged was a marked distance between peer educators and unions. When asked to rate how supportive a variety of different company players were, peer educators ranked union officials much lower than occupational nurses and HIV/AIDS managers. This was not entirely surprising, but what was surprising was that peer educators felt that their line managers or supervisors gave them as much—or as little—support as union officials, something that remained the case even when peer educators who were not union members are excluded from this rating (Table 14 in Appendix 1). Since unions are there on behalf of their members, while supervisors' role is to ensure that production objectives are achieved, this "parity of support" between union officials and supervisors toward peer educators is startling.

After pointing to cases of shop stewards who were active peer educators, criticism of the union in regards to HIV/AIDS activities was sometimes harsh. An African female peer educator in Autostar who was a union member explained:

> To tell the truth they [shop stewards] are not active, but most of the time management are focusing on them [in the HIV/AIDS program]. They

> [shop stewards] say they are busy, but I don't know what they are doing. They don't come with us on community visits. [Or] they come late, asking if they are going to get something. They just come to clock in for their voucher [a monthly token of R50 given by this company for those active in the peer educator program]. We don't see support from them. We've [peer educators] complained [to management] in meetings that the shop stewards are not active, but nothing has changed to date.

In a group interview of peer educators in the same company, a union member said: "I'd like to see the union doing something. They could make a difference, but they have no program of their own. The union is supposed to be for the people, but we only see them in meetings. There is no motivation from the union side...Let us fight for life too [and not only money]."

In several companies there were partnership agreements between management and the unions on company HIV/AIDS programs, but for many peer educators this did not filter down. In general, across the five companies researched, peer educators noted unions' institutional absence from the work they were doing.

Many in the South African union movement recognize and are troubled by the union's limited response to HIV/AIDS. In July 2007 the research unit of COSATU, the country's main union federation, produced a document that highlighted the role of unions in forcing government to provide antiretroviral drugs in the public sector. It also discussed discrimination against HIV-positive workers by other employees and the limited value, in practice, of workers' rights around HIV/AIDS. "Cases of abuse and discrimination [against] HIV/AIDS [infected] workers have become rampant despite the existence of policies prohibiting such behaviour." The report acknowledged that this "depict[s] the weakness of labour in ensuring that employers comply with the regulations advocated by ILO [International Labour Organisation] and National [Department of] Labour policies." Overall, the document noted, "Despite the high levels of HIV/AIDS in South Africa, unions' response to HIV and AIDS in South Africa has been minimal and *ad hoc*" (Guliwe 2007).

This inaction exists even though unions have long been aware of the issue. In 1992 COSATU produced a video, *AIDS: A Union Issue* (Hodes 2007), and it has discussed the disease at the highest levels of union leadership. A 1998 joint statement from the three largest union federations

(COSATU, FEDUSA, and NACTU) indicated a clear understanding of the threat that HIV/AIDS posed to its members and proposed a response.

> We, the representatives of organized labour in South Africa, comprising the Congress of South African Trade Unions (COSATU), the Federation of Unions of South Africa (FEDUSA), the National Council of Trade Unions (NACTU), as well as independent trade unions, acknowledge:
>
> - The HIV/AIDS epidemic affects the economically active people in our country, South Africa.
> - The proportions to which the disease is spreading and the serious challenges it poses to the country's development and future.
> - Poor living conditions and low wages are factors that make it difficult for many people to change behaviour that puts them at risk of HIV infection.
> - Our response, therefore, must be to campaign for HIV prevention and care with the same determination and energy with which we fight many other working class struggles. We say AIDS must he made a priority issue for every trade union member. Campaigns to stop AIDS must be discussed at every trade union meeting.

Why then is there so much union inertia about HIV/AIDS?

Understanding Union Inertia over HIV/AIDS

Union inaction seems particularly disheartening when one considers that, unlike South African corporate management that has been largely insulated from direct contact with the AIDS epidemic, union members have, to date, borne the brunt of it. Union inaction is in part a product of the complicated history of apartheid and its end.

In post-apartheid South Africa, unions had to deal with very particular problems. First, many union leaders were recruited to help lead the new democratic state. With open political organization all but impossible for blacks under apartheid, the trade unions carved out a space in the industrial sphere where organization was legal and, albeit grudgingly, tolerated. Not surprisingly, many saw the newly emerging unions as a vehicle for mobilizing resistance to apartheid. The result was an extraordinarily strong leadership cadre. With the transition to democracy, many of these trade union leaders moved into parliament and positions in provincial and local government. Additionally, many union leaders, who remained committed to working-class interests, moved into the Department of Labour where they felt that could better implement the labor market reforms; earning the Pretoria-based Department of Labour the sardonic nickname "COSATU's Pretoria office" among business leaders.

Alongside this move of union leaders into government, companies accelerated their own process of bringing union leaders into junior or supervisory management positions. For companies this kind of recruitment met two goals: Companies were able to change the demographic profile of their workforce (something that new employment equity legislation required, see Chapter 2) while simultaneously removing the most capable shop stewards from union leadership.

Widespread illiteracy and innumeracy—one of the most enduring legacies of apartheid—has undermined union attempts to develop leadership cadres to replace those it lost to government and management. Even when unions have trained replacements, this often does nothing more than provide individuals with a platform to move on (and up). While the post-1994 labor legislation is decidedly pro-labor, unions have often been unable to take advantage of it because of the complexity of engagement with processes with which they are unfamiliar. Skills development, cooperation over productivity gains, and employment equity require unions to engage jointly with management over what should be issues of mutual interest. Stripped of skilled officials, unions have generally been unable to move beyond the more straightforward strategy of opposing management over traditional industrial relations concerns such as pay and working conditions.

While these constraints on organized labor are relevant in understanding the limits of any trade union response to the AIDS epidemic, they do not fully explain the unions' failure to provide more support to peer educators than company supervisors. What else accounts for this?

Cultural differences between unions' modus operandi and that of peer educators helps explain unions' inaction on this issue. As John Kelly has outlined (1998), unions operate by mobilizing a constituency to make demands on another social group whose policies or practices they oppose. Thus, unions have demanded that their members have access to antiretroviral treatment. Unions have also used their institutional weight to support the demands of pressure groups such as the Treatment Action Campaign (TAC) that petitioned government to provide antiretroviral drugs in public-sector hospitals that workers and their families rely on. Typically, then, unions convince individuals to form collective groups that can through pressure and action achieve collective gain.

By contrast, peer educators tend to work at the individual rather than collective level. Peer educators' emphasis on the individual requires that oneself change and not the social "other." Rather than mobilizing enough collective power to force concessions from another group, peer educators seek to assist individuals to change what they do in their own lives.

Unions do, of course, deal with individuals when the rights that have been secured for all members are violated. But around HIV/AIDS, while legal rights are in place, their enforcement is not easy. A story told by Juliet Hennings in Bestbuyco (whom we met in Chapter 3), helps illustrate this. Two staff members in her store had gossiped about the HIV-positive status of a coworker. Because of this, the woman's new boyfriend discovered her status before she had felt ready to tell him herself. Juliet then gathered the peer educators together and openly confronted the two women responsible for what turned had turned out to be a destructive act. Although Hennings wanted to make their conduct the subject of a disciplinary hearing, a shop steward, while firmly behind her on the principle, did not want a conflict between union members to be dealt with in the company's disciplinary process. They thus settled on an assurance from the women that the gossip would not happen again. This example illustrates that rights-based safeguards against discrimination have to be imposed by active agency and that stigmatization around HIV/AIDS can be horizontal as well as vertical. In this case the union's ability to act as an enforcing agency was compromised because both stigmatizer and stigmatized were union members. Only the moral agency of the peer educator was able to assert the rights of the individual and impose sanctions.

Contrasting the collective and individually focused activity of unions and peer educators helps explain why each has different strengths and weaknesses in responding to HIV/AIDS. A peer educator in Autocircle, for example, explained that his union was party to the company's HIV/AIDS program but was reluctant to raise the issue when meeting their members. "The members don't want to hear them [on HIV/AIDS], unions avoid the issue—it would cause chaos," he commented. That's because, like other

South Africans we have encountered, union members have many varied views of the meaning and solution to HIV/AIDS. Unions, as agents of collective action, have mobilized their constituencies to stage front-stage encounters with management (and sometimes the state) to improve wages, benefits, and working conditions. They place a premium on internal unity and function particularly well when there is a clearly distinguishable opponent on whom they can make demands. This means that within unions some differences, such as class, are legitimate, in fact desirable, because they are projected outward. Other differences, internal to a union's membership, while just as real are unwelcome because they divide rather than unite. As far as possible, such internal differences are suppressed in the name of front-stage unity. Many of these differences are salient backstage, but are for the most part contained, stifled, and hidden.

Gender differences are an example of internal differences that are often suppressed. Even where a particular union is largely male, the class that these members are drawn from and the backstage spaces they inhabit consist of both men and women. In South Africa, the need for gender equality is, in public discourse, taken for granted, and unions have progressive policies in this regard. Yet, for all the talk of "gender mainstreaming," little is actually done and the gender offices of unions, if they exist at all, are marginal to unions' key concerns. The reason is obvious: if unions took gender seriously enough to shift the status quo of gender relations in the backstage spaces of their members, this would provoke a civil war that would deflect attention from other critical issues. As long as gender equality is confined to resolutions, and token gestures, members can get on with their, often deeply gendered and deeply unequal, daily lives; the boat is not rocked.

Unions' relation to HIV/AIDS reflects the same dynamic. Beyond HIV/AIDS treatment and protection from discrimination, to venture into the HIV/AIDS issue further risks unleashing controversy and contention among union members. This kind of conflict may weaken a union when it wants to confront management about other workplace issues. In the South African context, it can also weaken a union that faces competition from rivals. In Mineco, for examples, several unions competed fiercely for members. In the section of the company research in 2006, there were six unions in the main bargaining unit. The majority union was hovering around 50 percent representation (something that gives a union considerable rights under South Africa's labor law), raising the possibility of rival unions overtaking it as some point. Peter Mopedi, who was also a shop steward, explained the dangers of rival unions in the company stealing members if he started to talk about AIDS. "You can't speak about something that people don't want to [speak about], because you look [at] the other union[s] [and] those people are going to take [your members] while you are talking about the AIDS.... [The members will say,] 'We don't want that, the only thing that we want is money. Stop talking about the AIDS.'"

This contest over HIV/AIDS is not only among union members but also among union shop stewards and officials who share the same backstage spaces. One shop steward at the mining company, who it turned out was also a traditional healer with a number of HIV-positive patients, was selected for me to interview in part because he had a good working relationship with the peer educator group. This relationship was genuine, and the shop steward was full of praise for the group's coordinator, Mokwena, because he was pushing peer education onto the agenda of the local management-union forum. Nevertheless, as previously raised in Chapter 4, even though this shop steward had participated in HIV/AIDS training, he still questioned the Western explanation for the disease.

> It get difficult for them [peer educators] whenever someone asks, "where does AIDS come from?" Because some of them doesn't know clearly that this has been developed by having sex with a [polluted] woman [i.e., the breaching of purification rituals]. But... because I'm a traditional healer then I understand what was the basic cause of this [HIV/AIDS]. Whenever [somebody's] wife dies, he [the husband] gonna sleep with another woman within two to three months. He doesn't believe that he must wait and clean his blood. Because the blood have got the maggot [pollution]. [As an example,] whenever I dies and they buried me, my blood [be]comes *vrot* [rotten] underground... and also the one which is in my [living] wife makes the very same thing as the one who has been buried. That's why we use the traditional medicines. We try to pump the blood of one who has been dead from the one who is alive.

Shop stewards and union officials are equally divided around HIV/AIDS in other important dimensions. Thus, if a union is to move beyond high-level conference resolutions and partnership agreements and address the details of getting members to change behavior over HIV/AIDS, they will inevitably engage competing worldviews among rank-and-file membership and leadership. With these constraints the typical union response to HIV/AIDS has been to pass appropriate resolutions and act on issues that are relatively uncontroversial to their membership: bargaining for treatment provision and taking a public position against management discrimination. Backstage space has been left alone.

Projecting the Unions' Voice Backstage

For peer educators, unions are an important potential ally that can help ensure that company programs operate as the HIV/AIDS policy stipulates; that is, that all workplace agents "walk the HIV/AIDS talk." Additionally, and importantly, unions and educators need to be speaking with the same voice. For unions this means not only "talking HIV/AIDS talk" front stage, but projecting that voice into backstage spaces. Only this will close psychological escape routes for those who seek out more palatable explanations and responses to the disease. This, of course, is not an easy thing to ask, and it is even harder to achieve. It is requesting unions to take sides on an issue that divides their members and the very network of officials and shop stewards that would have to drive such a process in backstage space.

Given this, the previously quoted union resolution that "campaigns to stop AIDS must be discussed at every trade union meeting," may not be appropriate. Ten years since the resolution was passed, this has not gone very far. Rather than repeating ineffectual front-stage performances, what is needed is a strategic alliance between unions and peer educators in the workplace that synergizes their respective strengths—the mobilization of collective power and the ability to reach and work with individuals.

A Strategy of Specialized Roles between Unions and Peer Educators

It was clear during my research that many peer educators in the mining company and other workplaces lacked both power and resources. Although this did not affect informal activities, it restricted their ability to mount campaigns or collaborate with other groups which, in turn, sapped their effectiveness and morale. At Mineco, peer educators, could, in theory, go to a liaison officer who would request resources from the company's

HIV/AIDS Office. In practice, during the five-month period of my research with the peer educator group, all requests—for refresher training for peer educators, training of new peer educators, as well as requests for "uniforms" (effectively shirts and caps)—were stalled. On two occasions the liaison officer attended meetings, acknowledged peer educators' problems, and promised to resolve them. At the end of my research period, one peer educator suggested in exasperation that the liaison officer be invited once again so that he "could make more promises to them."

When the peer educators asked local managers to provide resources for a community clean-up project in nearby informal settlements, this was also turned down. Peer educators wanted to use a company truck to collect trash that filled the settlement's road and alleys. They also wanted to convert old oil drums into rubbish bins that would be painted with AIDS logos. Such a campaign would obviously bring peer educators into contact with community members. Mokwena, the group peer educator coordinator, explained their rationale: "If the people see that we care then they can listen to us. They will love us. They will be close to us. So if we speak to them, then they will understand us. But if they see that they are suffering, but we are doing nothing, we don't even come and visit and speak to them, then they think 'Okay, you are just like them. You don't care about us.'" The company's refusal to agree to the peer educators' request led them to jettison the project undermining the group's attempts to make itself relevant to local communities.

To mobilize both internally and outside the company, Mokwena asked for a seat on the local Partnership Forum, a joint consultative body largely made up of management and union representatives. This was granted, however, Mokwena quickly realized that just having a seat on the Forum was not going to ensure that he could get the help peer educators needed. Under pressure to contain costs, managers were reluctant to meet requests for resources, and without union backing for Mokwena's requests it was obvious that his seat would be little more than token. Through direct talks with union leaders, he thus began to educate the unions on HIV/AIDS in general and the role and needs of peer educators in particular. He brought a Person Living Openly with HIV/AIDS (PWA) to talk to the union and tried to exert pressure on unions by informing them about progress other, competitor unions had made on HIV/AIDS. He noted that when making or hosting a presentation either at a union meeting or at the

Partnership Forum, the critical response he was looking for was simple: Did union leaders ask him questions? For Mokwena, this was the first sign that an audience was beginning to grapple with the issues he presented.

With union support, the value of the peer educators' single seat on the Forum was magnified. The peer educator group was able to leverage more resources from management that would support their formal and informal work through training and capacity building, securing the right to give formal talks in the workplace, and obtaining resources to run community projects. The strategic partnership that was formed allowed unions to do what they did best—support claims on management that needed, because of their collective power, to be taken seriously. Peer educators could then exploit the benefits the unions had won by doing what they did best—talking with individuals at work and in the community.

Opening Up Contestation within Unions over HIV/AIDS

By promoting union-peer educator alliances, peer educators force unions to critically examine their attitudes and policies toward HIV/AIDS. These alliances can also add to the ranks of peer educators. Thus, Mokwena describes what happened when a trade unionist, Thabo Nonyane, visited his office the day after he had brought a nursing sister to talk to the Partnership Forum to talk about HIV/AIDS and peer educators.

> Thabo came to congratulate me for bringing the professional nurse to the Partnership Forum. He also wants to be trained as a peer educator to enable him to speak to the people of his union during meetings. And to introduce HIV/AIDS and Wellness Programs to his church.
>
> I was very happy because Thabo was one of the people who asked a lot of questions at the Partnership Forum. I really need strong leaders like him to be trained as peer educators. I realize that our managers/supervisors and unionists think they know [about HIV/AIDS], although they don't.

When unions publicly back peer educators as part of a strategic workplace alliance around HIV/AIDS, a valuable signal is sent—one that may, however, be only weakly received in backstage space. To address issues more effectively here, unions need to engage in the risky process of challenging their members' differing beliefs and practices about HIV/AIDS. This is a gradual and complicated process that also involves other powerful institutions and actors—notably South African churches and traditional healers.

Churches and the Response to HIV/AIDS

Most peer educators are religious; almost 80 percent of the six hundred surveyed peer educators reported attending religious services at least twice a month, and it was clear from interviews that many were extremely active in the life of their churches or other religious organizations (see Chapter 3). Having become peer educators, they saw the silence of churches on HIV/AIDS and, more generally, sex as a critical problem. Joe Rantete in Mineco, referring to his own church, put it, "The church is not doing enough in the fight against the pandemic. They only want to pray for those who are involved."

For many peer educators, churches, like unions, represent a potentially powerful ally in the fight for behavioral change—one that has also not fully mobilized. As Mokwena, during a group discussion on the role of churches and HIV/AIDS, put it: "The churches have been silent for a long time. They don't want [to talk about] condoms, but they are burying their own people [from HIV/AIDS]. We can go deep into churches. They have loyal people who can help us."

Rantete went further to talk about the failure of the church in responding to those who came to it for help on sex and HIV/AIDS with "stony silence."

> I believe that if the pastors and priests can include the issue of HIV/AIDS and sex in the theological programs this will make people more aware of this pandemic virus. The church is regarded as a conscience of humanity and the custodian of moral values, therefore if churches break the silence on sex and HIV/AIDS instead of stony silence or a counsel of [sexual] repression when people turn to the church for direction on sexuality, we will win against this virus. Putting a blanket on the subject of sex sabotages any serious attempt in fighting HIV/AIDS.

As Rantete indicates, the silence from churches around sex is often based on rigid moral codes that do not address the actual sexual practices of many church members. Sticking dogmatically to these ideal codes can, as Rantete put it, result in "simplistic answers that HIV/AIDS is God's punishment for the immoral corruption of humankind." Some churches went further to suggest that if HIV/AIDS was a punishment from God, then prayer could cure people of the disease.

> My wife and I were listening to a pastor on a local [Setswana language] community radio station. People from his church were claiming that the word of God had healed their sickness. They were weak, HIV-positive, but now they are cured by the pastor.... Some members of the pastor's church testified that Jesus is the Anti Retroviral Treatment... I know that religion can strengthen someone's faith. Christians know that Jesus died for every one of us. By accepting him while in this life is like preparing for life after death, but no prayer or religion can cure AIDS.

Alternative explanations of HIV/AIDS need to be challenged, and for this to be successful churches need to break the silence and address AIDS in the context of their own congregations' daily lives. This is not easy because congregations are often divided about what should be done about HIV/AIDS. Here, a peer educator's account of what is happening in his own church illustrates the difficulty:

> The assistant of the Reverend sometimes when he sees that there is a lot of people and after the service he used to say [to] the parents they must teach the children about HIV/AIDS. They mustn't be afraid to talk about [HIV/AIDS]. [But] some other parents they say, "No, this is rubbish. We can't say, we can't talk to children [about] HIV/AIDS. How can I face my children and say 'When you sleep with your girlfriend or boyfriend you must use this and this, this.'< hr>" They say, "This is nonsense." There's some people who don't understand. They say "No! We're misleading our children." Because they say we teach the children to go and sleep together with their boyfriends or girlfriends.

Churches in South Africa, while not all-powerful, are critical in dealing with the AIDS epidemic for at least two key reasons. First, when pulpit messages correspond to the realities of AIDS—that is, acknowledge that church members are being infected with HIV and are dying of AIDS—this delegitimizes alternative explanations of the disease. Second, and perhaps more important, when church leaders promote lay (peer) activity within church congregations—through women's meetings, choirs, and cell meetings—this allows the message about HIV/AIDS to reach the backstage spaces to which church leadership has only limited access.

Traditional Healers, Alternative Health Beliefs, and the Response to HIV/AIDS

Outside mine hostels one sees a typical scene that is replicated across South Africa wherever street traders set up shop: healers and their sales agents hawking herbal remedies for every conceivable illness and problem. Today, those who have or fear contracting HIV/AIDS are some of the most eager buyers. In the contest over explaining and advising on HIV/AIDS, one of the most difficult challenges a peer educator faces is dealing with alternative therapies that run directly counter to Western medical experts' explanations and advice about what has caused the epidemic and what to do about it. In backstage space peer educators enter the ring to do battle with opponents often well above their own weight—healers and hawkers who draw on sources that, for many South Africans, are far more powerful than the information produced by a raft of Western scientific experts: the ancestors, traditional knowledge and beliefs, or God.

At one of Mineco's group meetings, Peter Mopedi raised how in his attempts to educate coworkers about HIV/AIDS, he constantly came up against sellers of Aloe Extra—an herbal tonic widely promoted though a network of agents in townships. Pitchmen and women for Nature's Health Products, the company that manufactures and sells Aloe Extra, would extol its virtues. Nature's Health Products is careful not to overstep the line and claim its products cure HIV/AIDS, but it comes close enough to imply that it does just that. Its Original Formula, claimed to be the "No. 1 Best Selling Health Drink in South Africa," and which contains "unique herbs used by traditional healers in South Africa for centuries" will, among other things, "strengthen your immune system." Alternatively, you can buy the company's Anvirem, a "natural antiviral remedy" that "supports and boosts immune system [and] helps in overcoming viral infection which can cause: weight loss, coughing, flu, boils, skin rashes, loss of appetite, lip sores, shingles, low energy [and] thrush" (Nature's Health Products ND). In townships and informal settlements, where the writ of advertising standards authorities is absent, the company's agents, working on commission, have free reign. The latest sales pitch, Mopedi reported, involved taking a glass of dirty water and putting in a small amount of the herbal tonic. The water would clear. It was explained that Aloe Extra would do the same in your blood, removing pollution, including HIV.

Other hawkers of herbal remedies regularly make similar claims about their products and HIV/AIDS. Attempting to scrape a living from commissions, they are constantly seeking sales. Tlouane, working in Minco's HR, complained that she'd had to eject one such salesperson. This saleswoman had come into her office and asked if she could talk to workers about her wares. Tlouane did not hesitate to refuse her request and tell her to leave immediately. "She must say it [the claims for her products] outside, not in the office where I'm telling people there is no cure for HIV/AIDS [other than containment with antiretroviral drugs]." She was nonetheless frustrated because she knew the woman would be able to approach people only a few meters from her office outside the building.

These peer educators were working assiduously to convince people to change their behavior but after they finished talking, all a coworker had to do was leave work and on sale were many "quick fixes" that, for a few Rands, claimed more than Western medicine had to offer. To make matters worse, some of those selling herbal remedies were retired nurses or other "wise" people. Peer educators, with their limited training and knowledge, might have difficulty countering people who had great credibility in the community and who were peddling a message that was far more attractive than the one peer educators were promoting.

This is why many peer educators, like those in the mining group, believe they have to work with traditional healers. Although convincing traditional healers and quack practitioners not to sell "cures" for AIDS may seem overly optimistic, Mokwena told me of a church member who had sold herbal remedies but stopped when one of his clients, also a church member, died after substituting his herbal remedy for diabetes medications. "He warned us [church members] to be careful of people who are selling medicines and tablets like him because they are confusing the people by telling them their medicines can cure HIV if you stop your treatment and drink their herbal medicines. The brother promised to be honest when dealing with people."

Peer educators realize that it will be very difficult to work with traditional healers in the current South African context. As we saw in Chapter 4, in South Africa, Western medicine has not replaced traditional healing; it has merely driven it underground. For this reason, unlike working with unions or churches, which operate in both front- and backstage spaces, traditional healers work exclusively in backstage space. They thus lack any formal structures of leadership and organization, functioning either individually or in scattered, often fractious, groups.

The lack of formal structures among traditional healers means that there is no leadership that peer educators can approach, and it is difficult for even enlightened healers to attempt to voice a coherent front-stage message around HIV/AIDS. Among traditional healers there is no equivalent to the union's network of branches, local officials, and shop stewards that provides channels that can reach into backstage spaces—a structure potentially replicated by church office bearers, deacons, and other lay leadership. While there has been an overreliance on leadership pronouncements among unions in responding to HIV/AIDS and a failure to drive down the issues into the membership, something that churches are replicating, the limited structure among traditional healers means that there are no systematic routes into backstage space. Moreover, there is no regulation of traditional healers who are in direct competition with each other.

Yet, despite these difficulties, getting traditional healers to speak in harmony with peer educators around HIV/AIDS is important. While it is unlikely that every traditional and spiritual healer, let alone the hawkers of supposed cures, can be brought on board, there are some who could. Sam Mangala in Mineco, who occupied a junior management position and was completing a bachelor's degree by correspondence, identified his religion as "traditional Northern Sotho" (i.e., traditional Sepedi, non-Christian beliefs). His mother was a traditional healer, and he explained what he thought might help control the epidemic:

> Doctors, medical doctors, maybe they think that the traditional healers are going to take bread away from them. But I don't think they should have that idea. If we look back to history itself, the Africans were with [traditional] medicine... They [medical doctors and traditional healers] need to supplement one another somehow. And they [traditional healers] should

> not be undermined...there are chancers [i.e., charlatans] in the field, but not all are chancers....I think [we need to] work hand in glove with traditional healers. That may work.

It will obviously be far easier to work with traditional healers if they have an organizational structure that will allow them to engage in a broader social discourse around HIV/AIDS and give them the ability to set standards of counseling, treatment, and care that will prevent individual healers bettering what they collectively agree upon. The Traditional Health Practitioners Act (Government of South Africa 2007) makes provision for the recognition, registration, and regulation of traditional healers in South Africa. When promulgated a range of structures will be put in place to oversee registration and regulation. Given the challenges of regulating practices that encompass social, pharmacological, psychological, and traditional knowledge in addition to the use of ancestral guidance, this will be difficult. But it is clearly an important step in aligning the voice of traditional healers around HIV/AIDS.

Conclusion: Harmonizing Voices in Backstage Space

Peer educators have access to backstage spaces, but it is clear that they are no more than one voice among many. Up against competing explanations of HIV and AIDS, told by people with equally appropriate linguistic repertoires and similar sociocultural familiarity, peer educators need support. This support needs to move from rhetoric delivered from front-stage platforms to the penetration of backstage spaces if individuals are to confront the implications of HIV/AIDS for themselves and for their own behavior.

Unions are an important influence on many South Africans. But unions have yet to respond to the epidemic outside of the familiar terrain of collective action. Attempts to overcome the paralysis of union leadership in grasping the need for individual behavioral change in the era of AIDS are instructive. In contrast to calls for more conferences and resolutions—which simply replicate previous attempts to implement flawed solutions—peer educators need the unions to project their voice into backstage space. Until this is the case, it will be all too easy for individuals to slide away from the difficult realities of dealing with HIV/AIDS.

For unions this will be challenging. Nevertheless, if the difficulty unions have in responding to HIV/AIDS is clearly identified, a start can be made. The first step is for unions to drive the issue of HIV/AIDS into lower leadership structures in ways that will raise internal difference and a difficult process of peer alignment around HIV/AIDS. Only then will unions be able to add their voice within the backstage social spaces where it is so clearly needed. Much the same is necessary with other important social voices, such as churches and traditional healing, though each one will have to take into account its particular structures and mission.

This process of harmonizing voices backstage is not a discovery of the limitations of individual change and a realization that collective action is necessary—though superficially it may resemble this. Peer educators may realize the limitations of their work with individuals, but this rises from backstage conflict around HIV/AIDS that will not, cannot, be resolved by collective action. As peer educators attempt to get others to project their voices backstage, this will involve lobbying if organizations are to be turned. But if peer educators abandon their quest for individual behavioral change and seek rather to capture unions, churches, traditional healers, and other social agents by means of resolutions of support, then their work will come to naught. The value of turning these institutions in support of individual behavioral change is the resonation of all voices *backstage*.

7

Social Space, Leadership, and Action

Peer Education and Behavioral Change

In South Africa, one in three women between the ages of twenty-five and twenty-nine and one in five men in their thirties are infected with HIV. South Africa is not alone in facing these levels of HIV infection; many other sub-Saharan African countries face similar or even higher prevalence rates. In developed countries AIDS is largely contained as a problem of marginal groups with specific factors rendering them vulnerable. In developing countries, such as India and China, the epidemic threatens to go on the march, as it is doing in the transitional economies of Eastern Europe and Russia. The epidemic is still globalizing, and its impact continues to unfold.

As the epidemic has taken on global dimensions, there has been dramatic progress in treatment but little in the prevention of HIV infection. In a 2007 World AIDS Day editorial entitled "HIV Treatment Proceeds as Prevention Research Confounds," the editors of *PLoS Medicine* argued that "interrupting HIV transmission remains one of the world's greatest scientific challenges." The acknowledgment is to be welcomed, but we should also understand that the vision of prevention that the *PLoS Medicine* editors put forward is one rooted in a biomedical paradigm: prevention as technical fixes—a vaccine, microbicidal gels, circumcision, or condoms—that can be used to prevent infection. This largely ignores the human processes of responding to AIDS. The challenge involved in prevention is really the challenge of profound shifts in both individual and social behavior.

This is true for many other health-related problems, not just HIV/AIDS. The developed world may be able to shrug off its marginal AIDS problem, but problems of diet, lifestyle, obesity, smoking, and alcohol present endemic or epidemic challenges that significantly detract from well-being. Some of these concerns are as much problems of affluence as of poverty. No matter what one's social position, health-related problems such as obesity, addiction, and lack of exercise can be changed only when individuals recognize the implications of ingrained habits.

Examining the practice of peer educators helps us understand this difficult quest for behavioral change. What workplace peer educators in South Africa can teach us about changing beliefs and behavior around HIV/AIDS can help us better understand challenges in responding to other behaviors that detract from health and well-being. This concluding chapter draws together what we have learned into a three-part model of peer-led behavioral change that incorporates social space, social leadership, and social action.

Social Space

Drawing and expanding on Erving Goffman's dramatic model of social interaction, we have identified three sites of human interaction related to HIV/AIDS (and quite possibly to much else): (1) *front-stage space,* where formal performances are typically given; (2) *backstage space,* where informal interventions can be made within the daily lives of peers; and (3) *liminal space,* where peer educator and peer slip away momentarily from the constraints of social order.

Front-stage performances are the easiest type of interaction to initiate. Modeled on the classroom lesson, the church sermon, and public speeches, these performances, whether by a socially distant expert or a peer before an audience, present information on HIV and AIDS but provide no guarantee that anything will change because such performances are largely unconnected to the lives of the audience. Most mass media communications on HIV/AIDS operate along similar principles. This does not mean that front-stage presentations on HIV/AIDS are not of value; they are, and they can be improved. In isolation, however, they are unlikely to reshape beliefs and behavior.

Focusing on front-stage spaces also ignores a vast hinterland of social interaction. Away from the staccato volleys of AIDS facts delivered through formal educational interventions there are countless moments when the same information can be woven into the routines of everyday life: at work, at leisure, at worship, or at the bus stop—anywhere. When peer educators operate in backstage spaces they contextualize factual information so that those they educate can relate this information to their beliefs, concerns, and actions.

Although backstage spaces may exclude the most obvious social divisions, it is fanciful to think that these spaces are tension free. Far from it: In these seemingly more private spaces, tension is rife. This is as true for the supposedly intimate space of the family as it is for local communities, church congregations, work, or other peer settings. The hope that informal activity by peer educators need only clarify what has not been grasped when presented from a front-stage platform is wildly optimistic. Sometimes it can, and peer educators need to be constantly watchful for such teachable moments. But, more often, the tight social order in backstage space makes open discussion difficult and behavioral change hazardous. This is not only because HIV/AIDS is a difficult issue to address, but because the multiple lines of division in backstage space are well entrenched and there are no institutionalized processes for their (re)negotiation. Bringing in any new issue, beyond the trivial, threatens already accommodated worldviews and positions.

Paul Farmer's study (1990, 1994, 1999) of the construction of a cultural model of AIDS in a Haitian village during the 1980s argues that it took approximately five years for the generation of a consensual schema of understanding. The difficulty that peer educators have in operating in their own backstage spaces would indicate that in South Africa we are still far from a consensual cultural model of AIDS. One explanation for Farmer's rapid timeline is that he overweighed the degree of consensus and underestimated the significance of variations that he identifies in the model (1999, 175–177). Alternatively, and not incompatibly, we can acknowledge the point made by anthropologists that the exact dynamics of the AIDS epidemic and how it is understood will vary by location (Preston-Whyte 1995; Schoepf 2001; Setel 1999). A Haitian village is not South Africa, nor should South Africa be seen as a unitary entity.

Perhaps the most illustrative contrast to the difficulty South African peer educators have in working in backstage space is the achievements of peer education in urban gay communities. In cities across the globe, gay male communities were particularly vulnerable to HIV infection when it first spread beyond its African origins in the late 1970s and early 1980s. Penetrative anal sex is an efficient route for HIV infection, extensive sexual networks linked many in these communities, and condoms, given their then-primary contraceptive function, were not part of the gay scene. As the first sites of response to AIDS, urban gay communities are credited with considerable success in changing sexual behavior and lowering infection rates (Kippax et al. 1993). The STOP AIDS project in San Francisco in the 1980s utilized peer education within a community-based response (Wohlfeiler 1997). Arvind Singhal and Everett Rogers (2003, 210) argue that the main lesson of STOP AIDS in San Francisco was, "customizing the design and delivery of a communication program on the basis of the characteristics of an intended audience segment [i.e., peer education]."

A randomized, controlled intervention, using peer communication among homosexual men in eight small U.S. cities found that "population-level risk behavior decreased significantly in the intervention cities compared with the controlled cities" (Kelly et al. 1997, 1500). The authors concluded that, "Popular and well-liked members of a community who systematically endorse and recommend risk-reduction behaviour can influence the sexual-risk practices of others in their social networks. Natural styles of communication, such as conversations, brought about population-level changes in risk behaviour" (1500)" Susan Kippax et al. (1993) found that the best predictors of behavioral change among gay men, along with knowledge of HIV transmission and educational level, were the correlated variables of residence and attachment to the gay community: something that would promote access by and to peers.

The tangible success of peer education programs among urban gay communities has been much more difficult to replicate elsewhere. As discussed in Chapter 1, what peer educators do has been poorly understood. Given what we now know about the activity of South African workplace peer educators, we can suggest why peer education among gay men in Sydney, London, San Francisco, and other cities across the world has been so effective.

The first thing to note is that the backstage social space of gay communities was less complex and less divided than that of the social spaces in which South African workers live, love, and labor. There is, obviously, only one gender within gay communities, and strongly gendered roles are rarely re-created within same-sex relationships (Bolton 1992). Additionally, these gay communities were, in comparison to wider society, also highly homogeneous along lines of race, education, and economic status (McKusick et al. 1990). High education and economic status are regarded as a factor supporting behavioral change, but this is not the point being made here. Rather, it is the similarity of community members around these characteristics that is being highlighted.

Of course, gay communities are not entirely homogeneous. For example, as Ralph Bolton (1992, 154) notes, "the gay community is divided between separatists and integrationists [with respect to straight society]" something that, through perspectives on promiscuity, sets up tensions over strategies to counter HIV transmission. However, overall, it is plausible to argue that the gay community of San Francisco is less complex than the situation of a Xhosa migrant worker employed on a mine in the North West Province, whose girlfriend lives in a nearby informal settlement, while his wife remains a thousand kilometers away in the Eastern Cape. Additionally, Graham, Bill, and Paul in San Francisco may have, by virtue of their education and economic status, less need to defend *particular* positions in backstage space in the face of AIDS than Isaac, Lydia, and Tandi in South Africa.

The realities of these complex divisions and tensions over HIV/AIDS backstage means that peer educators, in South Africa at least, have emphasized slipping out of order into temporary and liminal spaces to effect change. Here, peer educator and peer can talk honestly and, as is often necessary, strategize about changes in peers' lives that stand a chance of success in the mist of everyday encounters. The need to step back into order armed with tricks, lies, and deceit reflects the difficulty of changing behavior when it comes to HIV/AIDS in South Africa. While change may be particularly hard when it comes to "this disease," other behavior linked to poor health—such as eating, smoking, and drinking—are also powerful human experiences that are entangled within social relationships and social positions. Slipping out of order is a pivotal step in how peer educators seek to turn behavior around AIDS. It is likely to provide a similar function for other health concerns around the globe.

A second difference between urban gay communities and those of black workers and their families in South Africa is how HIV/AIDS relates to front-stage divisions. Many homosexual men made a conscious choice to move to gay centers from more heterogeneous—and less tolerant—communities. This allowed gays to create a sense of collective identity directly linked to sexuality. Such a collective identity was then openly expressed in public, front-stage encounters; for example, when a gay group lobbied a city council or otherwise discussed the AIDS crisis. This openly expressed collective identity supported the efforts of peer education in gay communities.

As we have seen, however, in South Africa there is no collective identity or set of shared beliefs about HIV/AIDS aligned to major social divisions. The salient collective identities involved in front-stage encounters between workers and management, or between workers' communities and the state, have nothing to do with sexuality. In South African workplaces, unions have struggled to respond to HIV/AIDS beyond what can be packaged into the existing framework of collective bargaining around wages, benefits, and working conditions. Questions of sexuality are largely confined, and controlled, backstage. Peer educators seeking to intervene around HIV/AIDS are unable to align their messages with wider community identities. Again, this may not be so different from other problems of wellness. For example, those concerned about alcohol must not work only against powerful commercial interests but also a widespread acceptance of alcohol as an essential and desirable part of social life. Such challenges demand, if they are to be successfully tackled, a much broader approach than peer educators alone can mount.

Social Leadership

One of the many things we learn from exploring the work of peer educators is the difference between authority and social leadership. Those in authority, such as company managers, are obeyed—at least in the letter—because disobedience is sanctioned. However progressive a workplace might be, this social fact undergirds the functioning of all organizations. As we saw in Chapter 4, managers and AIDS experts have limited effectiveness when they try to promote behavior change among the workforce not only because of linguistic and cultural barriers but also because they are authority figures. In workplace relationships, characterized by unequal power, the risk and reality is that, should their policies and practices around HIV/AIDS be ineffective, these "emperors" will not be told that they wear no clothes. When it comes to educating employees on matters of personal behavior, they will be "leaders" without followers.

Peer educators are therefore asked to perform leadership roles. Depending on whether peer educator programs are conceived and designed as vertical or horizontal communication processes, this can take very different forms. If peer educators are viewed as conduits in a vertical transmission stream through which AIDS experts get their messages down to target populations, then the leadership roles peer educators are being asked to perform are, at best, compromised, at worst, a sham. They are being told both what to do and how to define success. There is little room for genuine leadership. Indeed, with this model of peer education in place, it is easy to see why South African workers might accuse peer educators of being pawns of management. However genuine, they are being asked to be the AIDS "boss boys" (i.e., Africans promoted into supervisory positions within apartheid workplaces to control the black workforce) and girls of management.

In practice most company programs incorporate a great deal of leeway for an alternative, horizontal model of peer education—even if this is the result of neglect as much as design. Peer educators may attempt to push packaged messages, but they will only be successful if dialogue is centered on the beliefs and concerns of peers. It is in achieving these forms of discourse that the linguistic and sociocultural access of peer educators is so vital. It is also central to their role as social leaders in promoting and supporting change in attitudes and behavior over HIV/AIDS. Such changes need to be brought about within the worldviews of their peers: a horizontal process of insider contestation over explanation and behavior. But we should not underestimate the difficultly of horizontal communication—a theme throughout this book. Sensing the potential of peer education, some argue that it should be used to develop a Freireian "critical consciousnesses" among peers who will challenge existing norms and conceive alternative ways of being (Campbell and MacPhail 2002).[1] Such aspirations are to be welcomed, but first we need to understand the social environment of peer educators before demanding that they so dramatically reconstruct their (and our) world.

Beyond the training of peer educators, the role of experts in horizontal communication strategies is to understand the debates peer educators are engaging in and channel appropriate knowledge, resources, and skills to support them. To use a metaphor: those responsible for peer education programs need to see themselves not as generals in command of an army but as the logistics corps maintaining supply lines that keep peer educators equipped, motivated, and able to conduct their work. Maintaining these supply lines requires, of course, a vertical channel of communication, but this is not one of command and control; rather, it is a line of contact enabling peer educators to explain what is happening backstage. Such a process allows a genuine partnership between companies and peer educators.

What we have seen is that achieving shifts in belief and behavior around HIV/AIDS is extremely difficult. Peer educators face open challenges and more subtle resistance. When confronted with either, as we saw in Chapter 5, they try to slip past these barriers. In practice, they support behavioral change without directly challenging the wider set of social and cultural relationships. Such behavior is not specific to peer education. Professional counselors do this on a formal basis around a wide range of issues. Indeed, all of us have had "quiet words" with family, friends, or colleagues or responded to requests to share a problem under circumstances similar to what I have described in this book as "slipping out of order."[2]

It is the multiplicity of perspectives held within everyday social spaces which prevents peer educators from engaging in more open and more aggressive activity or tempers the effectiveness of bold, but likely

1. Paulo Freire (1921–1997), a Brazilian educationalist, promoted a critical theory of education that opposed the idea of students being empty vessels to be filled with facts and argued that the teacher-learner relationship should be one of reciprocity.

2. There may be occasions when slipping out of order is not supportive. The soliciting of a bribe by a traffic cop involves a careful process requiring privacy and confidentiality. Here, however, the intention is not to assist the motorist who has violated a traffic regulation but to "solve" the problem the motorist has as a result of this violation with an easier solution from which the corrupt policeman benefits.

counterproductive, attempts to openly dominate backstage spaces with their message. Peer educators know that work colleagues and community members can easily desert them, psychologically if not physically, for others promoting alternative, more attractive explanations of AIDS. The social leadership peer educators display at the worksite or community level needs to be matched by similarly committed leadership from those in diverse positions of social and political authority. As we saw in Chapter 6, high-level leadership in all social institutions—including unions, churches, and traditional healers—needs to speak with one voice if such escape routes are to be closed. The failure of leadership in South Africa to date reveals the importance of this united voice. The same charge could well be leveled elsewhere when it comes to AIDS as well as many other problems that require an individual to bring about change within social settings.

Social Action

The question of what social action can be taken in response to HIV/AIDS is important, and will remain so as long as medical science has no cure for this disease. A key theme of this book has been to distinguish processes of collective action from individual behavioral change. This dichotomy of action repertoires is a perennial concern for those seeking to bring about change. The balance of what peer educators are doing in response to HIV/AIDS focuses on changing the individual. That does not mean that their work is not a form of social action.

Of course, the response to HIV/AIDS must include classic collective mobilization. The Treatment Action Campaign (TAC) has certainly proved this. Through widespread mobilization TAC pressurized the South African state to provide antiretroviral drugs. This approach worked not because it is a universally applicable model but because there *was* a "quick fix"—antiretroviral drugs—available. It also worked because TAC was able to mobilize a constituency (HIV-positive people and a range of allies such as unions) along existing front-stage divisions—that of the state and the population—using demonstrations, legal action, and the media. It did this while having to make minimal headway in backstage spaces. Indeed, we have learned that getting people to *take* antiretroviral drugs is a different problem—which often requires backstage change. The point that we should draw from this example is that confronting AIDS will require a range of social action. And if this is true of AIDS, it will be true of other health concerns.

Achieving individual change is almost certainly harder than achieving collective change when it comes to HIV/AIDS. It is difficult to encourage individual behavioral change not only because of what is at stake—sex, pleasure, power, comfort, elation, escape—but also because these behaviors are deeply embedded in complex social relationships. Many of those working toward the prevention of HIV infection believe that behavior cannot be changed by individuals away from group norms. Vera Paiva (1995, 112) argues that unless "socially constructed prejudices and fears" are broken down by members of a community, then "calls for individual responsibility are a waste of time." Based on this perception, a number of academic activists and practitioners have stressed that behavioral change programs must be integrated into community responses to the disease (Altman 1994; Kippax et al. 1993; Paiva 2000; Wohlfeiler 1997). Typically, this means involving the community by bringing people together in focus groups, workshops, or town hall meetings.

Involving communities in any response to HIV/AIDS is critical, but we need to question how to best accomplish this activity. What this book has demonstrated is that communities are not composed of individuals who share the same beliefs and customs even if they have the same skin color or ethnic background. To imagine a community as a cohesive group of people who, when brought together to listen to experts, will leave the room united in a different set of social relationships is fanciful. As we have seen, such performances win polite applause that may hearten the speaker but accomplish little else in daily lives. Because peer educators don't organize town hall meetings, or march, or carry placards and shout slogans, peer education may not look like community participation. Yet the heart of peer education is individual change rooted in a clear sense of community and social relationships. To dismiss peer education because it doesn't conform to our stereotypical understanding of social action (drawn heavily from the model and images of collective mobilization and public demands) is to narrow our understanding of social action. To do so discards an important way in which the collective and individual approaches to bringing about behavioral change can be integrated.

Peer educators are well aware of how socioeconomic conditions structure and constrain individuals' sexual behavior, but they have little power to do much about this. Given the failure of higher echelons of social leadership to respond to the epidemic, peer educators' efforts have been focused on spheres of activity that they believe they can influence: changing individuals' behavior within current contexts. In doing this they are acutely aware of how socially established norms inhibit their activity. Yet, their response has not been to throw up their hands in despair because they believe no one can change until everyone has changed. In practice rather than theory, they are seeking to negotiate ways around the difficulties encountered in backstage space. In doing so, their quest provides us with another form of social action in the fight against AIDS.

What Would Success Sound Like?

As peer educators continue to exercise leadership and engage in their version of social action, their companies and society are constantly trying to assess their effectiveness, evaluate their accomplishments, and define their "success" or "failure." Thus, the final question we must address is: For peer educators, what is success, how does one define the impact of a peer education program?

In reflecting on this question, it should be clear that peer educators are not—by themselves—going to turn the AIDS epidemic in South Africa or elsewhere. Nonetheless, they can make a major contribution—if they are properly understood and supported.

Any unified model of HIV transmission needs, within each particular context, to (1) account for the socioeconomic conditions that frame human relationships and sexual networks, (2) acknowledge the importance of sexuality to the human condition, and (3) grasp the cultural understandings of HIV/AIDS that exist within the population. Successfully slowing the rate of HIV transmission requires the use of such a model along with feasible methods of achieving behavioral change. In South Africa, and probably elsewhere, this will involve, among other things, reforming the migrant labor system, validating sex and sexuality, and aligning folk and scientific understandings of HIV and AIDS. Alongside such a program, there remains a need for comprehensive interventions around treatment, care, and support.

The contribution that peer educators can bring to this huge enterprise is quite simple: They can get people to talk. Their primary mission is not to make speeches, lectures, or presentations, but to listen and talk with other individuals. By participation in conversations with their peers, they generate other conversations, conversations that in turn generate further conversations that they will never hear. It is easy to underestimate the value of this fundamental human activity, especially when in search of the one quick fix that will "cure" a crisis. When those who want a silver bullet rush to evaluate interventions they typically hand out questionnaires and seek "better" responses to questions. They want to know if more condoms have been used, whether testing and treatment is up, or infection rates down. What this account of peer education has demonstrated is that such approaches to measuring the success of interventions miss the very foundation on which success rests. When it comes to behavioral change, talking to each other comes before anything else, and, beyond trivial superficialities, talking is not easy.

Instead of giving up or pursuing ever-diminishing returns by repeating previously ineffective communication strategies, the peer educators described in this book have pushed ahead. To do this, they have had to lower expectations. Instead of trying to find that elusive magic bullet that stops the epidemic in its tracks, they have engaged in tiny acts of resistance. They sow seeds of doubt as to whether a sexual partner can be trusted, offer information, suggest a trick that will make sex safer, silence a whisper, befriend an HIV-positive colleague and thus challenge the stigma of HIV/AIDS, help one person find the courage to test, let someone cry. All this is possible only because they have done the most important thing of all: listened before speaking.

Conversations that allow people to speak about AIDS aloud in intimate social spaces are critical to normalizing the epidemic. And normalization is the greatest challenge in bringing this epidemic to an end. Only if we can normalize AIDS can individuals change behavior without recourse to lies, tricks, deceit, or open defiance of those closest to them. Peer educators need to initiate and maintain conversations that will reconfigure the contours of backstage space and permit discussion on HIV/AIDS.

Peer educators are ahead of most of us in confronting AIDS. We should acknowledge their commitment and their contribution. But we should not put them on a pedestal. If we are to normalize the epidemic, then the peer educators that we have met in this book are but outriders of a much larger force. In a normalized epidemic we will all be peer educators.

Appendix 1

TABLES

TABLE 1. Employees and Peer Educators in Five Companies, 2005

Company	Employees (permanent and nonpermanent)	Active Peer Educators (estimated)	Ratio: Peer Educator to Employees
Autocircle	3,500	45	1:78
Autostar	4,000	85	1:47
Bestbuyco	41,500	800	1:52
Finco	29,500	450	1:66
Mineco	44,500	400	1:111
Total	123,00	1,780	1:69

Sources: Interviews and Company Employment Equity Reports (2005).

TABLE 2. Research Conducted on HIV/AIDS in the Workplace and Workplace Peer Educators

Sector	Number Full-time Employees (in South Africa)	Date of Research	Research Conducted
Petrochemicals	26,000	2001–2002	Interviews with 41 managers, occupational health practitioners (OHPs), employees responsible for HIV/AIDS programs, and unionists
			Questionnaire completed by 19 business units
		2003	Observation of 7 AIDS committee meetings
			Interviews with 35 managers, OHPs, employees responsible for HIV/AIDS programs, consultants, and unionists
			Observation of 1 peer educator training session
		2003–2005	Observation of 5 HIV voluntary counseling and testing days
All major sectors	3,500–50,000	2002–2003	Questionnaire survey completed by 28 large South African companies
Information technology	35,000	2003–2004	Interviews with 46 managers, OHPs, employees responsible for HIV/AIDS programs, and unionists
Health care	18,000		Interviews with 17 peer educators (or equivalents)
			Interviews with 25 rank-and-file employees
			Observation of 1, 2-day peer educator training session
Manufacturing (plastics)	250	2004	Interviews with 17 managers, OHPs, employees responsible for HIV/AIDS programs, and unionists
Manufacturing (beverages)	100		Interviews with 6 peer educators
			Observation of 1 peer educator training session
Manufacturing (engineering)	240		

Auto (Autocircle)	3,500	2005	Questionnaire completed by 614 peer educators
Auto (Autostar)	4,000		Interviews with 29 managers, OHPs, trade unionists, and trainers
Financial (Finco)	29,500		Interviews with 75 peer educators and/or peer educator coordinators
Mining (Mineco)	44,500		Observation of 3 peer educator training sessions
Retail (Bestbuyco)	41,500		
Mining (unit)	9,000	2006	Research diaries kept by 7 peer educators
Part of mining			Interviews of 8 peer educators
company studied			Interviews of 5 managers, OHPs, and unionists
in 2005			Observation of 5 peer educator meetings
			Site visits to mining hostel, informal settlement, and underground working environment

TABLE 3. How Employees Become Peer Educators

What *best* describes the way in which you became a peer educator?	Percent
1. I started to conduct peer educator activities on my own.	4.2
2. I was elected by my coworkers as a peer educator.	21.5
3. I volunteered to be a peer educator.	50.0
4. I was asked by another peer educator/somebody involved in HIV/AIDS to be a peer educator and agreed.	6.5
5. I was sent on peer educator training by my manager/supervisor and then became a peer educator.	9.6
6. I was asked by a manager/supervisor to be a peer educator and agreed.	5.1
7. I was told by a manager/supervisor to be a peer educator and agreed.	2.2
8. I was told by a manager/supervisor that I should be a peer educator and had no choice but to agree.	1.1

Note: $N = 552$.

Source: Peer Educator Survey 2005.

TABLE 4. Comparison of Employees and Peer Educators by Race and Gender (permanent and nonpermanent employees)

Gender	**Male (%)**					**Female (%)**				
Race	**African**	**colored**	**Indian**	**white**	**Total**	**African**	**colored**	**Indian**	**white**	**Total**
Employees	44.0	5.1	1.9	9.8	**60.8**	17.3	10.0	3.4	8.5	**39.2**
Peer educators	38.1	2.4	0.9	1.9	**44.4**	35.7	11.7	3.3	6.0	**55.6**
Over- or underrepresentation	-13	-53	-53	-81	**-27.0**	+104	+17	-3	-29	**+41.8**

Note: *N* (Employees) = 123,055; *N* (Peer Educators) = 580.

Sources: Peer Educator Survey (2005) and Company Employment Equity Reports (2005).

TABLE 5. Employees and Peer Educators by Occupational Level (permanent employees only)

Occupational Level	Company Workforce (%)	Peer Educators (%)	Over- or Underrepresentation (%)
Top, senior, and middle management and professionals	7.4	5.6	-24.3
Skilled technical workers, junior management, supervisors, foremen/women, and superintendents	20.6	20.1	-2.4
Semi-skilled and unskilled workers	72.0	74.4	+3.3

Note: *N* (Employees) = 102,009; *N* (Peer Educators) = 598. Company Employment Equity Reports do not provide a breakdown of occupational levels for nonpermanent employees.

Sources: Peer Educator Survey (2005) and Company Employment Equity Reports (2005).

TABLE 6. Topics Discussed During Informal Activity by Peer Educators in Mineco

Topic	As 1st Topic	As 2nd Topic	As 3rd Topic	Number of Times Topic Discussed	Topic as a Percentage of Total Topics Raised
Condoms or femidoms	47	8	6	61	14.3
Open talk on HIV/AIDS	45	16	0	61	14.3
Tuberculosis (TB)	35	2	0	37	8.7
Voluntary counseling and testing (VCT)	20	12	4	36	8.5
Mobilization around HIV/AIDS	21	13	1	35	8.2
Adult relationships	17	11	1	29	6.8
Support for peers	22	3	2	27	6.3
Infection routes for HIV and prevention	13	9	4	26	6.1
Antiretroviral drugs	14	6	4	24	5.7
Living with HIV	3	7	0	10	2.3
Other diseases	4	3	1	8	1.9
Origins of HIV/AIDS	5	2	1	8	1.9
General information on HIV/AIDS	7	1	0	8	1.9
Other sexually transmitted infections	4	2	1	7	1.6
General wellness issues	5	1	1	7	1.6
Domestic disputes/violence	0	6	0	6	1.4
Fear/stigma	0	3	3	6	1.4
Referral/securing access to health provision (not VCT)	3	1	0	4	0.9
Sexual abuse	2	0	0	2	0.5
Adult–child relationships	0	2	0	2	0.5
Disclosure (HIV-positive)	0	2	0	2	0.5
Other	19	1	1	21	4.9
Total	286	110	30	426	100

Source: Peer Educator Diaries 2006.

TABLE 7. Location of Informal Activity by Peer Educators in Mineco

Location of Informal Activity	Number Reported	Percentage of Total
Work	103	43.1
Community (could be in peer educator's home if involved nonfamily members)	80	33.5
Extended Family (could be outside the home if involved family members)	45	18.8
Church	11	4.6
Total	239	100

Note: Caution should be exercised in reading these categorizations; locations are rarely neatly separated. Thus, for example, decisions have to be made in coding a conversation in which a peer educator visited a sick colleague at home; had a conversation while walking back with a neighbour from church; or was involved in a discussion with members of a company football team on the way to a fixture in the community. See also Appendix 2 for a discussion on categorizing formal and informal discussions.

Source: Peer Educator Diaries 2006.

TABLE 8. Marital Status of Peer Educators

Marital Status	Male (%)	Female (%)	All (%)
Married/long-term partner	61.7	44.3	52.0
Divorced	3.0	11.4	7.7
Widow(er)	2.3	3.0	2.7
Single	33.0	41.3	37.6
Total	100	100	100

N = 598.

Source: Peer Educator Survey 2005.

TABLE 9. Occupations by Race for Five Companies (permanent employees only)

Occupational Level	Black (African, colored, and Indian) (%)	African (%)	White (%)	N =
Top management	16.2	9.4	83.8	382
Senior management	19.7	7.8	80.3	1,753
Professionally qualified and experienced specialists and middlemanagement	32.4	15.8	67.6	5,388
Skilled technical workers, junior management, supervisors, foremen, and superintendents	50.3	24.6	49.7	21,022
Semi-skilled and discretionary decision makers	90.0	77.7	10.0	48,082
Unskilled and defined decision makers	97.9	78.8	2.1	25,385
Total				102,012
South African population, ages 15–59 years	**90.4**	**78.3**	**9.6**	**28.47 million**

Sources: Company employment equity reports (2005) and Statistics South Africa (2006).

TABLE 10. Occupations by Race for Mineco (permanent employees only)

Occupational Level	Black (African, colored, and Indian) (%)	African (%)	White (%)	N =
Top management	6.7	6.7	93.3	15
Senior management	6.5	5.9	93.5	306
Professionally qualified and experienced specialists and middle management	24.4	15.3	85.2	1,517
Skilled technical workers, junior management, supervisors, foremen, and superintendents	40.6	39.3	59.4	4,908
Semi-skilled and discretionary decision makers	96.8	96.6	3.2	32,642
Unskilled and defined decision makers	98.0	97.9	2.0	4,837
South African population, ages 15–59 years	**90.4**	**78.3**	**9.6**	**28.47 million**

Sources: Company Employment Equity Report (2005) and Statistics South Africa (2006).

TABLE 11. Employees and Peer Educators by Race for Five Companies

All five companies	Black (African, colored, and Indian)	African (%)	White (%)
All employees (*N* = 123,055)	81.7	61.3	18.3
Peer educators (*N* = 580)	92.1	73.8	7.9

Sources: Company Employment Equity Reports (2005) and Peer Educator Survey 2005

TABLE 12. Employees and Peer Educators by Race for Mineco

Mining Company	Black (African, colored, and Indian)	African (%)	White (%)
All employees (*N* = 44,494)	87.0	86.7	13.0
Peer educators (*N* = 158)	94.3	93.1	5.7

Source: Company Employment Equity Report (2005) and Peer Educator Survey 2005.

TABLE 13. Stimulus for Informal Interaction between Peer Educators and Peers

Stimulus for Informal Interaction	Number of Informal Interactions	Percentage of Total
Known at work as a colleague/peer educator	70	30.8
Known within community or within family as a peer educator	65	28.6
Identified by T-shirt, badge, etc.	17	7.5
Media coverage of HIV/AIDS	17	7.5
Formal talk on HIV/AIDS by peer educator	16	7.0
Funeral	10	4.4
Pictures in peer educator's office	10	4.4
Job function (e.g., human resource issue)	10	4.4
Other	12	5.3
Total	227	100

Source: Peer Educator Diaries 2006.

TABLE 14. Peer Educators' Perceptions of Support for Their Activity

I get the support I need for my peer educator activity from the . . .	**All/Trade Unionists (only)**	**Strongly Agree (%)**	**Agree (%)**	**Neutral (%)**	**Disagree (%)**	**Strongly Disagree (%)**	**N/A**	***N* =**
Occupational nurses	All	42.8	26.4	12.9	7.7	3.0	7.1	560
	TU members	**41.8**	**29.1**	**12.2**	**7.8**	**2.8**	**6.3**	426
Managers responsible for the company's	All	32.2	31.1	16.3	8.9	6.1	5.4	559
HIV/AIDS policy and programs	**TU members**	**31.0**	**31.7**	**15.2**	**9.5**	**6.7**	**6.0**	420
Immediate supervisors and managers	All	25.1	31.6	14.3	14.1	9.2	5.7	545
	TU members	**24.1**	**30.9**	**15.1**	**14.8**	**9.3**	**5.8**	411
Trade union officials or office bearers	All	19.3	24.3	15.7	15.0	9.4	16.3	534
	TU members	**21.1**	**26.0**	**16.2**	**16.2**	**7.8**	**12.8**	408

Source: Peer Educator Survey 2005.

Appendix 2

Methodology

This book draws on some six years of research on company HIV/AIDS programs, which is summarized in Table 2 (see Appendix 1). This appendix details the research most extensively utilized in this book in six large companies.

Chapter 2 and a section of Chapter 5 draw on material collected between 2001 and 2005 in Deco, a company in the petrochemical sector. I started to research Deco's response to HIV/AIDS in 2001 in an exploratory manner. It was clear that South African companies were going to have to respond to the AIDS epidemic, and the limited corporate response in South Africa at that time indicated that it was likely to become a matter of urgency.

A number of South African companies that I approached in late 2000 were unwilling to provide access, primarily because of the sensitive nature of HIV/AIDS. Access was gained to Deco because, by chance, the company HIV/AIDS manager knew me though unrelated research. On the strength of this, she assisted in the long and complex process of persuading the company to give me research access. Although the research was conducted at no cost to the company, a nine-page legal agreement was eventually negotiated. Despite the fact that the legal document mimicked the "value-free" language in my research proposal, it was quickly evident that the research process would be used by the company HIV/AIDS manager to motivate a greater response from the company. Over the research period (2001–2005), I developed close working relationships with a number of Deco employees who were attempting to implement HIV/AIDS programs. They were invaluable in helping me understand the dynamics of the company, the motivations of individuals, and, frequently, opening up further research access. I conducted approximately seventy-five interviews with managers, trade unionists, medical personnel, and those individuals who were running HIV/AIDS programs in the company. Critically, in addition to these formal interviews, I attended meetings of the company's AIDS Forum and various workshops and HIV/AIDS-related events.

The bulk of the book, outside of Chapter 2, draws on two research projects conducted in 2005 and 2006 that specifically focused on peer educators. The first project, conducted between January and November 2005, sought to provide an overview of peer educator activity within five major companies—Autocircle, Autostar, Bestbuyco, Finco, and Mineco. These companies were selected on the basis of having significant peer educator programs, representing different economic sectors, and being willing to grant research access. This research had four major components.

First, in-depth interviews were conducted with 29 "key players" such as managers, occupational health practitioners, trade unionists, and trainers to establish the nature of company HIV/AIDS programs and the role of peer educators within these—or at least what these key players perceived them to be.

Second, a questionnaire was sent to all known peer educators in these companies though the companies' internal mail systems. Questionnaires were available in English, Isixhosa, Setswana, and Sepedi. In total 614 completed questionnaires were returned; an overall response rate of 35 percent, which ranged widely among individual companies, from 22 to 85 percent, depending on logistical capacity and, probably, the accuracy of estimated numbers of active peer educators.

Third, in-depth interviews were conducted with 75 workplace peer educators (some also acting as local peer educator coordinators) in six of the country's nine provinces. Interviews were semi-structured and lasted for approximately one hour. Most were done on an individual basis, but three small-group interviews were conducted with three or four peer educators. Interviews probed what peer educators were actually doing within HIV/AIDS programs and the barriers they faced in this regard, their motivations, their understanding of their own agency and behavioral change, and their views on workplace peer education and its possible future. The selection of peer educators was done at a local level by peer educator coordinators on the basis of a request for active peer educators representing a spectrum of race and gender and, where appropriate, differently sized workplaces and unionized and nonunionized employees. Typically around four peer educators would be interviewed at any one site. Sometimes, these were drawn from a number of smaller sites that had only one or two peer educators, for example, in Finco's branch operations. The request for a demographic range almost certainly meant an overrepresentation of white peer educators. Though their inclusion in the interview schedules sometimes also appeared to be a matter of presenting "trophy whites" given the general absence of whites from the ranks of peer educators (See Chapters 3 and 4).

The fourth component consisted of a small number of participatory observations. These included a two-day peer training workshop attended by 40 of Finco's peer educators and two one-day workshops attended by 25 and 120 peer educators, in Autocircle and Bestbuyco, respectively.

Following this research project, I chose to focus on the informal activity of peer educators because it seemed that this was where the most significant, and least understood, activity was taking place. The second project, based in one operation of Mineco where there was an active peer educator group, was conducted between May and September 2006. This project also consisted of four components. First, I attended the monthly meeting of the peer educator group as an observer. Five such meetings were attended. Between meetings, I maintained contact with the coordinator of the group, who provided logistical support, advice, and insights.

Second, the members of this peer educator group were asked to keep a daily diary of their informal activity. This consisted of a brief record of any interactions that occurred that day and a more complete record of one of these interactions. Seven peer educators kept these diaries which began in mid-May and finished at the end of August. An eighth peer educator kept a diary over a number of months, but this was not used because of concerns over its accuracy. Not all seven peer educators submitted complete diaries for all of this period—in total 20.5 months of diary entries were submitted. Peer educators were encouraged to indicate "no activity" when this was the case—but this was not always done, leaving uncertainty over blank entries. Peer educators were encouraged to write in the language of their choice. Only one chose to write in a language other than English (Setswana), which was translated. The work of keeping the diaries was recognized from the outset as onerous. By agreement, an honorarium was given, on completion of the project, to each peer educator who kept a research diary. Certificates of participation were awarded to those who kept diaries at the end of the project.

Much of the data contained in the diaries was qualitative in nature, consisting primarily of the peer educators' own accounts, or narratives, of their activity. Nevertheless, summarizing all interactions that they had each day, specific pieces of data that were requested in the standard diary page, and interpretations made by the researcher when reading the diary entries allowed some statistical data to be collected.

In total the seven peer educators recorded 343 interactions. However, of these entries, 52 recorded formal activity—addressing groups of people with largely prepared information. While most of these 52 reported interactions were at work and fit neatly into the idea of a formal presentation, a small number were in churches or at funerals (and often involving large numbers of people—as many as 300). From some perspectives these community-based interactions are different from the regular formal presentations given to coworkers by peer educators—for example, they often address people at a particular collective moment that itself may be directly linked to HIV/AIDS—at a routine shift or team meeting. Rigorously categorizing between formal and informal activity in this way can be questioned. Nevertheless, in seeking to specifically capture informal activity, this division between formal and informal (rather than work and community setting) was maintained.

By contrast to these 52 formal interactions, 16 interactions were classified as "mixed," in that formal activity led directly into informal activity with particular individuals from the group addressed. These interactions have been kept in the analysis—with the emphasis on the informal rather than formal component of the interaction.

Of the 286 interactions utilized for the analysis of informal activity (270 informal and 16 mixed), 185 were recorded in depth using a one-page template, to which additional pages were sometimes added, and 101 noted only location, the form of interaction (usually indicating the number of people involved), length of interaction, and topic discussed. Since interactions could involve more than one topic, a total of 426 topics were categorized by the researcher as forming the content of these 286 interactions.

Third, in-depth interviews were conducted with eight peer educators, of whom six had kept research diaries. Interviews drew on individuals' diary entries and sought to explore issues raised in these. Interviews with peer educators lasted between one and a half and three hours. Additionally, interviews of approximately one hour's duration were conducted with two managers, three trade unionists, and a nursing sister based at the site.

Fourth, and finally, I made three site visits to understand the environment in which the peer educators operated. These consisted of the mine hostel, an informal settlement, and the underground working environment.

Ethical permission for both research projects was obtained from the Wits University Human Research Ethics (Non-Medical) Committee: protocol numbers HO50310 and 60602. I strove to act ethically and fairly in my interactions with peer educators and others in the course of this research. I am, however, doubtful whether the "jumping though hoops" that was necessary to comply with the sometimes obscure requests of the ethics committee actually assisted in the practice (rather than formal facade) of acting ethically in often messy fieldwork environments.

Both research projects were written up in the form of research reports (Dickinson 2006a and 2007). Additionally, I made a number of presentations and wrote two journal articles (Dickinson 2006b, 2006c) based on the first research project. A sabbatical period that provided an extended period for reflection and reading enabled me to move beyond these formats and to think more deeply about what peer educators were doing—as this book attempts to describe.

My thinking, and the thesis put forward in this book, has also been framed by ten years of extensive contact with friends and acquaintances in Katlehong, a large township to the southeast of Johannesburg, and a two-month stay in a Free State township during 2007. Without my own informal activity in township communities (albeit of a very different nature to that I describe peer educators conducting in this book), it would have been much harder to understand what peer educators were telling me.

References

Abdool Karim, Quarraisha, Eleanor Preston-Whyte, Nkozazana Zuma, Zena Stein, Ida Susser, and Neetha Morar. 1994. Women and AIDS in Natal/KwaZulu, South Africa: Determinants of the Adoption of HIV Protective Behavior. Washington: International Centre for Research on Women.

Abdool Karim, Quarraisha. 2005. Heterosexual Transmission of HIV—The Importance of a Gendered Perspective in HIV Prevention. In *HIV/AIDS in South Africa,* edited by S. S. Abdool Karim and Q. Abdool Karim. Cambridge: Cambridge University Press.

AIDS Law Project. 2000. Your Victory Is Our Victory: The Case of "A" v South African Airways: AIDS Law Project. Johannesburg: University of the Witwatersrand.

Altman, Dennis. 1994. *Power and Community: Organizational and Cultural Responses to AIDS.* Southport, UK: Taylor and Francis.

Barnett, Tony, and Alan Whiteside. 2002. *AIDS in the Twenty-First Century: Disease and Globalization.* Basingstoke: Palgrave/Macmillan.

Baylies, Carolyn, Janet Bujra, and the-Gender-and-AIDS-Group. 2000. *AIDS, Sexuality, and Gender in Africa: Collective Strategies and Struggles in Tanzania and Zambia.* London: Routledge.

Bogart, Laura, and Sheryl Thornburn. 2005. Are HIV/AIDS Conspiracy Beliefs a Barrier to HIV Prevention among African Americans? *Journal of Acquired Immune Deficiency Syndrome* 38 (2):213–218.

Bolton, Ralph. 1992. AIDS and Promiscuity: Muddles in the Models of HIV Prevention. *Medical Anthropology* 14:145–223.

Brink, Brian. 2003. Response to HIV/AIDS in South Africa: A Business Perspective. *Labour Markets and Social Frontiers (South African Reserve Bank)* 4:9–13.

Brink, Brian, and L. Clausen. 1987. The Acquired Immune Deficiency Syndrome. *Journal of the Mine Medical Officers Association of South Africa* 63 (433): 10–17.

Bujra, Janet. 2006. Sex Talk: AIDS and the Transformation of Mutuality and Power in Africa. Paper read at Sixteenth International Sociology Conference World Congress of Sociology, 23–29 July, at Durban.

Business Day. 2002. Taming the Hurricane (Editorial). *Business Day,* 12 September, 15.

Cairns, Murray, David Dickinson, and Wendy Orr. 2006. Wits University's Response to HIV/AIDS: Flagship Programme or "Tramp Steamer"? *African Journal of AIDS Research* 5 (2):159–166.

Campbell, Catherine, and Catherine MacPhail. 2002. Peer Education, Gender, and the Development of Critical Consciousness: Participatory HIV Prevention by South African Youth. *Social Science and Medicine* 55:331–345.

Campbell, Catherine, and Brian Williams. 1999. Beyond the Biomedical and Behavioural: Towards an Integrated Approach to HIV Prevention in the Southern African Mining Industry. *Social Science and Medicine* 48:1625–1639.

Centre for the Support of Peer Education (CSPE). 2008. CSPE & ME: How Is It Different? *Face to Face* 3 (3):3.

Chambers, Robert. 1994. Participatory Rural Appraisal (PRA): Analysis of Experience. *World Development* 22 (9):1253–1268.

Chavunduka, G. L. 1986. The Organisation of Traditional Medicine in Zimbabwe. In *The Professionalisation of African Medicine,* edited by M. Last and G. Chavunduka. Manchester: Manchester University Press.

Clarke, Elizabeth, and Kathryn Strachan. 2000. *Everybody's Business: The Enlightening Truth About HIV/AIDS.* Cape Town: Metropolitan.

Colvin, Mark. 2000. Sexually Transmitted Infections in Southern Africa: A Public Health Crisis. *South African Journal of Science* 96 (6):335–339.

Congress of South African Trade Unions (COSATU), the Federation of Unions of South Africa (FEDUSA), and the National Council of Trade Unions (NACTU). *Pledge by Representatives of Workers* 1998. www.cosatu.org.za/docs/2000/hivbook.htm [accessed 12 October 2007].

Connelly, Patrick. 2004. Can Small and Medium Sized Enterprises Provide HIV/AIDS Services to their Employees? Constraints and Opportunities. Paper read at African-Asian Society, 21 April, Johannesburg.

De la Dehesa, G. 1999. The Challenges Facing President Mbeki's Government. *Business Day,* 18 June.

De Waal, Alex. 2006. *AIDS and Power: Why There Is No Political Crisis—Yet.* London: Zed Books.

Department of Health. 1998. Guidelines for Developing a Workplace Policy and Programme on HIV/AIDS and STDs. Pretoria: Department of Health.

——. 1999. The Electricity Supply Commission of South Africa (Eskom). In *HIV/AIDS Best Practice Series.* Pretoria: HIV/AIDS and STD Directorate, Department of Health.

——. 2003a. National HIV and Syphilis Antenatal Sero-Prevalence Survey in South Africa: 2002. Pretoria: Department of Health.

——. 2003b. The Traditional Health Practitioners Bill, 2003. Pretoria: Department of Health.

——. 2008. National HIV and Syphilis Prevalence Survey South Africa: 2007. Pretoria: Department of Health.

Department of Labour. 2000. *Code of Good Practice on Key Aspects of HIV/AIDS and Employment.* Pretoria: Department of Labour.

——. 2003. *HIV/AIDS Technical Assistance Guidelines.* Pretoria: Department of Labour.

Desmond, C., K. Michael, and J. Gow. 2000. The Hidden Battle: HIV/AIDS in the Family and Community. Durban: Health Economics and HIV/AIDS Research Division, University of Natal.

Dickinson, David. 2003. Managing HIV/AIDS in the South African Workplace: Just Another Duty? *South African Journal of Economic and Management Science* 6 (1):25–49.

——. 2004a. Corporate South Africa's Response to HIV/AIDS: Why So Slow? *Journal of Southern African Studies* 30 (3):627–650.

——. 2004b. People Living Openly with HIV/AIDS in the Workplace. *South African Labour Bulletin* 28 (2):59–62.

——. 2004c. Narratives of Life and Death: Voluntary Counselling and Testing Programmes in the Workplace. Paper read at WISER/CRESP Symposium: Life and Death in a Time of AIDS: The Southern African Experience, 14/16 October, Wits University, Johannesburg.

——. 2005. AIDS, Order, and "Best Practice" in South African Companies: Managers, Peer Educators, Traditional Healers, and Folk Theories. *African Journal of AIDS Research* 4 (1):11–20.

——. 2006a. Workplace HIV/AIDS Peer Educators in South African Companies. In *Wits Business School Working Papers.* Johannesburg: Wits Business School, University of the Witwatersrand.

——. 2006b. Fighting for Life: HIV/AIDS Peer Educators as New Industrial Relations Actors? *British Journal of Industrial Relation* 44 (4):697–718.

——. 2006c. Smokescreen or Opening a Can of Worms? Workplace HIV/AIDS Peer Education and Social Protection in South Africa. *African Studies* 65 (2):321–342.

——. 2007. Talking About AIDS: A Study of Informal Activities Undertaken by Workplace HIV/AIDS Peer Educators in a South African Company. In *Wits Business School Working Papers.* Johannesburg: Wits Business School, University of the Witwatersrand.

Dickinson, David, and Duncan Innes. 2004. Fronts or Front-lines? HIV/AIDS and Big Business in South Africa. *Transformation* 55:28–54.

Dickinson, David, Pule de Roland Phillips, and Rachel Tau. 2008. Working with Peer Educators to Identify and Respond to Risky Sexual Networks. Paper read at *South African Business Coalition on HIV & AIDS, 2nd Private Sector Conference on HIV and AIDS,* 5/6 November, Emperors Palace, Gauteng, South Africa.

Dickinson, David, and Marion Stevens. 2005. Understanding the Response of Large South African Companies to HIV/AIDS. *Journal of Social Aspects of HIV/AIDS* 2 (2):286–295.

Evans-Pritchard, E. E. 1977 [1937]. *Witchcraft, Oracles, and Magic Among the Azande.* Oxford: Clarendon Press.

Family Health International. 2002. *Workplace HIV/AIDS Programmes: An Action Guide for Managers.* www.fhi.org [accessed 30 November 2004].

Farmer, Paul. 1990. Sending Sickness: Sorcery, Politics, and Changing Concepts of AIDS in Rural Haiti. *Medical Anthropology Quarterly* 4 (1):6–27.

——. 1994. AIDS-Talk and the Constitution of Cultural Models. *Social Science and Medicine* 38 (6):801–809.

——. 1999. *Infections and Inequalities: The Modern Plagues.* Berkeley: University of California Press.

Feierman, Steven. 1985. Struggle for Control: The Social Roots of Health and Healing in Modern Africa. *African Studies Review* 28 (2 and 3).

Fourie, Pieter. 2006. *The Political Management of HIV and AIDS in South Africa: One Burden Too Many?* Houndmills, UK: Palgrave Macmillan.

——. 2007. The Relationship Between the AIDS Pandemic and State Fragility. *Global Change, Peace & Security* 19 (3):281–300.

Gevisser, Mark. 2007. *Thabo Mbeki: The Dream Deferred.* Johannesburg: Jonathan Ball.

Global Business Council on HIV/AIDS. 2002. *Employees & HIV/AIDS: Action for Business Leaders.* Available from www.businessfightsaids.org [accessed 4 December 2003].

Gluckman, Max. 1956. *Custom and Conflict in Africa.* Oxford: Blackwell.

Goffman, Erving. 1958. *The Presentation of Self in Everyday Life.* Edinburgh: Bateman Press.

——. 1961. *Asylums: Essays on the Social Situation of Mental Patients and Other Inmates.* London: Penguin.

——. 1966. *Behaviour in Public Places.* New York: The Free Press.

Gordon, Gill. 1995. Participation, Empowerment, and Sexual Health in Africa. In *Community Empowerment: A Reader in Participation and Development,* edited by M. Mayo and G. Craig. London: Zed Books.

Government of South Africa. 1995. *Labour Relations Act: Act 66 of 1995.*

——. 2007. *Traditional Health Practitioners Act: Act 22 of 2007.*

Grundlingh, L. 2001. A Critical Historical Analysis of Government Responses to HIV/AIDS in South Africa as Reported in the Media, 1983–1994. Paper read at AIDS in Context Conference, 4–7 April, University of the Witwatersrand, Johannesburg.

Guliwe, Thulani. 2007. Unions and Bargaining Councils Neglect HIV/AIDS. *South African Labour Bulletin* 31 (3):57–58.

Gupta, Geeta Rao. 2002. How Men's Power Over Women Fuels the HIV Epidemic. *British Medical Journal* 324:183–184.

Hammond-Tooke, David. 1989. *Rituals and Medicine: Indigenous Healing in South Africa.* Johannesburg: AD Donker.

Hochschild, Arlie. 1983. *The Managed Heart: Commercialization of Human Feeling.* Berkeley: University of California Press.

Hodes, Rebecca. 2007. HIV/AIDS in South African Documentary Film, c. 1990–2000. *Journal of Southern African Studies* 33 (1):153–171.

Human Sciences Research Council (HSRC). 2005. Nelson Mandela/HSRC Study of HIV/AIDS: South African National HIV Prevalence, Behavioural Risk and Mass Media. Cape Town: HSRC.

Hunter, Mark. 2007. The Changing Political Economy of Sex in South Africa: The Significance of Unemployment and Inequality to the Scale of the AIDS Pandemic. *Social Science and Medicine* 64:689–700.

Iliffe, John. 2006. *The African AIDS Epidemic: A History.* Oxford: James Currey.

ING Barings. 2000. Economic Impact of AIDS in South Africa: A Dark Cloud on the Horizon. ING Barings.

International Labour Organisation (ILO). 2000. HIV/AIDS: A Threat to Decent Work, Productivity and Development. Geneva: ILO.

——. 2001. An ILO Code of Practice on HIV/AIDS and the World of Work. Geneva: ILO.

Jelly, S. 2003. Why It Pays to Fight HIV/AIDS. *Sunday Times,* 20 July.

Jordan, B. 2001. Too Little, Too Late as AIDS Grips Firms. *Sunday Times,* 24 July.

Keeton, Claire. 2003. Focus on AIDS: Mines' Aids Program Saves Money and Lives. *Sunday Times,* 19 January.

Kelly, Jeffrey A., Debra A. Murphy, Kathleen J. Sikkema, Timothy L. McAuliffe, Roger A. Roffman, Laura J. Solomon, Richard A. Winett, Seth C. Kalichaman, and Commuity-HIV-Prevention-Research-Collaborative. 1997. Randomised, Controlled, Community-level HIV-prevention Intervention for Sexual-risk Behaviour Among Homosexual Men in US Cities. *Lancet* 350:1500–1505.

Kelly, John. 1998. *Rethinking Industrial Relations: Mobilization, Collectivism, and Long Waves.* London: Routledge.

Kerrigan, Deanna, and Ellen Weiss. 2000. *Peer Education and HIV/AIDS: Past Experience, Future Directions.* Washington, DC: Population Council. Available online at www.popcouncil.org/horizons [accessed 22 May 2009].

Kippax, Susan, R. W. Connell, G. W. Dowsett, and June Crawford. 1993. *Sustaining Safe Sex: Gay Communities Respond to AIDS.* London: The Flamer Press.

Klonoff, Elizabeth, and Hope Landrine. 1999. Do Blacks Believe That HIV/AIDS Is a Government Conspiracy Against Them? *Preventative Medicine* 28:451–457.

Klugman, Barbara. 2000. Sexual Rights in Southern Africa: A Beijing Discourse or a Strategic Necessity? *Health and Human Rights* 4 (2):144–173.

Labonte, R. 1994. Health Promotion and Empowerment: Reflections on Professional Practice. *Health Education Quarterly* 21:253–268.

Laverack, Glenn, and Nina Wallerstein. 2001. Measuring Community Empowerment: A Fresh Look at Organisational Domains. *Health Promotion International* 16 (2):179–185.

Le Roux, Magdel. 2003. *The Lemba: A Lost Tribe of Israel in Southern Africa?* Pretoria: University of South Africa.

Leclerc-Madlala, Suzanne. 2002. On the Virgin Cleansing Myth: Gendered Bodies, AIDS, and Ethnomedicine. *African Journal of AIDS Research* 1 (2):87–95.

——. 2005. Popular Responses to HIV/AIDS and Policy. *Journal of Southern African Studies* 31 (4):845–856.

Lein, Laura, and Marvin B. Sussman. 1983. *The Ties that Bind: Men's and Women's Social Networks.* New York: Haworth Press.

Low-Beer, Daniel, and Rand L. Stoneburner. 2003. Behaviour and Communication Change in Reducing HIV: Is Uganda Unique? *African Journal of AIDS Research* 2 (1):9–21.

——. 2004. Social Communication and AIDS Population Behaviour Changes in Uganda Compared to Other Countries. Johannesburg: *Communicating AIDS Needs Project,* Centre for AIDS Development Research and Evaluation (Cadre).

Lurie, Mark N. 2004. Migration, Sexuality, and the Spread of HIV/AIDS in Rural South Africa. In *Migration Policy Series,* edited by J. Crush. Cape Town: Southern African Migration Project.

MacCormack, Carol. 1986. The Articulation of Western and Traditional Systems of Health Care. In *The Professionalisation of African Medicine,* edited by M. Last and G. Chavunduka. Manchester: Manchester University Press.

Mamdani, Mahmood. 1996. *Citizen and Subject: Contemporary Africa and the Legacy of Colonialism.* London: Jame Currey.

Marais, Hein. 2000. *To the Edge: AIDS Review 2000.* Pretoria: Centre for the Study of AIDS, University of Pretoria.

Marks, Shula. 2002. An Epidemic Waiting to Happen? The Spread of HIV/AIDS in South Africa in Social and Historical Perspective. *African Studies* 61 (1):13–26.

Mayo, Marjorie, and Gary Craig. 1995. Community Participation and Empowerment: The Human Face of Structural Adjustment or Tools for Democratic Transformation? In *Community Empowerment: A Reader in Participation and Development,* edited by Marjorie Mayo and Gary Craig. London: Zed Books.

McKusick, Leon, Thomas J. Coates, Stephen F. Morin, Lance Pollack, and Colleen Hoff. 1990. Longtitudinal Predictors of Reductions in Unprotected Anal Intercourse Among Gay Men in San Francisco: The AIDS Behavioral Research Project. *American Journal of Public Health* 80 (8):978–893.

Meel, B. L. 2003. The Myth of Child Rape as a Cure for HIV/AIDS in Transkei: A Case Report. *Medical Science and the Law* 43 (1):85–88.

Moodie, Dunbar, with Vivienne Ndatshe. 1994. *Going for Gold: Men, Mines and Migration.* Johannesburg: Wits University Press.

Nattrass, Nicoli. 2004. *The Moral Economy of AIDS in South Africa.* Cambridge: Cambridge University Press.

Nature's Health Products. *Home Page* http://www.natureshealth.co.za [accessed 3 October 2007].

New Academy of Business. 2001. Empowerment and Positive Engagement: The Eskom Response to HIV/AIDS. New Academy of Business.

Newmann, S., P. Sarin, N. Kumarasamy, E. Amalraj, M. Rogers, P. Madhivanan, T. Flanigan, S. Cu-Uvin, S. McGarvey, K. Mayer, and S. Solomon. 2000. Marriage, Monogamy, and HIV: A Profile of HIV-Infected Women in South India. *International Journal of STD & AIDS* 11:250–253.

Niehaus, Isak, with Gunvor Jonsson. 2005. Dr. Wouter Basson, Americans, and Wild Beasts: Men's Conspiricy Theories of HIV/AIDS in the South African Lowveld. *Medical Anthropology* 24:179–208.

NOSA. 2003. *HIV/AIDS Management System Guideline Document.* www.nosa.co.za [accessed 25 November 2005].

Olson, Mancur. 1965. *The Logic of Collective Action.* Cambridge, MA: Harvard University Press.

Packard, Randall. 1990. *White Plague, Black Labor: Tuberculosis and the Political Economy of Health and Disease in South Africa.* Pietermaritzburg: University of Natal Press.

Paiva, Vera. 1995. Sexuality, AIDS, and Gender Norms Among Brazilian Teenagers. In *Culture and Sexual Risk: Anthropological Perspectives on AIDS,* edited by H. ten Brummelhuis and G. Herdt. Amsterdam: Gordon and Breach.

———. 2000. Gendered Scripts and the Sexual Scene: Promoting Sexual Subjects Among Brazilian Teenagers. In *Framing the Sexual Subject: The Politics of Gender, Sexuality, and Power,* edited by R. Parker, R. M. Barbosa, and P. Aggleton. Berkeley: University of California Press.

Panford, S., M. Nyaney, S. Amoach, and N. Aidoo. 2001. Using Folk Media in HIV/AIDS Prevention in Rural Ghana. *American Journal of Public Health* 91 (10):1559–1562.

Parker, Warren. 2004. *Rethinking Conceptual Approaches to Behaviour Change: The Importance of Context.* http://www.cadre.org.za/files/CANBehaviour.pdf [accessed 11 March 2007].

PLoS Medicine Editors. 2007. HIV Treatment Proceeds as Prevention Research Confounds. *PLoS Medicine* 4 (12), http://medicine.plosjournals.org.

Preston-Whyte, E. M. 1995. Half-way There: Anthropology and Interention-orientated AIDS Research in KwaZulu/Natal, South Africa. In *Culture and Sexual Risk: Anthropological Perspectives on AIDS,* edited by H. Ten Brummelhuis and G. Heardt. Amsterdam: Gordon and Breach.

Randall, C. 2002. Impacts and Response of Industries, Workplaces and Sectors of the South African Economy. In *HIV/AIDS, Economics and Governance in South Africa: Key Issues in Understanding Response.* Johannesburg: Cadre/USAID/Joint Centre for Political and Economic Studies.

Rehle, T., O. Shisana, V. Pillay, K. Zuma, A. Puren, and W. Parker. 2007. National HIV Incidence Measures—New Insights into the South African Epidemic. *South African Medical Journal* 97 (3):194–199.

Rehle, T., and O. Shisana. 2003. Epidemiological and Demographic HIV/AIDS Projections: South Africa. *African Journal of AIDS Research* 2 (1):1–8.

Rogers, Everett. 1962. *Diffusion of Innovations.* 1st ed. New York: Free Press.

———. 2003. *Diffusion of Innovations.* 5th ed. New York: Free Press.

Rosen, S., J. Simon, D. Thea, and J. Vincent. 2000. Care and Treatment to Extend the Working Lives of HIV-positive Employees: Calculating the Benefits to Business. *South African Journal of Science* 96 (6):300–304.

Rusconi, R. 2000. *The Impact of HIV/AIDS on the Workforce.* www.sanlam.co.za [accessed 2 November 2002].

Sanger, David, and Donald McNeil Jr. 2004. Bush Backs Condom Use to Prevent Spread of AIDS. *New York Times,* 24 June.

SAPA (South African Press Association). 2001. DA Slams Govt's Handling of AIDS Crisis. *Business Day,* 2 December.

SAPA and I-Net Bridge. 2000. Anglo Chairman Sees Reasons for Optimism in SA. *Business Day,* 20 November.

Schneider, Helen, and Didier Fassin. 2002. Denial and Defiance: A Socio-Political Analysis of AIDS in South Africa. *AIDS* 16 (Supplement 4):S45–S51.

Schneider, Helen, and Joanne Stein. 2001. Implementing AIDS Policy in Post-apartheid South Africa. *Social Science and Medicine* 52 (5):723–731.

Schoepf, Brooke G. 2001. International AIDS Research in Anthropology: Taking a Critical Perspective on the Crisis. *Annual Review of Anthropology* 30: 335–361.

Scott, James C. 1990. *Domination and the Arts of Resistance: Hidden Transcripts.* New Haven: Yale University Press.

Setel, Philip W. 1999. *A Plague of Paradoxes: AIDS, Culture, and Demography in Northern Tanzania.* Chicago: University of Chicago Press.

Shepherd, Jonathan, Katherine Weare, and Glenn Turner. 1997. Peer-led Sexual Health Promotion with Young Gay and Bisexual Men—Results of the HAPEER Project. *Health Education* 97 (6):204–212.

Shisana, O., K. Peltzer, N. Zungu-Dirway, and J. Louw. 2005. *The Health of Our Educators.* Cape Town: HSRC Press.

Singhal, Arvind, and Everett M. Rogers. 2003. *Combating AIDS: Communication Strategies in Action.* New Delhi, India: Sage.

Sobo, Eilsa J. 1995. *Choosing Unsafe Sex: AIDS-Risk Denial Among Disadvantaged Women.* Philadelphia: University of Pennsylvania Press.

South African Business Coalition on HIV/AIDS (SABCOHA). 2002. Evaluation of Workplace Responses to HIV/AIDS in South Africa. Johannesburg: SABCOHA.

——. 2004. The Economic Impact of HIV/AIDS on Business in South Africa 2003. Johannesburg: SABCOHA.

South African Institute of Race Relations (SAIRR). 2008. *South Africa Survey 2007/2008.* Johannesburg: SAIRR.

South African National AIDS Committee (SANAC). 2007. HIV & AIDS and STI Strategic Plan for South Africa 2007–2011. Pretoria: SANAC.

Sprague, Courtenay. 2008. Women's Health, HIV/AIDS, and the Workplace in South Africa. *African Journal of AIDS Research* 7 (3):341–352.

Stadler, Jonathan. 2003. Rumor, Gossip, and Blame: Implications for HIV/AIDS Prevention in the South African Lowveld. *AIDS Education and Prevention* 15 (4):357–368.

Statistics South Africa. 2002. The South African Labour Market: Selected Time-based Social and International Comparisons. Pretoria: Statistics South Africa.

——. 2004. Census 2001: Primary Tables South Africa. Pretoria: Statistics South Africa.

——. 2006. Mid-year Population Estimates: 2005. Pretoria: Statistics South Africa.

——. 2008a. Mid-year Population Estimates: 2008. Pretoria: Statistics South Africa.

——. 2008b. Income and Expenditure of Households: 2005/2006. Pretoria: Statistics South Africa.

Stevens, Marion, Renay Weiner, and Siphelo Mapolisa. 2003. AIDS and the Workplace: What Are Managers in South Africa doing? Paper read at first South African HIV/AIDS Conference, 3—6 August 2003, Durban.

Stevens, Marion, Renay Weiner, Siphelo Mapolisa, and David Dickinson. 2005. Management Responses to HIV/AIDS in South African Workplaces: A Baseline Survey. *South African Journal of Economic and Management Science* 8 (3):287–299.

Sunter, Clem. 1987. *The World and South Africa in the 1990s.* Cape Town: Human & Rousseau Tafelberg.

——. 1992. *The New Century: Quest for the High Road.* Cape Town: Human & Rousseau Tafelberg.

——. 1996. *The High Road: Where Are We Now?* Cape Town: Human & Rousseau Tafelberg.

Susser, Ida, and Zena Stein. 2000. Culture, Sexuality, and Women's Agency in the Prevention of HIV/AIDS in Southern Africa. *American Journal of Public Health* 90 (7):1042–1048.

Truth and Reconciliation Commission. 1998. Institutional Hearing: Business and Labour. Chapter 2 in *Truth and Reconciliation Commission of South Africa Report (Vol. 4).* Cape Town: CTP Books.

Turner, Glenn, and Jonathan Shepherd. 1999. A Method in Search of a Theory: Peer Education and Health Promotion. *Health Education Research* 14 (2):235–247.

Turner, Victor. 1974. *Dramas, Fields, and Metaphors: Symbolic Action in Human Society.* Ithaca, NY: Cornell University Press.

UNAIDS. 2000. The Business Response to HIV/AIDS: Impact and Lessons Learned. Geneva: UNAIDS, The Global Business Council on HIV/AIDS, and The Prince of Wales Business Leaders Forum.

——. 2003. UNAIDS Fact Sheet: Sub-Saharan Africa. www.unaids.org [accessed 5 April 2005].

UNAIDS and WHO. 2007. AIDS Epidemic Update 2007. Geneva: UNAIDS and WHO.

United Nations Development Programme (UNDP). 1993. *Human Development Report 1993: People's Participation.* Oxford: Oxford University Press.

United Nations Population Fund (UNFPA). 2002. Communication for Development Roundtable Report: Focus on HIV/AIDS Communication and Evaluation. New York: UNFPA.

U.S. Agency for International Development (USAID). 2002. What Happened in Uganda? Declining HIV Prevalence, Behavior Change, and the National Response. Washington: USAID.

Valente, Thomas W., and Rebecca L. Davis. 1999. Accelerating the Diffusion of Innovations Using Opinion Leaders. *The Annals of the American Acadamy of Political and Social Science* 566:55–67.

Washington, Harriet. 2007. Why Africa Fears Western Medicine. *New York Times,* July 31.

Webb, Douglas. 1997. *HIV and AIDS in Africa.* London: Pluto.

Whelan, Ronald, David Dickinson, and Tessa Murray. 2008. Use and Neglect of Best-Practice HIV/AIDS Progamme Guides by South African Companies. *African Journal of AIDS Research* 7 (3):375–388.

Whiteside, Alan, and Clem Sunter. 2000. *AIDS: The Challenge for South Africa.* Cape Town: Human & Rousseau Tafelberg.

Williams, Lewis, Ronald Labonte, and Mike O'Brian. 2003. Empowering Social Action Through Narratives of Identity and Culture. *Health Promotion International* 18 (1):33–40.

Willian, S. 2004. Recent Changes in the South African Government's HIV/AIDS Policy and Its Implementation. *African Affairs* 103 (410):109–117.

Wohlfeiler, Dan. 1997. Community Organizing and Community Building among Gay and Bisexual Men. In *Community Organizing and Community Building for Health,* edited by M. Minkler. New Brunswick, NJ: Rutgers University Press.

Wolf, R. Cameron., and K. C. Bond. 2002. Exploring Similarity between Peer Educators and Their Contacts and AIDS-protective Behaviours in Reproductive Health Programmes for Adolescents and Young Adults in Ghana. *AIDS Care* 14 (3) 361–373.

World Bank. 1996. *The World Bank Participation Sourcebook*. http://www.worldbank.org/wbi/sourcebook/sbhome.htm [accessed 14 November 2008].

World Health Organization (WHO). 2001. Legal Status of Traditional Medicine and Complementary/Alternative Medicine: A Worldwide Review. Geneva: WHO.

——. 2002. WHO Traditional Medicine Strategy 2002–2005. Geneva: WHO.

Young, Michael P. 2002. Confessional Protest: The Religious Birth of U.S. National Social Movements. *American Sociological Review* 67 (5):660–688.

Index

Italic page numbers indicate tables.